MW01120756

Collector's Library

PLATO

PLATO

SELECTIONS FROM
*Protagoras, Republic
Phaedrus, Gorgias*

Collector's Library

This edition published in 2004 in the
Collector's Library of Essential Thinkers
an imprint of CRW Publishing Limited
69 Gloucester Crescent, London NW1 7EG
Re-issued in the Collector's Library Series in 2009

ISBN 978 1 905716 71 5

1 3 5 7 9 10 8 6 4 2

Typeset in Great Britain by Antony Gray
Printed and bound in China by Imago

Contents

Introduction	7
Key Dates	19
Further Reading	20
PROTAGORAS	21
REPUBLIC	85
BOOK ONE	87
BOOK TWO	132
BOOK THREE	159
BOOK FOUR	168
BOOK FIVE	210
BOOK SIX	261
BOOK SEVEN	281
BOOK EIGHT	292
BOOK NINE	334
BOOK TEN	362
PHAEDRUS	383
GORGIAS	403

Introduction

WHAT IS AND WHAT OUGHT TO BE

The world in general does not have a very high opinion of philosophers. We think of them as sitting around in university departments, at best discussing the meanings of words, at worst discussing what it would mean for a word to have a meaning, supposing it *could* have one. What they should be doing, we feel, is giving give us guidance on how we should live our lives, and we are disappointed when they do not.

For this state of affairs we can perhaps blame David Hume, who pointed out, rather more than two hundred and fifty years ago, that you cannot (logically) derive statements about how people ought to behave from statements about how the world is arranged. Put simply, you cannot derive 'ought' from 'is':

> In every system of morality which I have hitherto met with, I have always remarked that the author proceeds for some time in the ordinary way of reasoning . . . when of a sudden I am surprised to find, that instead of . . . *is*, and *is not*, I meet with no proposition that is not connected with an *ought*, or an *ought not*. This change is imperceptible; but is, however, of the last consequence. For as this ought or ought not expresses some new relation or affirmation, it is necessary that . . . a reason should be given . . . how this new relation can be a deduction from others

7

which are entirely different from it. (*Treatise of Human Nature* 3, 1, 1)

Most philosophers have agreed with Hume, which is perhaps why they stopped offering moral guidance. However, in the real world we frequently *do* derive ought from is, with or without a logical justification. In fact, we do it all the time. We see a world full of beauty and wonder, and it seems a crime not to try and appreciate it as fully and as broadly as we can. If we know people are starving, it is hard not to feel that something should be done about feeding them. In each case, it is seeing how things are which prompts a feeling about how we ought to behave.

The good thing about ancient philosophy in general – and Plato in particular – is that (in a pre-Hume era) you can see how the questions it asks relate to one another, and how they relate to the most fundamental question, 'How should we live?' Plato commands our admiration because he so eminently relates how we *ought* to behave to what *is* real and what we can know.

ANCIENT AND MODERN PHILOSOPHY

For Plato, the answer to the question 'How should we live?' was given by his friend and mentor Socrates, who, for all his protestations that he did not know anything, had an unshakeable conviction that there were moral truths and moral realities. Of these truths, two were of overriding importance. The first, which found its way into Christianity 400 years later, and has been immensely influential ever since, was that we are never justified in harming anyone (the prevailing view being that we should help our friends and harm our enemies). The second was that goodness and knowledge are the same thing, that people do wrong simply because they fail to understand what is good and what is bad. Few people these days would accept this as a moral truth, perhaps, but for Socrates and Plato it was fundamental.

Unlike many philosophers, Socrates was a living embodiment of his own beliefs. He did not merely say you should never act unjustly. He himself risked his life precisely by refusing to act unjustly – opposing first the democracy, and then the oligarchy which overthrew it, within the space of a couple of years. He could have been put to death on either occasion, and indeed he was put to death (under the democracy) not many years later. One of the questions – perhaps the central question – which interested Plato was, where did this moral certainty which Socrates possessed come from?

MORAL CERTAINTY AND THE THEORY OF FORMS

When we say we know something, it may be something which is necessarily true, or something which simply happens to be true. That $2 + 2 = 4$ is necessarily true, because once the numbers have been defined in the way they have been defined, it is logically absurd for $2 + 2$ to equal anything else. That Paris is the capital of France, on the other hand, or a town in Texas, or Helen of Troy's lover, just happens to be true. It would not be logically absurd for it to be otherwise.

It seemed to Plato that for Socrates moral truths were as certain as the necessary truths of mathematics, and more certain than contingent truths such as how many stadia it is from Marathon to Athens. Once we understand what beauty, goodness and justice are, we can see they *must* exist, just as 2 + 2 *must* equal 4. It follows from this, in Plato's view, that beauty, goodness and justice must have greater reality than the things we see, hear and touch.

The theory Plato developed to account for this is known as the Theory of Forms (or Theory of Ideas). At its simplest level, the theory explains why we give the same name (for example, 'tree' or 'dog') to objects which differ from one another to a greater or lesser degree. According to Plato, we call things trees because they all in some way participate in, or share in, 'treeness'. The theory is summarised in six words, with absolute accuracy and clarity, by Stephen Dedalus in James Joyce's *Ulysses*: 'Horseness is the whatness of allhorse.'

It is hard for us not to picture the forms or ideas as abstract definitions, but for Plato they were substantial entities which were more real than the everyday trees and dogs which take their names from them. And just as the forms of things were more real than the things themselves, so the forms of what we think of as abstractions (beauty, goodness, justice) were more real than the forms of everyday things. The most real of all is the form of the good, which is almost synonymous, in Plato's philosophy, with god.

If the forms are eternal and unchanging, and our knowledge of them does not come from experience, where does it come from? From recollection, is Plato's answer. Souls are continually being reborn in a thousand-year cycle. In the periods between lives, free of the body, they acquire knowledge of the forms, but then lose this knowledge when they are reborn.

The wise person's life is a continuous attempt to recapture lost knowledge.

At the end of the *Republic* there is a description (the myth of Er) of the souls dying, being judged and punished, and choosing new lives for themselves. The description is both moving and witty, with a superb thumbnail portrait of Odysseus searching and searching for a humdrum, uneventful life, and his delight when he finds it. If you are not sure you are going to read all the selections in this volume, do at the very least read the final part of *Republic* Book Ten.

PLATO'S IMAGES

This is in fact the key to Plato as a whole. The Theory of Forms is open to all sorts of objections. Plato raises some himself in later dialogues, and Aristotle came up with others. Nor are the arguments for the theory ever set out very convincingly; it is simply assumed as a basis for everything else. What we find inspiring are the conviction that moral truths are the most real thing there is, and the captivating images Plato employs to illustrate what he has to say. I shall briefly refer to three of these images: the cave, the charioteer and the shipowner.

The cave

Plato distrusted the senses. The senses tell you about what is shifting and impermanent, whereas the knowledge gained by reason is of things which are eternal and unchanging (the forms). In the allegory of the cave at the beginning of *Republic* Book Seven, he compares humans who rely on their senses to prisoners watching shadows on the wall of the cave where they are imprisoned. Here is his description, which is worth quoting at some length:

> Behold! human beings housed in an underground cave, which has a long entrance open towards the light and as wide as the interior of the cave; here they have been from their childhood, and have their legs and necks chained, so that they cannot move and can only see before them, being prevented by the chains from turning round their heads. Above and behind them a fire is blazing at a distance, and between the fire and the prisoners there is a raised way; and you will see, if you look, a low wall built along the way, like the screen which marionette players have in front of them, over which they show the puppets.
>
> I see.
>
> And do you see, I said, men passing along the wall carrying all sorts of vessels, and statues and figures of animals made of wood and stone and various materials, which appear over the wall? While carrying their burdens, some of them, as you would expect, are talking, others silent.
>
> You have shown me a strange image, and they are strange prisoners.
>
> Like ourselves, I replied; for in the first place do you think they have seen anything of themselves, and of one another, except the shadows which the fire throws on the opposite wall of the cave?
>
> How could they do so, he asked, if throughout their lives they were never allowed to move their heads?
>
> And of the objects which are being carried in like manner they would only see the shadows?

Yes, he said.

And if they were able to converse with one another, would they not suppose that the things they saw were the real things?

Very true.

And suppose further that the prison had an echo which came from the other side, would they not be sure to fancy when one of the passers-by spoke that the voice which they heard came from the passing shadow?

No question, he replied.

To them, I said, the truth would be literally nothing but the shadows of the images.

That is certain.

The charioteer

In the struggle between reason, which is searching for knowledge, and the appetites or desires which distract it from the search, there is also a third player – that part of our nature which is spirited and passionate. This third part of the soul has the potential for good or evil, and can be enlisted as an ally either by the reason or the appetites. In the *Republic* an analogy is drawn between these three parts of the soul and the three classes in Plato's ideal state – the rulers, the warriors or guardians, and the remainder of the population.

We might also compare Plato's picture of the soul with that of Freud. Freud's soul too is in three parts: the ego, the id, and the superego. The superego more or less corresponds to Plato's reason, and the id to Plato's appetites. Unlike Plato, Freud believes it is harmful to suppress the appetites, so his ego represents a compromise between the ideal proposed by the superego and the demands of the appetites.

Appetites, for Freud, are like a mountain stream: obstruct it in one place, and it will overflow more damagingly somewhere else. For Plato, an appetite grows with what it feeds on, and is therefore best not fed at all.

Here, from the *Phaedrus*, is Plato's picture of the soul as a charioteer (the reason) driving two winged horses – one of them ruly, one unruly. The unruly horse represents the appetites. The charioteer is trying to drive in the realm of the gods, high in the heavens; the appetites and desires are forever dragging the chariot back down to earth.

> Now the horses and the charioteers of the gods are all of them noble and of noble descent, but those of other races are mixed. First, you must know that the human charioteer drives a pair; and next, that one of his horses is noble and of noble breed, and the other is ignoble and of ignoble breed; ... [the soul] which follows god best and is likest to him lifts the head of the charioteer into the outer world, and is carried round in the revolution, troubled indeed by the steeds, and with difficulty beholding true being; while another only rises and falls, and sees, and again fails to see by reason of the unruliness of the steeds. The rest of the souls are also longing after the upper world and they all follow, but not being strong enough they are carried round below the surface, plunging, treading on one another, each striving to be first; and there is confusion and perspiration and the extremity of effort; and many of them are lamed or have their wings broken through the ill driving of the charioteers ...

The shipowner

Plato had a strong antipathy to democracy – democracy in Athens being very different from what we call democracy. An Athenian would not have regarded our societies as democracies, because our political decisions are not taken by the people. They did have a useful word (*isonomia*: equality of rights) for societies like ours, but for some reason we do not use it. In Athens decisions *were* taken by the Athenian people. The assembly (of adult males) met four times a month, and voted on all major issues. There are some advantages to this system (you cannot take a country to war against the wishes of its people), but not when decisions are made in haste and coloured by emotion.

Briefly, Athens lost a war it was impossible for them to lose by twice allowing the fleet on which they depended for survival to be destroyed. In each case the destruction was a result of a bad decision by the Athenian assembly. First they sent out a major expedition to Sicily, when conquering Sicily would not have helped them to defeat the Spartans. And after (surprisingly) recovering from the disaster which befell this expedition, they took it into their heads to put all their military commanders – or as many of them as they could lay their hands on – to death. Shortly afterwards their remaining fleet was destroyed, through the incompetence of the new commanders. The Athenian democracy also, of course, put Socrates to death – something for which Plato was never going to forgive it.

The trouble with democracy, in his view, is that decisions are made by people with no knowledge.

Here is his picture (*Republic* Book Six) of democracy:

> Imagine then a fleet or a ship in which the owner is
> sailing, and he is taller and stronger than any of the
> crew, but he is a little deaf and has a similar
> infirmity in sight, and his knowledge of navigation
> is not much better. The sailors are quarrelling with
> one another about the steering – everyone is of
> opinion that he has a right to steer, though he has
> never learned the art of navigation and cannot tell
> who taught him or when he learned . . . They throng
> about the owner, begging and praying him to
> commit the helm to them; and if at any time they do
> not prevail, but others are preferred to them, they
> kill the others or throw them overboard . . . Him
> who is their partisan and cleverly aids them in their
> plot for getting the ship out of the owner's hands
> whether by force or persuasion, they compliment
> with the name of sailor, pilot, able seaman . . . but
> that the true pilot must pay attention to the year and
> seasons and sky and stars and winds, and whatever
> else belongs to his art, if he intends to be really
> qualified for the command of a ship – this has never
> seriously entered into their thoughts.

We might reply to Plato that it is not only a
democracy which can make these kinds of mistakes.
Hitler lost World War II in exactly the same way – by
making an unnecessary attack on the Soviet Union, a
country he had no need to attack, and by not trusting
his own generals. So these are mistakes which can be
as easily made by a dictator as by a democracy.

PLATO AND PRACTICAL POLITICS

Plato's approach to politics was in many ways very remote from ours. He had no time for democracy, as we have seen, and his ideal was a set of political arrangements under which nothing would ever change, and everybody would agree about how things should be. By contrast, we assume that people will not agree, and that politics consists of a set of arrangements for what happens when they disagree. We can tolerate disagreement because we have no recent experience of civil war. In ancient Greece, civil war was an ever-present threat, and its avoidance was the first political priority for everybody.

There are, nonetheless, echoes of Plato in modern political theory. The agreement of all classes in society is an idea which resurfaces in John Rawls's *A Theory of Justice*, where a just society is held to be one which is agreed to be just by people who have no idea into what stratum of the society they will be born.

Nor are his ideas always quite as far-fetched as they sound. Take the philosopher-ruler, for example. 'Until philosophers are kings in their cities, or the kings and princes of this world have the spirit and power of philosophy . . . and those commoner natures who pursue either to the exclusion of the other are compelled to stand aside, cities will never have rest from their evils – no, nor the human race, as I believe – and then only will this our ideal state have a possibility of life and behold the light of day.' (*Republic* Book Five)

Such was Plato's ideal of the philosopher-ruler. He thinks it sounds far-fetched, though he did make one attempt to realise his ideal. In 367 BCE, at the age of sixty, he went to Syracuse in Sicily, having been invited to come and tutor the young ruler, Dionysius II. As it turned out, Dionysius failed to qualify on either count, having not the slightest talent either for philosophy or for ruling.

We too find the idea of the philosopher-ruler far-fetched. And yet, 500 years after Plato, the emperor Marcus Aurelius did show a talent for both. He was a Stoic philosopher of some note, and a just, competent and energetic emperor. The historian Gibbon described the Roman Empire under his rule as 'the period in the history of the world, during which the condition of the human race was most happy and prosperous'.

TOM GRIFFITH

Key dates

469 BCE   Socrates born

431 BCE   The Peloponnesian War begins between Athens and Sparta, and continues for 27 years

427 BCE   Plato born

415 BCE   Athens sends a major expedition to Sicily

413 BCE   Loss of the Athenian expedition to Sicily

404 BCE   Athens (again) loses her fleet. She surrenders to Sparta. Establishment of a pro-Spartan oligarchy (the Thirty Tyrants)

403 BCE   The oligarchy is overthrown, and democracy restored

399 BCE   Socrates put to death by the Athenians

387 BCE   Plato founds the Academy

367 BCE   Plato's first visit to Dionysius, tyrant of Syracuse

361 BCE   Plato's second visit to Dionysius, tyrant of Syracuse

347 BCE   Plato dies

Further reading

Aristotle, *Ethics*

Aristotle, *Politics*

Berkeley, *Treatise Concerning the Principles of Human Knowledge*

Descartes, *Discourse on Method*

Hegel, *The Philosophy of Right*

Hobbes, *Leviathan*

Hume, *A Treatise of Human Nature*

Locke, *Essay Concerning Human Understanding*

Plato, *Symposium*

Plato, *Apology*

Popper, *The Open Society and Its Enemies*

Note: Standard editions of these books are available in most larger public libraries and also in college bookshops. Most titles are also available in recent paperback editions.

PROTAGORAS

PROTAGORAS

Persons of the dialogue
SOCRATES, *who is the narrator of the dialogue*
   to his companion
HIPPOCRATES, ALCIBIADES *and* CRITIAS
PROTAGORAS, HIPPIAS *and* PRODICUS (*sophists*)
CALLIAS, *a wealthy Athenian*
SCENE: *The house of Callias*

COMPANION: Where do you come from, Socrates?
And yet I need hardly ask the question, for I know that
you have been in chase of the fair Alcibiades. I saw him
the day before yesterday; and he had got a beard like a
man – and he is a man, as I may tell you in your ear.
But I thought that he was still very charming.
SOCRATES: What of his beard? Are you not of Homer's
opinion, who says 'Youth is most charming when the
beard first appears'? And that is now the charm of
Alcibiades.
COMPANION: Well, and how do matters proceed? Have
you been visiting him, and was he gracious to you?
SOCRATES: Yes, I thought that he was very gracious;
and especially today, for I have just come from him,
and he has been helping me in an argument. But shall
I tell you a strange thing? I paid no attention to him,
and several times I quite forgot that he was present.
COMPANION: What is the meaning of this? Has anything happened between you and him? For surely you
cannot have discovered a fairer love than he is;
certainly not in this city of Athens.

SOCRATES: Yes, much fairer.

COMPANION: What do you mean – a citizen or a foreigner?

SOCRATES: A foreigner.

COMPANION: Of what country?

SOCRATES: Of Abdera.

COMPANION: And is this stranger really in your opinion a fairer love than the son of Cleinias?

SOCRATES: And is not the wiser always the fairer, sweet friend?

COMPANION: But have you really met, Socrates, with some wise one?

SOCRATES: Say rather, with the wisest of all living men, if you are willing to accord that title to Protagoras.

COMPANION: What! Is Protagoras in Athens?

SOCRATES: Yes; he has been here two days.

COMPANION: And do you just come from an interview with him?

SOCRATES: Yes; and I have heard and said many things.

COMPANION: Then, if you have no engagement, suppose that you sit down and tell me what passed, and my attendant here shall give up his place to you.

SOCRATES: To be sure; and I shall be grateful to you for listening.

COMPANION: Thank you, too, for telling us.

SOCRATES: That is thank you twice over. Listen then: Last night, or rather very early this morning, Hippocrates, the son of Apollodorus and the brother of Phason, gave a tremendous thump with his staff at my door; some one opened to him, and he came rushing in and bawled out: Socrates, are you awake or asleep? I knew his voice, and said: Hippocrates, is that you? And do you bring any news?

Good news, he said; nothing but good.

Delightful, I said; but what is the news? And why have you come hither at this unearthly hour?

He drew nearer to me and said: Protagoras is come.

Yes, I replied; he came two days ago: have you only just heard of his arrival?

Yes, by the gods, he said; but not until yesterday evening. At the same time he felt for the truckle-bed, and sat down at my feet, and then he said: Yesterday quite late in the evening, on my return from Oenoe whither I had gone in pursuit of my runaway slave Satyrus, as I meant to have told you, if some other matter had not come in the way; on my return, when we had done supper and were about to retire to rest, my brother said to me: Protagoras is come. I was going to you at once, and then I thought that the night was far spent. But the moment sleep left me after my fatigue, I got up and came hither direct.

I, who knew the very courageous madness of the man, said: What is the matter? Has Protagoras robbed you of anything?

He replied, laughing: Yes, indeed he has, Socrates, of the wisdom which he keeps from me.

But, surely, I said, if you give him money, and make friends with him, he will make you as wise as he is himself.

Would to heaven, he replied, that this were the case! He might take all that I have, and all that my friends have, if he pleased. But that is why I have come to you now, in order that you may speak to him on my behalf; for I am young, and also I have never seen nor heard him; (when he visited Athens before I was but a child); and all men praise him, Socrates; he is reputed to be the most accomplished of speakers. There is no reason why we should not go to him at once, and then we shall find him at home. He lodges, as I hear, with Callias the son of Hipponicus: let us start.

I replied: Not yet, my good friend; the hour is too early. But let us rise and take a turn in the court and wait about there until daybreak; when the day breaks, then we will go. For Protagoras is generally at home, and we shall be sure to find him; never fear. Upon this we got up and walked about in the court, and I thought that I would make trial of the strength of his resolution. So I examined him and put questions to him. Tell me, Hippocrates, I said, as you are going to Protagoras, and will be paying your money to him, what is he to whom you are going, and what will he make of you? If, for example, you had thought of going to Hippocrates of Cos, the Asclepiad, and were about to give him your money, and someone had said to you: 'You are paying money to your namesake Hippocrates, O Hippocrates; tell me, what is he that you give him money?' how would you have answered?

I should say, he replied, that I gave money to him as a physician.

And what will he make of you?

A physician, he said.

And if you were resolved to go to Polycleitus the Argive, or Pheidias the Athenian, and were intending to give them money, and some one had asked you: 'What are Polycleitus and Pheidias, and why do you give them this money?' how would you have answered?

I should have answered, that they were statuaries.

And what will they make of you?

A statuary, of course.

Well now, I said, you and I are going to Protagoras, and we are ready to pay him money on your behalf. If our own means are sufficient, and we can gain him with these, we shall be only too glad; but if not, then we are to spend the money of your friends as well. Now suppose, that while we are thus enthusiastically pursuing our object someone were to say to us: 'Tell me, Socrates, and you Hippocrates, what is Protagoras, and why are you going to pay him money?' how should we answer? I know that Pheidias is a sculptor, and that Homer is a poet; but what appellation is given to Protagoras? How is he designated?

They call him a sophist, Socrates, he replied.

Then we are going to pay our money to him in the character of a sophist?

Certainly.

But suppose a person were to ask this further question: And how about yourself? What will Protagoras make of you, if you go to see him?

He answered, with a blush upon his face (for the day was just beginning to dawn, so that I could see him): Unless this differs in some way from the former instances, I suppose that he will make a sophist of me.

By the gods, I said, and are you not ashamed at having to appear before the Hellenes in the character of a sophist?

Indeed, Socrates, to confess the truth, I am.

But you should not assume, Hippocrates, that the instruction of Protagoras is of this nature: may you not learn of him in the same way that you learned the arts of the grammarian, or musician, or trainer, not with the view of making any of them a profession, but only as a part of education, and because a private gentleman and freeman ought to know them?

Just so, he said; and that, in my opinion, is a far truer account of the teaching of Protagoras.

I said: I wonder whether you know what you are doing?

And what am I doing?

You are going to commit your soul to the care of a man whom you call a sophist. And yet I hardly think that you know what a sophist is; and if not, then you do not even know to whom you are committing your soul and whether the thing to which you commit yourself be good or evil.

I certainly think that I do know, he replied.

Then tell me, what do you imagine that he is?

I take him to be one who knows wise things, he replied, as his name implies.

And might you not, I said, affirm this of the painter and of the carpenter also? Do not they, too, know wise things? But suppose a person were to ask us: in what are the painters wise? We should answer: in what relates to the making of likenesses, and similarly of other things. And if he were further to ask: what is the wisdom of the sophist, and what is the manufacture over which he presides? how should we answer him?

How should we answer him, Socrates? What other answer could there be but that he presides over the art which makes men eloquent?

Yes, I replied, that is very likely true, but not enough; for in the answer a further question is involved: of what does the sophist make a man talk eloquently? The player on the lyre may be supposed to make a man talk eloquently about that which he makes him understand, that is about playing the lyre. Is not that true?

Yes.

Then about what does the sophist make him eloquent? Must not he make him eloquent in that which he understands?

Yes, that may be assumed.

And what is that which the sophist knows and makes his disciple know?

Indeed, he said, I cannot tell.

Then I proceeded to say: Well, but are you aware of the danger which you are incurring? If you were going to commit your body to someone who might do good or harm to it, would you not carefully consider and ask the opinion of your friends and kindred, and deliberate many days as to whether you should give him the care of your body? But when the soul is in question, which you hold to be of far more value than the body, and upon the good or evil of which depends the well-being of your all – about this you never consulted either with your father or with your brother or with any one of us who are your companions. But no sooner does this foreigner appear, than you instantly commit your soul to his keeping. In the evening, as you say, you hear of him, and in the morning you go to him, never deliberating or taking the opinion of anyone as to whether you ought to entrust yourself to him or not; you have quite made up your mind that you will at all hazards be a pupil of Protagoras, and are prepared to expend all the property of yourself and of your friends in carrying out at any price this determination, although, as you admit, you do not know him, and have never spoken with him: and you call him a sophist, but are manifestly ignorant of what a sophist is; and yet you are going to commit yourself to his keeping.

When he heard me say this, he replied: No other inference, Socrates, can be drawn from your words.

I proceeded: Is not a sophist, Hippocrates, one who deals wholesale or retail in the food of the soul? To me that appears to be his nature.

And what, Socrates, is the food of the soul?

Surely, I said, knowledge is the food of the soul; and we must take care, my friend, that the sophist does not deceive us when he praises what he sells, like the dealers wholesale or retail who sell the food of the body; for they praise indiscriminately all their goods, without knowing what are really beneficial or hurtful: neither do their customers know, with the exception of any trainer or physician who may happen to buy of them. In like manner those who carry about the wares of knowledge, and make the round of the cities, and sell or retail them to any customer who is in want of them, praise them all alike; though I should not wonder, O my friend, if many of them were really ignorant of their effect upon the soul; and their customers equally ignorant, unless he who buys of them happens to be a physician of the soul. If, therefore, you have understanding of what is good and evil, you may safely buy knowledge of Protagoras or of anyone; but if not, then, O my friend, pause, and do not hazard your dearest interests at a game of chance. For there is far greater peril in buying knowledge than in buying meat and drink: the one you purchase of the wholesale or retail dealer, and carry them away in other vessels, and before you receive them into the body as food, you may deposit them at home and call in any experienced friend who knows what is good to be eaten or drunken, and what not, and how much, and when; and then the danger of purchasing them is not so great. But you cannot buy the wares of knowledge and carry them away in another vessel; when you have paid for them you must receive them into the soul and go your way, either greatly harmed or greatly benefited; and therefore we should deliberate and take counsel with our elders; for we are still young – too young to determine such a matter.

And now let us go, as we were intending, and hear Protagoras; and when we have heard what he has to say, we may take counsel of others; for not only is Protagoras at the house of Callias, but there is Hippias of Elis, and, if I am not mistaken, Prodicus of Ceos, and several other wise men. To this we agreed, and proceeded on our way until we reached the vestibule of the house; and there we stopped in order to conclude a discussion which had arisen between us as we were going along; and we stood talking in the vestibule until we had finished and come to an understanding. And I think that the doorkeeper, who was a eunuch, and who was probably annoyed at the great inroad of the sophists, must have heard us talking. At any rate, when we knocked at the door, and he opened and saw us, he grumbled: They are sophists – he is not at home; and instantly gave the door a hearty bang with both his hands.

Again we knocked, and he answered without opening: Did you not hear me say that he is not at home, fellows?

But, my friend, I said, you need not be alarmed; for we are not sophists, and we are not come to see Callias, but we want to see Protagoras; and I must request you to announce us. At last, after a good deal of difficulty, the man was persuaded to open the door.

When we entered, we found Protagoras taking a walk in the cloister; and next to him, on one side, were walking Callias, the son of Hipponicus, and Paralus, the son of Pericles, who, by the mother's side, is his half-brother, and Charmides, the son of Glaucon. On the other side of him were Xanthippus, the other son of Pericles, Philippides, the son of Philomelus; also Antimoerus of Mende, who of all the disciples of Protagoras is the most famous, and intends to make sophistry his profession. A train of listeners followed him; the greater part of them appeared to be foreigners, whom Protagoras had brought with him out of the various cities visited by him in his journeys, he, like Orpheus, attracting them his voice, and they following. I should mention also that there were some Athenians in the company. Nothing delighted me more than the precision of their movements: they never got into his way at all; but when he and those who were with him turned back, then the band of listeners parted regularly on either side; he was always in front, and they wheeled round and took their places behind him in perfect order. After him, as Homer says, 'I lifted up my eyes and saw' Hippias the Elean sitting in the opposite cloister on a chair of state, and around him were seated on benches Eryximachus, the son of Acumenus, and Phaedrus the Myrrhinusian, and Andron the son of Androtion, and there were strangers whom he had brought with him from his native city of Elis, and some others: they were putting to Hippias certain physical and astronomical questions, and he, ex cathedra, was determining their several questions to them, and discoursing of them.

Also, 'my eyes beheld Tantalus', for Prodicus the Cean was at Athens: he had been lodged in a room which, in the days of Hipponicus, was a storehouse; but, as the house was full, Callias had cleared this out and made the room into a guest-chamber. Now Prodicus was still in bed, wrapped up in sheepskins and bedclothes, of which there seemed to be a great heap; and there was sitting by him on the couches near, Pausanias of the deme of Cerameis, and with Pausanias was a youth quite young, who is certainly remarkable for his good looks, and, if I am not mistaken, is also of a fair and gentle nature. I thought that I heard him called Agathon, and my suspicion is that he is the beloved of Pausanias. There was this youth, and also there were the two Adeimantuses, one the son of Cepis, and the other of Leucolophides, and some others. I was very anxious to hear what Prodicus was saying, for he seems to me to be an all-wise and inspired man; but I was not able to get into the inner circle, and his fine deep voice made an echo in the room which rendered his words inaudible. No sooner had we entered than there followed us Alcibiades the beautiful, as you say, and I believe you; and also Critias the son of Callaeschrus. On entering we stopped a little, in order to look about us, and then walked up to Protagoras, and I said: Protagoras, my friend Hippocrates and I have come to see you.

Do you wish, he said, to speak with me alone, or in the presence of the company?

Whichever you please, I said; you shall determine when you have heard the purpose of our visit.

And what is your purpose? he said.

I must explain, I said, that my friend Hippocrates is a native Athenian; he is the son of Apollodorus, and of a great and prosperous house, and he is himself in natural ability quite a match for anybody of his own age. I believe that he aspires to political eminence; and this he thinks that conversation with you is most likely to procure for him. And now you can determine whether you would wish to speak to him of your teaching alone or in the presence of the company.

Thank you, Socrates, for your consideration of me. For certainly a stranger finding his way into great cities, and persuading the flower of the youth in them to leave company of their kinsmen or any other acquaintances, old or young, and live with him, under the idea that they will be improved by his conversation, ought to be very cautious; great jealousies are aroused by his proceedings, and he is the subject of many enmities and conspiracies. Now the art of the sophist is, as I believe, of great antiquity; but in ancient times those who practised it, fearing this odium, veiled and disguised themselves under various names, some under that of poets, as Homer, Hesiod, and Simonides, some, of hierophants and prophets, as Orpheus and Musaeus, and some, as I observe, even under the name of gymnastic-masters, like Iccus of Tarentum, or the more recently celebrated Herodicus, now of Selymbria and formerly of Megara, who is a first-rate sophist. Your own Agathocles pretended to be a musician, but was really an eminent sophist; also Pythocleides the Cean; and there were many others; and all of them, as I was saying, adopted these arts as veils or disguises because they were afraid of the odium which they would incur. But that is not my way, for I do not believe that they effected their purpose, which was to deceive the government, who were not blinded by them; and as to the people, they have no understanding, and only repeat what their rulers are pleased to tell them. Now to run away, and to be caught in running away, is the very height of folly, and also greatly increases the exasperation of mankind; for they regard him who runs away as a rogue, in addition to any other objections which they have to him; and therefore I take an entirely opposite course, and acknowledge myself to be a sophist and instructor of mankind; such an open acknowledgement appears to me to be a better sort of caution than concealment. Nor do I neglect other precautions, and therefore I hope, as I may say, by the favour of heaven that no harm will come of the acknowledgment that I am a sophist. And I have been now many years in the profession – for all my years when added up are many: there is no one here present of whom I might not be the father. Wherefore I should much prefer conversing with you, if you want to speak with me, in the presence of the company.

As I suspected that he would like to have a little display and glorification in the presence of Prodicus and Hippias, and would gladly show us to them in the light of his admirers, I said: But why should we not summon Prodicus and Hippias and their friends to hear us?

Very good, he said.

Suppose, said Callias, that we hold a council in which you may sit and discuss. This was agreed upon, and great delight was felt at the prospect of hearing wise men talk; we ourselves took the chairs and benches, and arranged them by Hippias, where the other benches had been already placed. Meanwhile Callias and Alcibiades got Prodicus out of bed and brought in him and his companions.

When we were all seated, Protagoras said: Now that the company are assembled, Socrates, tell me about the young man of whom you were just now speaking.

I replied: I will begin again at the same point, Protagoras, and tell you once more the purport of my visit: this is my friend Hippocrates, who is desirous of making your acquaintance; he would like to know what will happen to him if he associates with you. I have no more to say.

Protagoras answered: Young man, if you associate with me, on the very first day you will return home a better man than you came, and better on the second day than on the first, and better every day than you were on the day before.

When I heard this, I said: Protagoras, I do not at all wonder at hearing you say this; even at your age, and with all your wisdom, if anyone were to teach you what you did not know before, you would become better no doubt: but please to answer in a different way – I will explain how by an example. Let me suppose that Hippocrates, instead of desiring your acquaintance, wished to become acquainted with the young man Zeuxippus of Heraclea, who has lately been in Athens, and he had come to him as he has come to you, and had heard him say, as he has heard you say, that every day he would grow and become better if he associated with him: and then suppose that he were to ask him, 'In what shall I become better, and in what shall I grow?' – Zeuxippus would answer, 'In painting.' And suppose that he went to Orthagoras the Theban, and heard him say the same thing, and asked him, 'In what shall I become better day by day?' he would reply, 'In flute-playing.' Now I want you to make the same sort of answer to this young man and to me, who am asking questions on his account. When you say that on the first day on which he associates with you he will return home a better man, and on every day will grow in like manner – in what, Protagoras, will he be better, and about what?

When Protagoras heard me say this, he replied: You ask questions fairly, and I like to answer a question which is fairly put. If Hippocrates comes to me he will not experience the sort of drudgery with which other sophists are in the habit of insulting their pupils; who, when they have just escaped from the arts, are taken and driven back into them by these teachers, and made to learn calculation, and astronomy, and geometry, and music (he gave a look at Hippias as he said this); but if he comes to me, he will learn that which he comes to learn. And this is prudence in affairs private as well as public; he will learn to order his own house in the best manner, and he will be able to speak and act for the best in the affairs of the state.

Do I understand you, I said; and is your meaning that you teach the art of politics, and that you promise to make men good citizens?

That, Socrates, is exactly the profession which I make.

Then, I said, you do indeed possess a noble art, if there is no mistake about this; for I will freely confess to you, Protagoras, that I have a doubt whether this art is capable of being taught, and yet I know not how to disbelieve your assertion. And I ought to tell you why I am of opinion that this art cannot be taught or communicated by man to man. I say that the Athenians are an understanding people, and indeed they are esteemed to be such by the other Hellenes. Now I observe that when we are met together in the assembly, and the matter in hand relates to building, the builders are summoned as advisers; when the question is one of shipbuilding, then the shipwrights; and the like of other arts which they think capable of being taught and learned. And if some person offers to give them advice who is not supposed by them to have any skill in the art, even though he be good-looking, and rich, and noble, they will not listen to him, but laugh and hoot at him, until either he is clamoured down and retires of himself; or if he persist, he is dragged away or put out by the constables at the command of the prytanes. This is their way of behaving about professors of the arts. But when the question is an affair of state, then everybody is free to have a say – carpenter, tinker, cobbler, sailor, passenger; rich and poor, high and low – anyone who likes gets up, and no one reproaches him, as in the former case, with not having learned, and having no teacher, and yet giving advice; evidently because they are under the impression that this sort of knowledge cannot be taught. And not only is this true of the state, but of individuals; the best and wisest of our citizens are unable to impart their political wisdom to others: as for example, Pericles, the father of these young men, who gave them excellent instruction in all that could be learned from masters, in his own department of politics neither taught them, nor gave them teachers; but they were allowed to wander at their own free will in a sort of hope that they would light upon virtue of their own accord. Or take another example: there was Cleinias the younger brother of our friend Alcibiades, of whom this very same Pericles was the guardian; and he being in fact under the apprehension that Cleinias would be corrupted by Alcibiades, took him away, and placed him in the house of Ariphron to be educated; but before six months had elapsed, Ariphron sent him back, not knowing what to do with him. And I could mention numberless other instances of persons who were good themselves, and never yet made anyone else good, whether friend or stranger. Now I, Protagoras, having these examples before me, am inclined to think that virtue cannot be taught. But then again, when I listen to your words, I waver; and am disposed to think that there must be something in what you say, because I know that you have great experience, and learning, and invention. And I wish that you would, if possible, show me a little more clearly that virtue can be taught. Will you be so good?

That I will, Socrates, and gladly. But what would you like? Shall I, as an elder, speak to you as younger men in an apologue or myth, or shall I argue out the question?

To this several of the company answered that he should choose for himself.

Well, then, he said, I think that the myth will be more interesting. Once upon a time there were gods only, and no mortal creatures. But when the time came that these also should be created, the gods fashioned them out of earth and fire and various mixtures of both elements in the interior of the earth; and when they were about to bring them into the light of day, they ordered Prometheus and Epimetheus to equip them, and to distribute to them severally their proper qualities. Epimetheus said to Prometheus: 'Let me distribute, and do you inspect.' This was agreed, and Epimetheus made the distribution. There were some to whom he gave strength without swiftness, while he equipped the weaker with swiftness; some he armed, and others he left unarmed; and devised for the latter some other means of preservation, making some large, and having their size as a protection, and others small, whose nature was to fly in the air or burrow in the ground; this was to be their way of escape. Thus did he compensate them with the view of preventing any race from becoming extinct. And when he had provided against their destruction by one another, he contrived also a means of protecting them against the seasons of heaven; clothing them with close hair and thick skins sufficient to defend them against the winter cold and able to resist the summer heat, so that they might have a natural bed of their own when they wanted to rest; also he furnished them with hoofs and hair and hard and callous skins under their feet. Then he gave them varieties of food – herb of the soil to some, to others fruits of trees, and to others roots, and to some again he gave other animals as food. And some he made to have few young ones, while those who were their prey were very prolific; and in this manner the race was preserved.

Thus did Epimetheus; who, not being very wise, forgot that he had distributed among the brute animals all the qualities which he had to give – and when he came to man, who was still unprovided, he was terribly perplexed. Now while he was in this perplexity, Prometheus came to inspect the distribution, and he found that the other animals were suitably furnished, but that man alone was naked and shoeless, and had neither bed nor arms of defence. The appointed hour was approaching when man in his turn was to go forth into the light of day; and Prometheus, not knowing how he could devise his salvation, stole the mechanical arts of Hephaestus and Athene, and fire with them (they could neither have been acquired nor used without fire), and gave them to man. Thus man had the wisdom necessary to the support of life, but political wisdom he had not; for that was in the keeping of Zeus, and the power of Prometheus did not extend to entering into the citadel of heaven, where Zeus dwelt, who moreover had terrible sentinels; but he did enter by stealth into the common workshop of Athene and Hephaestus, in which they used to practise their favourite arts, and carried off Hephaestus' art of working by fire, and also the art of Athene, and gave them to man. And in this way man was supplied with the means of life. But Prometheus is said to have been afterwards prosecuted for theft, owing to the blunder of Epimetheus.

Now man, having a share of the divine attributes, was at first the only one of the animals who had any gods, because he alone was of their kindred; and he would raise altars and images of them. He was not long in inventing articulate speech and names; and he also constructed houses and clothes and shoes and beds, and drew sustenance from the earth. Thus provided, mankind at first lived dispersed, and there were no cities. But the consequence was that they were destroyed by the wild beasts, for they were utterly weak in comparison of them, and their art was only sufficient to provide them with the means of life, and did not enable them to carry on war against the animals: food they had, but not as yet the art of government, of which the art of war is a part. After a while the desire of self-preservation gathered them into cities; but when they were gathered together, having no art of government, they evil entreated one another, and were again in process of dispersion and destruction. Zeus feared that the entire race would be exterminated, and so he sent Hermes to them, bearing reverence and justice to be the ordering principles of cities and the bonds of friendship and conciliation. Hermes asked Zeus how he should impart justice and reverence among men: should he distribute them as the arts are distributed; that is to say, to a favoured few only, one skilled individual having enough of medicine or of any other art for many unskilled ones? 'Shall this be the manner in which I am to distribute justice and reverence among men, or shall I give them to all?' 'To all,' said Zeus; 'I should like them all to have a share; for cities cannot exist, if a few only share in the virtues, as in the arts. And further, make a law by my order, that he who has no part in reverence and justice shall be put to death, for he is a plague of the state.'

And this is the reason, Socrates, why the Athenians and mankind in general, when the question relates to carpentering or any other mechanical art, allow but a few to share in their deliberations; and when any one else interferes, then, as you say, they object, if he be not of the favoured few; which, as I reply, is very natural. But when they meet to deliberate about political virtue, which proceeds only by way of justice and wisdom, they are patient enough of any man who speaks of them, as is also natural, because they think that every man ought to share in this sort of virtue, and that states could not exist if this were otherwise. I have explained to you, Socrates, the reason of this phenomenon.

And that you may not suppose yourself to be deceived in thinking that all men regard every man as having a share of justice or honesty and of every other political virtue, let me give you a further proof, which is this. In other cases, as you are aware, if a man says that he is a good flute- player, or skilful in any other art in which he has no skill, people either laugh at him or are angry with him, and his relations think that he is mad and go and admonish him; but when honesty is in question, or some other political virtue, even if they know that he is dishonest, yet, if the man comes publicly forward and tells the truth about his dis- honesty, then, what in the other case was held by them to be good sense, they now deem to be madness. They say that all men ought to profess honesty whether they are honest or not, and that a man is out of his mind who says anything else. Their notion is, that a man must have some degree of honesty; and that if he has none at all he ought not to be in the world.

I have been showing that they are right in admitting every man as a counsellor about this sort of virtue, as they are of opinion that every man is a partaker of it. And I will now endeavour to show further that they do not conceive this virtue to be given by nature, or to grow spontaneously, but to be a thing which may be taught, and which comes to a man by taking pains. No one would instruct, no one would rebuke, or be angry with those whose calamities they suppose to be due to nature or chance; they do not try to punish or to prevent them from being what they are; they do but pity them. Who is so foolish as to chastise or instruct the ugly, or the diminutive, or the feeble? And for this reason: because he knows that good and evil of this kind is the work of nature and of chance; whereas if a man is wanting in those good qualities which are attained by study and exercise and teaching, and has only the contrary evil qualities, other men are angry with him, and punish and reprove him. Of these evil qualities one is impiety, another injustice, and they may be described generally as the very opposite of political virtue. In such cases any man will be angry with another, and reprimand him – clearly because he thinks that by study and learning, the virtue in which the other is deficient may be acquired.

If you will think, Socrates, of the nature of punishment, you will see at once that in the opinion of mankind virtue may be acquired; no one punishes the evil-doer under the notion, or for the reason, that he has done wrong – only the unreasonable fury of a beast acts in that manner. But he who desires to inflict rational punishment does not retaliate for a past wrong which cannot be undone; he has regard to the future, and is desirous that the man who is punished, and he who sees him punished, may be deterred from doing wrong again. He punishes for the sake of prevention, thereby clearly implying that virtue is capable of being taught. This is the notion of all who retaliate upon others either privately or publicly. And the Athenians, too, your own citizens, like other men, punish and take vengeance on all whom they regard as evil-doers; and hence, we may infer them to be of the number of those who think that virtue may be acquired and taught. Thus far, Socrates, I have shown you clearly enough, if I am not mistaken, that your countrymen are right in admitting the tinker and the cobbler to advise about politics, and also that they deem virtue to be capable of being taught and acquired.

There yet remains one difficulty which has been raised by you about the sons of good men. What is the reason why good men teach their sons the knowledge which is gained from teachers, and make them wise in that, but do nothing towards improving them in the virtues which distinguish themselves? And here, Socrates, I will leave the apologue and resume the argument. Please to consider: is there or is there not some one quality of which all the citizens must be partakers, if there is to be a city at all? In the answer to this question is contained the only solution of your difficulty; there is no other. For if there be any such quality, and this quality or unity is not the art of the carpenter, or the smith, or the potter, but justice

and temperance and holiness and, in a word, manly
virtue – if this is the quality of which all men must be
partakers, and which is the very condition of their
learning or doing anything else, and if he who is
wanting in this, whether he be a child only or a grown-
up man or woman, must be taught and punished,
until by punishment he becomes better, and he who
rebels against instruction and punishment is either
exiled or condemned to death under the idea that he
is incurable – if what I am saying be true, good men
have their sons taught other things and not this, do
consider how extraordinary their conduct would
appear to be. For we have shown that they think
virtue capable of being taught and cultivated both in
private and public; and, notwithstanding, they have
their sons taught lesser matters, ignorance of which
does not involve the punishment of death: but greater
things, of which the ignorance may cause death and
exile to those who have no training or knowledge of
them – aye, and confiscation as well as death, and,
in a word, may be the ruin of families – those things,
I say, they are supposed not to teach them – not to
take the utmost care that they should learn. How
improbable is this, Socrates!

Education and admonition commence in the first
years of childhood, and last to the very end of life.
Mother and nurse and father and tutor are vying with
one another about the improvement of the child as
soon as ever he is able to understand what is being said
to him: he cannot say or do anything without their
setting forth to him that this is just and that is unjust;
this is honourable, that is dishonourable; this is holy,
that is unholy; do this and abstain from that. And if he
obeys, well and good; if not, he is straightened by

threats and blows, like a piece of bent or warped wood. At a later stage they send him to teachers, and enjoin them to see to his manners even more than to his reading and music; and the teachers do as they are desired. And when the boy has learned his letters and is beginning to understand what is written, as before he understood only what was spoken, they put into his hands the works of great poets, which he reads sitting on a bench at school; in these are contained many admonitions, and many tales, and praises, and encomia of ancient famous men, which he is required to learn by heart, in order that he may imitate or emulate them and desire to become like them. Then, again, the teachers of the lyre take similar care that their young disciple is temperate and gets into no mischief; and when they have taught him the use of the lyre, they introduce him to the poems of other excellent poets, who are the lyric poets; and these they set to music, and make their harmonies and rhythms quite familiar to the children's souls, in order that they may learn to be more gentle, and harmonious, and rhythmical, and so more fitted for speech and action; for the life of man in every part has need of harmony and rhythm. Then they send them to the master of gymnastic, in order that their bodies may better minister to the virtuous mind, and that they may not be compelled through bodily weakness to play the coward in war or on any other occasion.

This is what is done by those who have the means, and those who have the means are the rich; their children begin to go to school soonest and leave off latest. When they have done with masters, the state again compels them to learn the laws, and live after the pattern which they furnish, and not after their own fancies; and just as in learning to write, the writing-master first draws lines with a style for the use of the young beginner, and gives him the tablet and makes him follow the lines, so the city draws the laws, which were the invention of good lawgivers living in the olden time; these are given to the young man, in order to guide him in his conduct whether he is commanding or obeying; and he who transgresses them is to be corrected, or, in other words, called to account, which is a term used not only in your country, but also in many others, seeing that justice calls men to account. Now when there is all this care about virtue private and public, why, Socrates, do you still wonder and doubt whether virtue can be taught? Cease to wonder, for the opposite would be far more surprising.

But why then do the sons of good fathers often turn out ill? There is nothing very wonderful in this; for, as I have been saying, the existence of a state implies that virtue is not any man's private possession. If so – and nothing can be truer – then I will further ask you to imagine, as an illustration, some other pursuit or branch of knowledge which may be assumed equally to be the condition of the existence of a state. Suppose that there could be no state unless we were all flute-players, as far as each had the capacity, and everybody was freely teaching everybody the art, both in private and public, and reproving the bad player as freely and openly as every man now teaches justice and the laws, not concealing them as he would conceal the other arts, but imparting them – for all of us have a mutual interest in the justice and virtue of one another, and this is the reason why everyone is so ready to teach justice and the laws; suppose, I say, that there were the same readiness and liberality among us in teaching

47

one another flute-playing, do you imagine, Socrates, that the sons of good flute-players would be more likely to be good than the sons of bad ones? I think not. Would not their sons grow up to be distinguished or undistinguished according to their own natural capacities as flute-players, and the son of a good player would often turn out to be a bad one, and the son of a bad player to be a good one, and all flute-players would be good enough in comparison of those who were ignorant and unacquainted with the art of flute-playing?

In like manner I would have you consider that he who appears to you to be the worst of those who have been brought up in laws and humanities, would appear to be a just man and a master of justice if he were to be compared with men who had no education, or courts of justice, or laws, or any restraints upon them which compelled them to practise virtue – with the savages, for example, whom the poet Pherecrates exhibited on the stage at the last year's Lenaean festival. If you were living among men such as the man-haters in his chorus, you would be only too glad to meet with Eurybates and Phrynondas, and you would sorrowfully long to revisit the rascality of this part of the world. You, Socrates, are discontented, and why? Because all men are teachers of virtue, each one according to his ability; and you say, Where are the teachers?

You might as well ask, Who teaches Greek? For of that too there will not be any teachers found. Or you might ask, Who is to teach the sons of our artisans this same art which they have learned of their fathers? He and his fellow-workmen have taught them to the best of their ability – but who will carry them further in their arts? And you would certainly have a difficulty, Socrates, in finding a teacher of them; but there would be no difficulty in finding a teacher of those who are wholly ignorant. And this is true of virtue or of anything else; if a man is better able than we are to promote virtue ever so little, we must be content with the result. A teacher of this sort I believe myself to be, and above all other men to have the knowledge which makes a man noble and good; and I give my pupils their money's-worth, and even more, as they themselves confess. And therefore I have introduced the following mode of payment: when a man has been my pupil, if he likes he pays my price, but there is no compulsion; and if he does not like, he has only to go into a temple and take an oath of the value of the instructions, and he pays no more than he declares to be their value.

Such is my apologue, Socrates, and such is the argument by which I endeavour to show that virtue may be taught, and that this is the opinion of the Athenians. And I have also attempted to show that you are not to wonder at good fathers having bad sons, or at good sons having bad fathers, of which the sons of Polycleitus afford an example, who are the companions of our friends here, Paralus and Xanthippus, but are nothing in comparison with their father; and this is true of the sons of many other artists. As yet I ought not to say the same of Paralus and Xanthippus themselves, for they are young and there is still hope of them.

Protagoras ended, and in my ear 'So charming left his voice, that I the while Thought him still speaking; still stood fixed to hear.' At length, when the truth dawned upon me, that he had really finished, not without difficulty I began to collect myself, and looking at Hippocrates, I said to him: O son of Apollodorus, how deeply grateful I am to you for having brought me hither; I would not have missed the speech of Protagoras for a great deal. For I used to imagine that no human care could make men good; but I know better now. Yet I have still one very small difficulty which I am sure that Protagoras will easily explain, as he has already explained so much. If a man were to go and consult Pericles or any of our great speakers about these matters, he might perhaps hear as fine a discourse; but then when one has a question to ask of any of them, like books, they can neither answer nor ask; and if any one challenges the least particular of their speech, they go ringing on in a long harangue, like brazen pots, which when they are struck continue to sound unless some one puts his hand upon them; whereas our friend Protagoras can not only make a good speech, as he has already shown, but when he is asked a question he can answer briefly; and when he asks he will wait and hear the answer; and this is a very rare gift. Now I, Protagoras, want to ask of you a little question, which if you will only answer, I shall be quite satisfied. You were saying that virtue can be taught; that I will take upon your authority, and there is no one to whom I am more ready to trust. But I marvel at one thing about which I should like to have my mind set at rest. You were speaking of Zeus sending justice and reverence to men; and several times while you were speaking, justice, and temperance, and holiness, and all these qualities, were described by you as if together they made up virtue. Now I want you to tell me truly whether virtue is one whole, of which justice and temperance and holiness are parts; or whether all these are only the names of one and the same thing: that is the doubt which still lingers in my mind.

There is no difficulty, Socrates, in answering that the qualities of which you are speaking are the parts of virtue which is one.

And are they parts, I said, in the same sense in which mouth, nose, and eyes, and ears, are the parts of a face; or are they like the parts of gold, which differ from the whole and from one another only in being larger or smaller?

I should say that they differed, Socrates, in the first way; they are related to one another as the parts of a face are related to the whole face.

And do men have some one part and some another part of virtue? Or if a man has one part, must he also have all the others?

By no means, he said; for many a man is brave and not just, or just and not wise.

You would not deny, then, that courage and wisdom are also parts of virtue?

Most undoubtedly they are, he answered; and wisdom is the noblest of the parts.

And they are all different from one another? I said. Yes.

And has each of them a distinct function like the parts of the face; the eye, for example, is not like the ear, and has not the same functions; and the other parts are none of them like one another, either in their functions, or in any other way? I want to know whether the comparison holds concerning the parts of virtue. Do they also differ from one another in themselves and in their functions? For that is clearly what the simile would imply.

Yes, Socrates, you are right in supposing that they differ.

Then, I said, no other part of virtue is like knowledge, or like justice, or like courage, or like temperance, or like holiness?

No, he answered.

Well then, I said, suppose that you and I enquire into their natures. And first, you would agree with me that justice is of the nature of a thing, would you not? That is my opinion: would it not be yours also?

Mine also, he said.

And suppose that some one were to ask us, saying, 'O Protagoras, and you, Socrates, what about this thing which you were calling justice, is it just or unjust?' – and I were to answer, just: would you vote with me or against me?

With you, he said.

Thereupon I should answer to him who asked me, that justice is of the nature of the just: would not you?

Yes, he said.

And suppose that he went on to say: 'Well now, is there also such a thing as holiness?' – we should answer, 'Yes,' if I am not mistaken?

Yes, he said.

Which you would also acknowledge to be a thing – should we not say so?

He assented.

'And is this a sort of thing which is of the nature of the holy, or of the nature of the unholy?' I should be angry at his putting such a question, and should say, 'Peace, man; nothing can be holy if holiness is not holy.' What would you say? Would you not answer in the same way?

Certainly, he said.

And then after this suppose that he came and asked us, 'What were you saying just now? Perhaps I may not have heard you rightly, but you seemed to me to be saying that the parts of virtue were not the same as one another.' I should reply, 'You certainly heard that said, but not, as you imagine, by me; for I only asked the question; Protagoras gave the answer.' And suppose that he turned to you and said, 'Is this true, Protagoras? And do you maintain that one part of virtue is unlike another, and is this your position?' – how would you answer him?

I could not help acknowledging the truth of what he said, Socrates.

Well then, Protagoras, we will assume this; and now supposing that he proceeded to say further, 'Then holiness is not of the nature of justice, nor justice of the nature of holiness, but of the nature of unholiness; and holiness is of the nature of the not just, and therefore of the unjust, and the unjust is the unholy': how shall we answer him? I should certainly answer him on my own behalf that justice is holy, and that holiness is just; and I would say in like manner on your behalf also, if you would allow me, that justice is either the same with holiness, or very nearly the same; and above all I would assert that justice is like holiness and holiness is like justice; and I wish that you would tell me whether I may be permitted to give this answer on your behalf, and whether you would agree with me.

He replied, I cannot simply agree, Socrates, to the proposition that justice is holy and that holiness is just, for there appears to me to be a difference between them. But what matter? If you please I please; and let us assume, if you will I, that justice is holy, and that holiness is just.

Pardon me, I replied; I do not want this 'if you wish' or 'if you will' sort of conclusion to be proven, but I want you and me to be proven: I mean to say that the conclusion will be best proven if there be no 'if'.

Well, he said, I admit that justice bears a resemblance to holiness, for there is always some point of view in which everything is like every other thing; white is in a certain way like black, and hard is like soft, and the most extreme opposites have some qualities in common; even the parts of the face which, as we were saying before, are distinct and have different functions, are still in a certain point of view similar, and one of them is like another of them. And you may prove that they are like one another on the same principle that all things are like one another; and yet things which are like in some particular ought not to be called alike, nor things which are unlike in some particular, however slight, unlike.

And do you think, I said in a tone of surprise, that justice and holiness have but a small degree of likeness?

Certainly not; any more than I agree with what I understand to be your view.

Well, I said, as you appear to have a difficulty about this, let us take another of the examples which you mentioned instead. Do you admit the existence of folly?

I do.

And is not wisdom the very opposite of folly?

That is true, he said.

And when men act rightly and advantageously they seem to you to be temperate?

Yes, he said.

And temperance makes them temperate?

Certainly.

And they who do not act rightly act foolishly, and in acting thus are not temperate?

I agree, he said.

Then to act foolishly is the opposite of acting temperately?

He assented.

And foolish actions are done by folly, and temperate actions by temperance?

He agreed.

And that is done strongly which is done by strength, and that which is weakly done, by weakness?

He assented.

And that which is done with swiftness is done swiftly, and that which is done with slowness, slowly?

He assented again.

And that which is done in the same manner, is done by the same; and that which is done in an opposite manner by the opposite?

He agreed.

Once more, I said, is there anything beautiful?

Yes.

To which the only opposite is the ugly?

There is no other.

And is there anything good?

There is.

To which the only opposite is the evil?

There is no other.

And there is the acute in sound?

True.

To which the only opposite is the grave?

There is no other, he said, but that.

Then every opposite has one opposite only and no more?

He assented.

Then now, I said, let us recapitulate our admissions. First of all we admitted that everything has one opposite and not more than one?

We did so.

And we admitted also that what was done in opposite ways was done by opposites?

Yes.

And that which was done foolishly, as we further admitted, was done in the opposite way to that which was done temperately?

Yes.

And that which was done temperately was done by temperance, and that which was done foolishly by folly?

He agreed.

And that which is done in opposite ways is done by opposites?

Yes.

And one thing is done by temperance, and quite another thing by folly?

Yes.

And in opposite ways?

Certainly.

And therefore by opposites: then folly is the opposite of temperance?

Clearly.

And do you remember that folly has already been acknowledged by us to be the opposite of wisdom?

He assented.

And we said that everything has only one opposite?

Yes.

Then, Protagoras, which of the two assertions shall we renounce? One says that everything has but one opposite; the other that wisdom is distinct from temperance, and that both of them are parts of virtue; and that they are not only distinct, but dissimilar, both in themselves and in their functions, like the parts of a face. Which of these two assertions shall we renounce? For both of them together are certainly not in harmony; they do not accord or agree: for how can they be said to agree if everything is assumed to have only one opposite and not more than one, and yet folly, which is one, has clearly the two opposites – wisdom and temperance? Is not that true, Protagoras? What else would you say?

He assented, but with great reluctance.

Then temperance and wisdom are the same, as before justice and holiness appeared to us to be nearly the same. And now, Protagoras, I said, we must finish the enquiry, and not faint. Do you think that an unjust man can be temperate in his injustice?

I should be ashamed, Socrates, he said, to acknowledge this, which nevertheless many may be found to assert.

And shall I argue with them or with you? I replied.

I would rather, he said, that you should argue with the many first, if you will.

Whichever you please, if you will only answer me and say whether you are of their opinion or not. My object is to test the validity of the argument; and yet the result may be that I who ask and you who answer may both be put on our trial.

Protagoras at first made a show of refusing, as he said that the argument was not encouraging; at length, he consented to answer.

Now then, I said, begin at the beginning and answer me. You think that some men are temperate, and yet unjust?

Yes, he said; let that be admitted.

And temperance is good sense?

Yes.

And good sense is good counsel in doing injustice?

Granted.

If they succeed, I said, or if they do not succeed?

If they succeed.

And you would admit the existence of goods?

Yes.

And is the good that which is expedient for man?

Yes, indeed, he said: and there are some things which may be inexpedient, and yet I call them good.

I thought that Protagoras was getting ruffled and excited; he seemed to be setting himself in an attitude of war. Seeing this, I minded my business, and gently said: When you say, Protagoras, that things inexpedient are good, do you mean inexpedient for man only, or inexpedient altogether? And do you call the latter good?

Certainly not the last, he replied; for I know of many things – meats, drinks, medicines, and ten thousand other things, which are inexpedient for man, and some which are expedient; and some which are neither expedient nor inexpedient for man, but only for horses; and some for oxen only, and some for dogs; and some for no animals, but only for trees; and some for the roots of trees and not for their branches, as for example, manure, which is a good thing when laid about the roots of a tree, but utterly destructive if thrown upon the shoots and young branches; or I may instance olive oil, which is mischievous to all plants, and generally most injurious to the hair of every animal with the exception of man, but beneficial to human hair and to the human body generally; and even in this application (so various and changeable is the nature of the benefit), that which is the greatest good to the outward parts of a man, is a very great evil to his inward parts: and for this reason physicians always forbid their patients the use of oil in their food, except in very small quantities, just enough to extinguish the disagreeable sensation of smell in meats and sauces.

When he had given this answer, the company cheered him. And I said: Protagoras, I have a wretched memory, and when any one makes a long speech to me I never remember what he is talking about. As then, if I had been deaf, and you were going to converse with me, you would have had to raise your voice; so now, having such a bad memory, I will ask you to cut your answers shorter, if you would take me with you.

What do you mean? he said: how am I to shorten my answers? Shall I make them too short?

Certainly not, I said.

But short enough?

Yes, I said.

Shall I answer what appears to me to be short enough, or what appears to you to be short enough?

I have heard, I said, that you can speak and teach others to speak about the same things at such length that words never seemed to fail, or with such brevity that no one could use fewer of them. Please therefore, if you talk with me, to adopt the latter or more compendious method.

Socrates, he replied, many a battle of words have I fought, and if I had followed the method of disputation which my adversaries desired, as you want me to do, I should have been no better than another, and the name of Protagoras would have been nowhere.

I saw that he was not satisfied with his previous answers, and that he would not play the part of

answerer any more if he could help; and I considered
that there was no call upon me to continue the
conversation; so I said: Protagoras, I do not wish to
force the conversation upon you if you had rather not,
but when you are willing to argue with me in such a
way that I can follow you, then I will argue with you.
Now you, as is said of you by others and as you say of
yourself, are able to have discussions in shorter forms
of speech as well as in longer, for you are a master of
wisdom; but I cannot manage these long speeches: I
only wish that I could. You, on the other hand, who
are capable of either, ought to speak shorter as I beg
you, and then we might converse. But I see that you
are disinclined, and as I have an engagement which
will prevent my staying to hear you at greater length
(for I have to be in another place), I will depart;
although I should have liked to have heard you.

Thus I spoke, and was rising from my seat, when
Callias seized me by the right hand, and in his left hand
caught hold of this old cloak of mine. He said: We
cannot let you go, Socrates, for if you leave us there
will be an end of our discussions: I must therefore beg
you to remain, as there is nothing in the world that I
should like better than to hear you and Protagoras
discourse. Do not deny the company this pleasure.

Now I had got up, and was in the act of departure.
Son of Hipponicus, I replied, I have always admired,
and do now heartily applaud and love your philosophical spirit, and I would gladly comply with your
request, if I could. But the truth is that I cannot. And
what you ask is as great an impossibility to me, as if
you bade me run a race with Crison of Himera, when
in his prime, or with some one of the long or day
course runners. To such a request I should reply that

I would fain ask the same of my own legs; but they refuse to comply. And therefore if you want to see Crison and me in the same stadium, you must bid him slacken his speed to mine, for I cannot run quickly, and he can run slowly. And in like manner if you want to hear me and Protagoras discoursing, you must ask him to shorten his answers, and keep to the point, as he did at first; if not, how can there be any discussion? For discussion is one thing, and making an oration is quite another, in my humble opinion.

But you see, Socrates, said Callias, that Protagoras may fairly claim to speak in his own way, just as you claim to speak in yours.

Here Alcibiades interposed, and said: That, Callias, is not a true statement of the case. For our friend Socrates admits that he cannot make a speech – in this he yields the palm to Protagoras: but I should be greatly surprised if he yielded to any living man in the power of holding and apprehending an argument. Now if Protagoras will make a similar admission, and confess that he is inferior to Socrates in argumentative skill, that is enough for Socrates; but if he claims a superiority in argument as well, let him ask and answer – not, when a question is asked, slipping away from the point, and instead of answering, making a speech at such length that most of his hearers forget the question at issue (not that Socrates is likely to forget – I will be bound for that, although he may pretend in fun that he has a bad memory). And Socrates appears to me to be more in the right than Protagoras; that is my view, and every man ought to say what he thinks.

[*after some argument about how the conversation should proceed, there follows a discussion of a passage*

61

*in one of Simondes' poems where the poet talks about
the difficulty of being good; this discussion holds little
interest for the modern reader, and has been omitted;
Socrates then drags a reluctant Protagoras back to the
question-and-answer he had objected to earlier]*

I said: I wish Protagoras either to ask or answer as he
is inclined; but I would rather have done with poems
and odes, if he does not object, and come back to the
question about which I was asking you at first,
Protagoras, and by your help make an end of that.
The talk about the poets seems to me like a commonplace entertainment to which a vulgar company have
recourse; who, because they are not able to converse
or amuse one another, while they are drinking, with
the sound of their own voices and conversation, by
reason of their stupidity, raise the price of flute-girls in
the market, hiring for a great sum the voice of a flute
instead of their own breath, to be the medium of
intercourse among them: but where the company are
real gentlemen and men of education, you will see no
flute-girls, nor dancing- girls, nor harp-girls; and they
have no nonsense or games, but are contented with
one another's conversation, of which their own voices
are the medium, and which they carry on by turns and
in an orderly manner, even though they are very
liberal in their potations. And a company like this of
ours, and men such as we profess to be, do not require
the help of another's voice, or of the poets whom you
cannot interrogate about the meaning of what they
are saying; people who cite them declaring, some that
the poet has one meaning, and others that he has
another, and the point which is in dispute can never
be decided. This sort of entertainment they decline,

and prefer to talk with one another, and put one another to the proof in conversation. And these are the models which I desire that you and I should imitate. Leaving the poets, and keeping to ourselves, let us try the mettle of one another and make proof of the truth in conversation. If you have a mind to ask, I am ready to answer; or if you would rather, do you answer, and give me the opportunity of resuming and completing our unfinished argument.

I made these and some similar observations; but Protagoras would not distinctly say which he would do. Thereupon Alcibiades turned to Callias, and said: Do you think, Callias, that Protagoras is fair in refusing to say whether he will or will not answer? For I certainly think that he is unfair; he ought either to proceed with the argument, or distinctly refuse to proceed, that we may know his intention; and then Socrates will be able to discourse with someone else, and the rest of the company will be free to talk with one another.

I think that Protagoras was really made ashamed by these words of Alcibiades, and when the prayers of Callias and the company were superadded, he was at last induced to argue, and said that I might ask and he would answer.

So I said: Do not imagine, Protagoras, that I have any other interest in asking questions of you but that of clearing up my own difficulties. For I think that Homer was very right in saying that 'When two go together, one sees before the other,' for all men who have a companion are readier in deed, word, or thought; but if a man 'sees a thing when he is alone,' he goes about straightway seeking until he finds someone to whom he may show his discoveries, and who may confirm him in them. And I would rather hold discourse with you than with anyone, because I think that no man has a better understanding of most things which a good man may be expected to understand, and in particular of virtue. For who is there but you? Who not only claim to be a good man and a gentleman, for many are this, and yet have not the power of making others good – whereas you are not only good yourself, but also the cause of goodness in others. Moreover such confidence have you in yourself, that although other sophists conceal their profession, you proclaim in the face of Hellas that you are a sophist or teacher of virtue and education, and are the first who demanded pay in return. How then can I do otherwise than invite you to the examination of these subjects, and ask questions and consult with you? I must, indeed. And I should like once more to have my memory refreshed by you about the questions which I was asking you at first, and also to have your help in considering them. If I am not mistaken, the question was this: are wisdom and temperance and courage and justice and holiness five names of the same thing? Or has each of the names a separate underlying essence and corresponding thing having a peculiar function, no one of them being like any other of them? And you replied that the five names were not the names of the same thing, but that each of them had a separate object, and that all these objects were parts of virtue, not in the same way that the parts of gold are like each other and the whole of which they are parts, but as the parts of the face are unlike the whole of which they are parts and one another, and have each of them a distinct function. I should like to know whether this is still your opinion; or if not, I will ask you to define your meaning, and I shall not take you to task if you now make a different statement. For I dare say that you may have said what you did only in order to make trial of me.

I answer, Socrates, he said, that all these qualities are parts of virtue, and that four out of the five are to some extent similar, and that the fifth of them, which is courage, is very different from the other four, as I prove in this way: you may observe that many men are utterly unrighteous, unholy, intemperate, ignorant, who are nevertheless remarkable for their courage.

Stop, I said; I should like to think about that. When you speak of brave men, do you mean the confident, or another sort of nature?

Yes, he said; I mean the impetuous, ready to go at that which others are afraid to approach.

In the next place, you would affirm virtue to be a good thing, of which good thing you assert yourself to be a teacher.

Yes, he said; I should say the best of all things, if I am in my right mind.

And is it partly good and partly bad, I said, or wholly good?

Wholly good, and in the highest degree.

Tell me then: who are they who have confidence when diving into a well?

I should say, the divers.

And the reason of this is that they have knowledge?

Yes, that is the reason.

And who have confidence when fighting on horseback – the skilled horseman or the unskilled?

The skilled.

And who when fighting with light shields – the peltasts or the nonpeltasts?

The peltasts. And that is true of all other things, he said, if that is your point: those who have knowledge are more confident than those who have no knowledge, and they are more confident after they have learned than before.

And have you not seen persons utterly ignorant, I said, of these things, and yet confident about them?

Yes, he said, I have seen such persons far too confident.

And are not these confident persons also courageous?

In that case, he replied, courage would be a base thing, for the men of whom we are speaking are surely madmen.

Then who are the courageous? Are they not the confident?

Yes, he said; to that statement I adhere.

And those, I said, who are thus confident without knowledge are really not courageous, but mad; and in that case the wisest are also the most confident, and being the most confident are also the bravest, and upon that view again wisdom will be courage.

Nay, Socrates, he replied, you are mistaken in your remembrance of what was said by me. When you asked me, I certainly did say that the courageous are the confident; but I was never asked whether the confident are the courageous; if you had asked me, I should have answered 'Not all of them': and what I did answer you have not proved to be false, although you proceeded to show that those who have knowledge are more courageous than they were before they had knowledge, and more courageous than others who have no knowledge, and were then led on to think that courage is the same as wisdom. But in this way of arguing you might come to imagine that strength is wisdom. You might begin by asking whether the strong are able, and I should say 'Yes'; and then whether those who know how to wrestle are not more able to wrestle than those who do not know how to wrestle, and more able after than before they had learned, and I should assent. And when I had admitted this, you might use my admissions in such a way as to prove that upon my view wisdom is strength; whereas in that case I should not have admitted, any more than in the other, that the able are strong, although I have admitted that the strong are able. For there is a difference between ability and strength; the former is given by knowledge as well as by madness or rage, but strength comes from nature and a healthy state of the body. And in like manner I say of confidence and courage, that they are not the same; and I argue that the courageous are confident, but not all the confident courageous. For confidence may be given to men by art, and also, like ability, by madness and rage; but courage comes to them from nature and the healthy state of the soul.

I said: You would admit, Protagoras, that some men live well and others ill?

He assented.

And do you think that a man lives well who lives in pain and grief?

He does not.

But if he lives pleasantly to the end of his life, will he not in that case have lived well?

He will.

Then to live pleasantly is a good, and to live unpleasantly an evil?

Yes, he said, if the pleasure be good and honourable.

And do you, Protagoras, like the rest of the world,

call some pleasant things evil and some painful things good? For I am rather disposed to say that things are good in as far as they are pleasant, if they have no consequences of another sort, and in as far as they are painful they are bad.

I do not know, Socrates, he said, whether I can venture to assert in that unqualified manner that the pleasant is the good and the painful the evil. Having regard not only to my present answer, but also to the whole of my life, I shall be safer, if I am not mistaken, in saying that there are some pleasant things which are not good, and that there are some painful things which are good, and some which are not good, and that there are some which are neither good nor evil.

And you would call pleasant, I said, the things which participate in pleasure or create pleasure?

Certainly, he said.

Then my meaning is, that in as far as they are pleasant they are good; and my question would imply that pleasure is a good in itself.

According to your favourite mode of speech, Socrates, 'Let us reflect about this,' he said; and if the reflection is to the point, and the result proves that pleasure and good are really the same, then we will agree; but if not, then we will argue.

And would you wish to begin the enquiry? I said; or shall I begin?

You ought to take the lead, he said; for you are the author of the discussion.

May I employ an illustration? I said. Suppose someone who is enquiring into the health or some other bodily quality of another: he looks at his face and at the tips of his fingers, and then he says, 'Uncover your chest and back to me that I may have a better view': that is the sort of thing which I desire in this speculation. Having seen what your opinion is about good and pleasure, I am minded to say to you: 'Uncover your mind to me, Protagoras, and reveal your opinion about knowledge, that I may know whether you agree with the rest of the world'. Now the rest of the world are of opinion that knowledge is a principle not of strength, or of rule, or of command: their notion is that a man may have knowledge, and yet that the knowledge which is in him may be overmastered by anger, or pleasure, or pain, or love, or perhaps by fear – just as if knowledge were a slave, and might be dragged about anyhow. Now is that your view? Or do you think that knowledge is a noble and commanding thing, which cannot be overcome, and will not allow a man, if he only knows the difference of good and evil, to do anything which is contrary to knowledge, but that wisdom will have strength to help him?

I agree with you, Socrates, said Protagoras; and not only so, but I, above all other men, am bound to say that wisdom and knowledge are the highest of human things.

Good, I said, and true. But are you aware that the majority of the world are of another mind; and that men are commonly supposed to know the things which are best, and not to do them when they might? And most persons whom I have asked the reason of this have said that when men act contrary to knowledge they are overcome by pain, or pleasure, or some of those affections which I was just now mentioning.

Yes, Socrates, he replied; and that is not the only point about which mankind are in error.

Suppose, then, that you and I endeavour to instruct

and inform them what is the nature of this affection which they call 'being overcome by pleasure,' and which they affirm to be the reason why they do not always do what is best. When we say to them: 'Friends, you are mistaken, and are saying what is not true,' they would probably reply: 'Socrates and Protagoras, if this affection of the soul is not to be called "being overcome by pleasure", pray, what is it, and by what name would you describe it?'

But why, Socrates, should we trouble ourselves about the opinion of the many, who just say anything that happens to occur to them?

I believe, I said, that they may be of use in helping us to discover how courage is related to the other parts of virtue. If you are disposed to abide by our agreement, that I should show the way in which, as I think, our recent difficulty is most likely to be cleared up, do you follow; but if not, never mind.

You are quite right, he said; and I would have you proceed as you have begun.

Well then, I said, let me suppose that they repeat their question, 'What account do you give of that which, in our way of speaking, is termed being overcome by pleasure?' I should answer thus: 'Listen, and Protagoras and I will endeavour to show you. When men are overcome by eating and drinking and other sensual desires which are pleasant, and they, knowing them to be evil, nevertheless indulge in them, would you not say that they were overcome by pleasure?' They will not deny this. And suppose that you and I were to go on and ask them again: 'In what way do you say that they are evil – in that they are pleasant and give pleasure at the moment, or because they cause disease and poverty and other like evils in the future? Would they still be evil, if they had no attendant evil consequences, simply because they give the consciousness of pleasure of whatever nature?' Would they not answer that they are not evil on account of the pleasure which is immediately given by them, but on account of the after consequences – diseases and the like?

I believe, said Protagoras, that the world in general would answer as you do.

And in causing diseases do they not cause pain? And in causing poverty do they not cause pain? They would agree to that also, if I am not mistaken.

Protagoras assented.

Then I should say to them, in my name and yours: 'Do you think them evil for any other reason, except because they end in pain and rob us of other pleasures?' There again they would agree?

We both of us thought that they would.

And then I should take the question from the opposite point of view, and say: 'Friends, when you speak of goods being painful, do you not mean remedial goods, such as gymnastic exercises, and military service, and the physician's use of burning, cutting, drugging, and starving? Are these the things which are good but painful?' They would assent to me?

He agreed.

'And do you call them good because they occasion the greatest immediate suffering and pain; or because, afterwards, they bring health and improvement of the bodily condition and the salvation of states and power over others and wealth?' They would agree to the latter alternative, if I am not mistaken?

He assented.

'Are these things good for any other reason except that they end in pleasure, and get rid of and avert pain? Are you looking to any other standard but pleasure and pain when you call them good?' They would acknowledge that they were not?

I think so, said Protagoras.

'And do you not pursue after pleasure as a good, and avoid pain as an evil?'

He assented.

'Then you think that pain is an evil and pleasure is a good: and even pleasure you deem an evil, when it robs you of greater pleasures than it gives, or causes pains greater than the pleasure. If, however, you call pleasure an evil in relation to some other end or standard, you will be able to show us that standard. But you have none to show.'

I do not think that they have, said Protagoras.

'And have you not a similar way of speaking about pain? You call pain a good when it takes away greater pains than those which it has, or gives pleasures greater than the pains: then if you have some standard other than pleasure and pain to which you refer when you call actual pain a good, you can show what that is. But you cannot.'

True, said Protagoras.

Suppose again, I said, that the world says to me: 'Why do you spend many words and speak in many ways on this subject?' Excuse me, friends, I should reply; but in the first place there is a difficulty in explaining the meaning of the expression 'overcome by pleasure'; and the whole argument turns upon this. And even now, if you see any possible way in which evil can be explained as other than pain, or good as other than pleasure, you may still retract. Are you satisfied, then, at having a life of pleasure which is without pain? If you are, and if you are unable to show any good or evil which does not end in pleasure and pain, hear the consequences: if what you say is true, then the argument is absurd which affirms that a man often does evil knowingly, when he might abstain, because he is seduced and overpowered by pleasure; or again, when you say that a man knowingly refuses to do what is good because he is overcome at the moment by pleasure. And that this is ridiculous will be evident if only we give up the use of various names, such as pleasant and painful, and good and evil. As there are two things, let us call them by two names – first, good and evil, and then pleasant and painful. Assuming this, let us go on to say that a man does evil knowing that he does evil. But someone will ask, Why? Because he is overcome, is the first answer. And by what is he overcome? the enquirer will proceed to ask. And we shall not be able to reply 'By pleasure,' for the name of pleasure has been exchanged for that of good. In our answer, then, we shall only say that he is overcome. 'By what?' he will reiterate. By the good, we shall have to reply; indeed we shall. Nay, but our questioner will rejoin with a laugh, if he be one of the swaggering sort, 'That is too ridiculous, that a man should do what he knows to be evil when he ought not, because he is overcome by good. Is that,' he will ask, 'because the good was worthy or not worthy of conquering the evil'? And in answer to that we shall clearly reply, 'Because it was not worthy'; for if it had been worthy, then he who, as we say, was overcome by pleasure, would not have been wrong. 'But how,' he will reply, 'can the good be unworthy of the evil, or the evil of the good? Is not the real explanation that they are out of proportion to one another, either as greater and smaller, or more and fewer?' This we cannot deny. 'And when you speak of being overcome – what do you mean,' he will say, 'but that you choose the greater evil in exchange for the lesser good?' Admitted. And now substitute the names of pleasure and pain for good and evil, and say, not as before, that a man does what is evil knowingly, but that he does what is painful knowingly, and because he is overcome by pleasure, which is unworthy to overcome. What measure is there of the relations of pleasure to pain other than excess and defect, which means that they become greater and smaller, and more and fewer, and differ in degree? For if anyone says: 'Yes, Socrates, but immediate pleasure differs widely from future pleasure and pain' – to that I should reply: 'And do they differ in anything but in pleasure and pain? There can be no other measure of them. And do you, like a skilful weigher, put into the balance the pleasures and the pains, and their nearness and distance, and weigh them, and then say which outweighs the other. If you weigh pleasures against pleasures, you of course take the more and greater; or if you weigh pains against pains, you take the fewer and the less; or if pleasures against pains, then you choose that course of action in which the painful is exceeded by the pleasant, whether the distant by the near or the near by the distant; and you avoid that course of action in which the pleasant is exceeded by the painful. Would you not admit, my friends, that this is true?' I am confident that they cannot deny this.

He agreed with me.

'Well then,' I shall say, 'if you agree so far, be so good as to answer me a question: do not the same magnitudes appear larger to your sight when near, and smaller when at a distance?' They will acknowledge that. And the same holds of thickness and number; also sounds, which are in themselves equal, are greater when near, and lesser when at a distance. They will grant that also. Now suppose happiness to consist in doing or choosing the greater, and in not doing or in avoiding the less, what would be the saving principle of human life? Would not the art of measuring be the saving principle; or would the power of appearance? Is not the latter that deceiving art which makes us wander up and down and take the things at one time of which we repent at another, both in our actions and in our choice of things great and small? But the art of measurement would do away with the effect of appearances, and, showing the truth, would fain teach the soul at last to find rest in the truth, and would thus save our life. Would not mankind generally acknowledge that the art which accomplishes this result is the art of measurement?

Yes, he said, the art of measurement.

Suppose, again, the salvation of human life to depend on the choice of odd and even, and on the knowledge of when a man ought to choose the greater or less, either in reference to themselves or to each other, and whether near or at a distance; what would be the saving principle of our lives? Would not knowledge – a knowledge of measuring, when the question is one of excess and defect, and a knowledge of number, when the question is of odd and even? The world will assent, will they not?

Protagoras himself thought that they would.

Well then, my friends, I say to them; seeing that the salvation of human life has been found to consist in the right choice of pleasures and pains – in the choice of

75

the more and the fewer, and the greater and the less, and the nearer and remoter, must not this measuring be a consideration of their excess and defect and equality in relation to each other?

This is undeniably true.

And this, as possessing measure, must undeniably also be an art and science?

They will agree, he said.

The nature of that art or science will be a matter of future consideration; but the existence of such a science furnishes a demonstrative answer to the question which you asked of me and Protagoras. At the time when you asked the question, if you remember, both of us were agreeing that there was nothing mightier than knowledge, and that knowledge, in whatever existing, must have the advantage over pleasure and all other things; and then you said that pleasure often got the advantage even over a man who has knowledge; and we refused to allow this, and you rejoined: 'O Protagoras and Socrates, what is the meaning of being overcome by pleasure if not this? Tell us what you call such a state.' If we had immediately and at the time answered 'Ignorance', you would have laughed at us. But now, in laughing at us, you will be laughing at yourselves: for you also admitted that men err in their choice of pleasures and pains; that is, in their choice of good and evil, from defect of knowledge; and you admitted further, that they err, not only from defect of knowledge in general, but of that particular knowledge which is called measuring. And you are also aware that the erring act which is done without knowledge is done in ignorance. This, therefore, is the meaning of being overcome by pleasure: ignorance, and that the greatest. And our friends Protagoras and Prodicus and Hippias declare that they are the physicians of ignorance; but you, who are under the mistaken impression that ignorance is not the cause, and that the art of which I am speaking cannot be taught, neither go yourselves, nor send your children, to the sophists, who are the teachers of these things – you take care of your money and give them none; and the result is, that you are the worse off both in public and private life: Let us suppose this to be our answer to the world in general. And now I should like to ask you, Hippias, and you, Prodicus, as well as Protagoras (for the argument is to be yours as well as ours), whether you think that I am speaking the truth or not?

They all thought that what I said was entirely true.

Then you agree, I said, that the pleasant is the good, and the painful evil. And here I would beg my friend Prodicus not to introduce his distinction of names, whether he is disposed to say pleasurable, delightful, joyful. However, by whatever name he prefers to call them, I will ask you, most excellent Prodicus, to answer in my sense of the words.

Prodicus laughed and assented, as did the others.

Then, my friends, what do you say to this? Are not all actions honourable and useful, of which the tendency is to make life painless and pleasant?

[Yes.]

The honourable work is also useful and good?

This was admitted.

Then, I said, if the pleasant is the good, nobody does anything under the idea or conviction that some other thing would be better and is also attainable, when he might do the better. And this inferiority of a man to himself is merely ignorance, as the superiority of a man to himself is wisdom.

They all assented.

And is not ignorance the having a false opinion and being deceived about important matters?

To this also they unanimously assented.

Then, I said, no man voluntarily pursues evil, or that which he thinks to be evil. To prefer evil to good is not in human nature; and when a man is compelled to choose one of two evils, no one will choose the greater when he may have the less.

All of us agreed to every word of this.

Well, I said, there is a certain thing called fear or terror; and here, Prodicus, I should particularly like to know whether you would agree with me in defining this fear or terror as expectation of evil.

Protagoras and Hippias agreed, but Prodicus said that this was fear and not terror.

Never mind, Prodicus, I said; but let me ask whether, if our former assertions are true, a man will pursue that which he fears when he is not compelled? Would not this be in flat contradiction to the admission which has been already made, that he thinks the things which he fears to be evil; and no one will pursue or voluntarily accept that which he thinks to be evil?

That also was universally admitted.

Then, I said, these, Hippias and Prodicus, are our premises; and I would beg Protagoras to explain to us how he can be right in what he said at first. I do not mean in what he said quite at first, for his first statement, as you may remember, was that whereas there were five parts of virtue none of them was like any other of them; each of them had a separate function. To this, however, I am not referring, but to the assertion which he afterwards made that of the five virtues four were nearly akin to each other, but

that the fifth, which was courage, differed greatly
from the others. And of this he gave me the following
proof. He said: 'You will find, Socrates, that some of
the most impious, and unrighteous, and intemperate,
and ignorant of men are among the most courageous;
which proves that courage is very different from the
other parts of virtue.' I was surprised at his saying this
at the time, and I am still more surprised now that I
have discussed the matter with you. So I asked him
whether by the brave he meant the confident. 'Yes,'
he replied, 'and the impetuous or goers.' (You may
remember, Protagoras, that this was your answer.)

He assented.

Well then, I said, tell us against what are the
courageous ready to go – against the same dangers as
the cowards?

No, he answered.

Then against something different?

Yes, he said.

Then do cowards go where there is safety, and the
courageous where there is danger?

Yes, Socrates, so men say.

Very true, I said. But I want to know against what do
you say that the courageous are ready to go – against
dangers, believing them to be dangers, or not against
dangers?

No, said he; the former case has been proved by you
in the previous argument to be impossible.

That, again, I replied, is quite true. And if this has
been rightly proven, then no one goes to meet what he
thinks to be dangers, since the want of self-control,
which makes men rush into dangers, has been shown
to be ignorance.

He assented.

And yet the courageous man and the coward alike go to meet that about which they are confident; so that, in this point of view, the cowardly and the courageous go to meet the same things.

And yet, Socrates, said Protagoras, that to which the coward goes is the opposite of that to which the courageous goes; the one, for example, is ready to go to battle, and the other is not ready.

And is going to battle honourable or disgraceful? I said.

Honourable, he replied.

And if honourable, then already admitted by us to be good; for all honourable actions we have admitted to be good.

That is true; and to that opinion I shall always adhere.

True, I said. But which of the two are they who, as you say, are unwilling to go to war, which is a good and honourable thing?

The cowards, he replied.

And what is good and honourable, I said, is also pleasant?

It has certainly been acknowledged to be so, he replied.

And do the cowards knowingly refuse to go to the nobler, and pleasanter, and better?

The admission of that, he replied, would belie our former admissions.

But does not the courageous man also go to meet the better, and pleasanter, and nobler?

That must be admitted.

And the courageous man has no base fear or base confidence?

True, he replied.

And if not base, then honourable?

He admitted this.

And if honourable, then good?

Yes.

But the fear and confidence of the coward or foolhardy or madman, on the contrary, are base?

He assented.

And these base fears and confidences originate in ignorance and uninstructedness?

True, he said.

Then as to the motive from which the cowards act, do you call it cowardice or courage?

I should say cowardice, he replied.

And have they not been shown to be cowards through their ignorance of dangers?

Assuredly, he said.

And because of that ignorance they are cowards?

He assented.

And the reason why they are cowards is admitted by you to be cowardice?

He again assented.

Then the ignorance of what is and is not dangerous is cowardice?

He nodded assent.

But surely courage, I said, is opposed to cowardice?

Yes.

Then the wisdom which knows what are and are not dangers is opposed to the ignorance of them?

To that again he nodded assent.

And the ignorance of them is cowardice?

To that he very reluctantly nodded assent.

And the knowledge of that which is and is not dangerous is courage, and is opposed to the ignorance of these things?

At this point he would no longer nod assent, but was silent.

And why, I said, do you neither assent nor dissent, Protagoras?

Finish the argument by yourself, he said.

I only want to ask one more question, I said. I want to know whether you still think that there are men who are most ignorant and yet most courageous?

You seem to have a great ambition to make me answer, Socrates, and therefore I will gratify you, and say, that this appears to me to be impossible consistently with the argument.

My only object, I said, in continuing the discussion, has been the desire to ascertain the nature and relations of virtue; for if this were clear, I am very sure that the other controversy which has been carried on at great length by both of us – you affirming and I denying that virtue can be taught – would also become clear. The result of our discussion appears to me to be singular. For if the argument had a human voice, that voice would be heard laughing at us and saying: 'Protagoras and Socrates, you are strange beings; there are you, Socrates, who were saying that virtue cannot be taught, contradicting yourself now by your attempt to prove that all things are knowledge, including justice, and temperance, and courage – which tends to show that virtue can certainly be taught; for if virtue were other than knowledge, as Protagoras attempted to prove, then clearly virtue cannot be taught; but if virtue is entirely knowledge, as you are seeking to show, then I cannot but suppose that virtue is capable of being taught. Protagoras, on the other hand, who started by saying that it might be taught, is now eager to prove it to be anything rather than knowledge; and if this is true, it must be quite incapable of being taught.' Now I, Protagoras, perceiving this terrible confusion of our ideas, have a great desire that they should be cleared up. And I should like to carry on the discussion until we ascertain what virtue is, whether capable of being taught or not, lest haply Epimetheus should trip us up and deceive us in the argument, as he forgot us in the story; I prefer your Prometheus to your Epimetheus, for of him I make use, whenever I am busy about these questions, in Promethean care of my own life. And if you have no objection, as I said at first, I should like to have your help in the enquiry.

Protagoras replied: Socrates, I am not of a base nature, and I am the last man in the world to be envious. I cannot but applaud your energy and your conduct of an argument. As I have often said, I admire you above all men whom I know, and far above all men of your age; and I believe that you will become very eminent in philosophy. Let us come back to the subject at some future time; at present we had better turn to something else.

By all means, I said, if that is your wish; for I too ought long since to have kept the engagement of which I spoke before, and only tarried because I could not refuse the request of the noble Callias.

So the conversation ended, and we went our way.

REPUBLIC

REPUBLIC

Persons of the dialogue
SOCRATES, *who is the narrator*
CEPHALUS
GLAUCON
THRASYMACHUS
ADEIMANTUS
CLEITOPHON
POLEMARCHUS
and others who are mute auditors

THE SCENE *is laid in the house of Cephalus at the Peiraeus; and the whole dialogue is narrated by Socrates the day after it actually took place to persons who are never named.*

BOOK ONE

I went down yesterday to the Peiraeus with Glaucon the son of Ariston, that I might offer up my prayers to the goddess; and also because I wanted to see in what manner they would celebrate the festival, which was a new thing. I was delighted with the procession of the inhabitants; but that of the Thracians was equally, if not more, beautiful. When we had finished our prayers and viewed the spectacle, we turned in the direction of the city; and Polemarchus the son of Cephalus chanced to catch sight of us from a distance when we had started on our way home, and told his servant to run and bid us wait for him. The servant took hold of me by the cloak behind, and said: Polemarchus desires you to wait.

I turned round, and asked him where his master was.

There he is, said the youth, coming after you, if you will only wait.

Certainly we will, said Glaucon; and in a few minutes Polemarchus appeared, and with him Adeimantus, Glaucon's brother, Niceratus the son of Nicias, and several others who had probably been at the procession.

Polemarchus said to me: I perceive, Socrates, that you and your companion are already on your way back to the city.

You are not far wrong, I said.

But do you see, he rejoined, how many we are?

Of course.

And are you stronger than all these? For if not, you will have to remain where you are.

May there not be the alternative, I said, that we may persuade you to let us go?

But can you persuade us, if we refuse to listen to you? he said.

Certainly not, replied Glaucon.

Then we are not going to listen; of that you may be assured.

Adeimantus added: Has no one told you of the torch-race on horseback in honour of the goddess which will take place in the evening?

With horses! I replied: That is a novelty. Will horsemen carry torches and pass them one to another during the race?

Yes, said Polemarchus, and not only so, but a festival will be celebrated lasting throughout the night, which you certainly ought to see. Let us rise soon after supper and see this festival; there will be a gathering of young men, and we will have a good talk. Stay then, and do not be perverse.

Glaucon said: I suppose, since you insist, that we must.

Let us do so if you wish, I replied.

Accordingly we went with Polemarchus to his house; and there we found his brothers Lysias and Euthydemus, and with them Thrasymachus the Chalcedonian, Charmantides the Paeanian, and Cleitophon the son of Aristonymus. There too was Cephalus the father of Polemarchus, whom I had not seen for a long time, and he now seemed a very old man. He was seated on a cushioned chair, and had a garland on his head, for he had been sacrificing in the court; and there were some other chairs in the room arranged in a semicircle, upon which we sat down by him. When he saw me, he saluted me eagerly, saying:

You don't come to see me, Socrates, as often as you ought: if I were still able to go and see you, I would not ask you to come to me. But at my age I can hardly get to the city, and therefore you should come oftener to the Peiraeus. For let me tell you, that the more the pleasures of the body fade away, the greater to me is the pleasure and charm of conversation. Do not then deny my request, but make our house your resort and keep company with these young men; we are old friends, and you will be quite at home with us.

I replied: There is nothing which for my part I like better, Cephalus, than conversing with aged men; for I regard them as travellers who have gone a journey which I too may have to go, and of whom I ought to enquire whether the way is smooth and easy, or rugged and difficult. And this is a question which I should especially like to ask of you, who have arrived at that

time which the poets call the 'threshold of old age' –
Is life harder towards the end, or what report do you
give of it?

I will tell you, Socrates, he said, what my own feeling
is. Men of my age flock together; we are birds of a
feather, as the old proverb says; and at our meetings
the tale of my acquaintance commonly is – 'I cannot
eat, I cannot drink; the pleasures of youth and love are
fled away: there was a good time once, but now that is
gone, and life is no longer life.' Some complain of the
slights which are put upon an old man by his relations,
and this sets them going upon a recital of evils, of
which old age is the cause. But to me, Socrates, these
complainers seem to blame that which is not really in
fault. For if old age were the cause, I too being old, and
every other old man, would have felt as they do. But
this is not my own experience, nor that of others whom
I have known. How well I remember the aged poet
Sophocles, when in answer to the question 'How does
love suit with age, Sophocles – are you still the man
you were?' 'Peace', he replied; 'most gladly have I
escaped the thing of which you speak; I feel as if I had
escaped from a mad and furious master.' His words
seem as good to me now as at the time when he uttered
them. For certainly old age has a great sense of calm,
and freedom from the things he mentions; when
the passions diminish and relax their hold, then, as
Sophocles says, we are freed from the grasp not of one
mad master only, but of many. The truth is, Socrates,
that these regrets and also the complaints about
relations, are to be attributed to the same cause,
which is not old age, but men's characters and
tempers; for he who is of a calm and happy nature will
hardly feel the pressure of age, but to him who is of

an opposite disposition youth and age are equally a burden.

I listened in admiration, and wanting to draw him out, that he might go on – Yes, Cephalus, I said; but I rather suspect that people in general are not convinced by you when you speak thus; they think that old age sits lightly upon you, not because of your happy disposition, but because you are rich, and wealth, it is often said, brings many consolations.

You are right, he replied; they are not convinced: and there is something in what they say; not, however, so much as they imagine. I might answer them as Themistocles answered the Seriphian who was abusing him and saying that he was famous, not for his own merits but because he was an Athenian: 'If you had been a native of my country and I of yours, neither of us would have been famous.' And to those who are not rich and are impatient of old age, the same reply may be made; for to the good poor man old age cannot be a light burden, nor can a bad rich man ever have peace with himself.

May I ask, Cephalus, whether your fortune was for the most part inherited or acquired by you?

Acquired? Socrates, do you want to know how much I acquired? In the art of making money I have been midway between my father and grandfather: for my grandfather, whose name I bear, doubled and trebled the value of his patrimony, that which he inherited being much what I possess now; but my father Lysanias reduced the property below what it is at present: and I shall be satisfied if I leave to these my sons not less but a little more than I received.

That was why I asked you the question, I replied, because I see that you have no excessive love for money, which is a characteristic rather of those who have inherited their fortunes than of those who have acquired them; the makers of fortunes have a second love of money as a creation of their own, resembling the affection of authors for their own poems, or of parents for their children, besides that natural love of it for the sake of use and profit which is common to them and all men. And hence they are very bad company, for they insist on measuring the value of things in terms of wealth.

That is true, he said.

Yes, that is very true, but may I ask another question? What do you consider to be the greatest blessing which you have reaped from your wealth?

One, he said, of which I could not expect easily to convince others. For let me tell you, Socrates, that when a man begins to think that his last hour is near, fears and cares enter into his mind which he never had before; the tales of a world below and the punishment which is exacted there for deeds done here were once a laughing-matter to him, but now he is tormented with the thought that they may be true: either from the weakness of age, or because he is now drawing nearer to that other place, and has a clearer view of these things, suspicions and alarms crowd thickly upon him, and he begins to reflect and consider any wrongs which he may have done to others. And when he finds that the sum of his transgressions is great he will many a time like a child start up in his sleep for fear, and he is filled with dark forebodings. But to him who has no injustice on his conscience, sweet hope, as Pindar charmingly says, is the kind nurse of his age:

'Hope', he says, 'cherishes the soul of him who lives

in justice and holiness, and is the nurse of his age and the companion of his journey; hope which is mightiest to sway the restless soul of man.'

How admirable are his words! And the great blessing of riches, I do not say to every man, but to a good and upright man, is, that he has had no occasion to deceive or to defraud others, even without intention; and that when he departs to the world below he is not in any apprehension about offerings due to the gods or debts which he owes to men. Now to this peace of mind the possession of wealth greatly contributes. It has, perhaps, many other advantages; but still, setting one thing against another, to a man of sense this is in my opinion the greatest.

Well said indeed, Cephalus, I replied; but as concerning justice, what is it? To speak the truth and to pay your debts – no more than this? May not these very actions be sometimes justly, and sometimes unjustly performed? Suppose that a friend when in his right mind has deposited arms with me and he asks for them when he is not in his right mind, ought I to give them back to him? No one would say that I ought or that I should be right in doing so, any more than they would say that I ought always to speak the truth to one who is in his condition.

You are quite right, he replied.

But then, I said, speaking the truth and paying your debts is not a correct definition of justice.

Quite correct, Socrates, if Simonides is to be believed, said Polemarchus interposing.

I fear, said Cephalus, that I must go now, for I have to look after the sacrifices, and I hand over the argument to the company.

Polemarchus, then, is your heir? I said.

To be sure, he answered, and went away laughing to the sacrifices.

Tell me then, O thou heir of the argument, what did Simonides say, and according to you truly say, about justice?

He said that the repayment of a debt is just, and in saying so he appears to me to be right.

I should be sorry to doubt the word of such a wise and inspired man, but his meaning, though probably clear to you, is the reverse of clear to me. For he certainly does not mean, as we were just now saying, that I ought to return a deposit of arms or of anything else to one who asks for it when he is not in his right senses; and yet a deposit cannot be denied to be a debt.

True.

Then when the person who asks me is not in his right mind, I am by no means to make the return?

That is true.

When Simonides said that the repayment of a debt was justice, it seems he did not mean to include that case?

Certainly not; for he thinks that a friend ought always to do good to a friend and never evil.

You mean that the return of a deposit of gold which is to the injury of the receiver, if the two parties are friends, is not the repayment of a debt – that is what you would imagine him to say?

Yes.

And enemies? Should we restore to them whatever we owe them?

By all means what we owe them, he said, and an enemy, I take it, owes to an enemy that which is due or proper to him, an evil.

Simonides, then, after the manner of poets, would

seem to have spoken darkly of the nature of justice; for he really meant to say that justice is the giving to each man what is proper to him, and this he termed a debt.

That must have been his meaning, he said.

Tell me, pray, I replied, if we asked him what due or proper thing is given by the art named medicine, and to whom, what answer do you think that he would make to us?

He would surely reply that medicine gives drugs and food and drink to human bodies.

And what due or proper thing is given by the art named cookery, and to what?

Seasoning to food.

And what is that which justice gives, and to whom?

If, Socrates, we are to be guided at all by the analogy of the preceding instances, then justice is the art which gives benefit to friends and injury to enemies.

He means, then, by justice doing good to friends and harm to enemies?

I think so.

And who is best able to do good to his friends and evil to his enemies in respect of sickness and health?

The physician.

Or when they are on a voyage, amid the perils of the sea?

The pilot.

And in what sort of actions or with a view to what result is the just man most able to do harm to his enemy and confer benefit upon his friend?

In going to war against the one and in making alliances with the other.

But when a man is well, my dear Polemarchus, there is no need of a physician?

No.

And he who is not on a voyage has no need of a pilot?

No.

Then in time of peace justice will be of no use?

I do not think that is quite true.

You think that justice may be of use in peace as well as in war?

Yes.

Like husbandry for the acquisition of corn?

Yes.

Or like shoemaking for the acquisition of shoes – that is what you mean?

Yes.

And what similar service would you say that justice can render, or what can it help us to acquire, in time of peace?

It serves for making contracts, Socrates.

And by contracts you mean partnerships?

Exactly.

But is the just man or the skilful player a more useful and better partner at a game of draughts?

The skilful player.

And in the laying of bricks and stones is the just man a more useful or better partner than the builder?

Quite the reverse.

Then in what sort of partnership is the just man a better partner than the builder and the harp-player, as in playing the harp the harp-player is certainly a better partner than the just man?

In a money partnership, I suppose.

Yes, Polemarchus, but surely not in the use of money when the partners contemplate the purchase or sale of a horse; a man who is knowing about horses would be better for that, would he not?

Certainly.

And when you want to buy a ship, the shipwright or the pilot would be better?

True.

Then what is that joint use of silver or gold, in which the just man is to be preferred to other partners?

When you want a deposit to be kept safely.

You mean when money is not wanted for use, but allowed to lie?

Precisely.

That is to say, justice is useful when the money which it supervises is useless?

That is the inference.

And when you want to keep a pruning-hook safe, then justice is useful to men severally or in association; but when you want to use it, then the art of the vine-dresser?

Clearly.

And when you want to keep a shield or a lyre, and not to use them, you would say that justice is useful; but when you want to use them, then the art of the soldier or of the musician?

Certainly.

And so of all other things; justice is useful when they are useless, and useless when they are being used?

That is the inference.

Then justice is not worth much, if it deals only with useless things. But let us consider this further point: is not he who can best strike a blow in a boxing match or in any kind of fighting best able to ward off a blow?

Certainly.

And he who is skilful in giving protection against a disease, is best able to implant it without being observed?

True.

And the good guard of a camp is also the man who is able to discover the designs of the enemy or forestall his actions?

Certainly.

Then he who is a good keeper of anything is also a good thief?

That, I suppose, is to be inferred.

Then if the just man is good at keeping money, he is good at stealing it.

That is implied in the argument.

Then after all the just man has turned out to be a kind of thief. And this is a lesson which I suspect you must have learnt out of Homer; for he, speaking of Autolycus, the maternal grandfather of Odysseus, who is a favourite of his, affirms that

'He was excellent above all men in theft and perjury'.

And so, you and Homer and Simonides seem to be agreed that justice is an art of theft; to be practised however 'for the benefit of friends and for the harm of enemies' – that was what you were saying?

No, certainly not that, though I do not now know what I did say; but I still think that justice is beneficial to friends and harmful to enemies.

Well, there is another question: By friends and enemies do we mean those who are really good and bad, or only seem so?

Surely, he said, a man may be expected to love those whom he thinks good, and to hate those whom he thinks evil.

Yes, but do not persons often err about good and evil: many who are not good seem to be so, and conversely?

That is true.

Then to them the good will be enemies and the evil will be their friends?

True.

And in that case they will be right in doing good to the evil and evil to the good?

Clearly.

But the good are just and would not do an injustice?

True.

Then according to your argument it is just to injure those who do no wrong?

Nay, Socrates; the doctrine is immoral.

Then I suppose that it is just to do good to the just and harm to the unjust?

I like that better.

But see the consequence: many a man who has misjudged his fellows has friends who are bad friends, and in that case he ought to do harm to them; and he has good enemies whom he ought to benefit; but, if so, we shall be saying the very opposite of that which we affirmed to be the meaning of Simonides.

Very true, he said; and I think that we had better correct an error into which we seem to have fallen in our definition of 'friend' and 'enemy'.

What definition, Polemarchus? I asked.

We assumed that he is a friend who seems to be or who is thought good.

And how is the error to be corrected?

We should rather say that he is a friend who is, as well as seems, good; and that he who seems only and is not good, only seems to be and is not a friend; and of an enemy the same may be said.

You would argue that the good are our friends and the bad our enemies?

Yes.

And instead of saying simply as we did at first, that it is just to do good to our friends and harm to our enemies, you would have us add, 'It is just to do good to our friends when they are good and harm to our enemies when they are evil'?

Yes, it appears to me that with that change our statement would be quite correct.

But ought the just to injure anyone at all?

Undoubtedly he ought to injure those who are both wicked and his enemies.

When horses are injured, are they improved or deteriorated?

The latter.

Deteriorated, that is to say, in the good qualities of horses, not of dogs?

Yes, of horses.

And dogs are deteriorated in the good qualities of dogs, and not of horses?

Of course.

And will not men who are injured be deteriorated in that which is the proper virtue of man?

Certainly.

And that human virtue is justice?

To be sure.

Then, my friend, men who are injured are of necessity made more unjust?

That is the result.

But can the musician by his art make men unmusical?

Certainly not.

Or the horseman by his art make them bad horsemen?

Impossible.

And can the just by justice make men unjust, or speaking generally, can the good by virtue make them bad?

Impossible.

Any more than heat can produce cold, or drought moisture; these are the effects of opposite causes?

Exactly.

Nor is it the effect of the good, but of its opposite, to cause harm?

Evidently.

And the just man is good?

Certainly.

Then to injure a friend or anyone else is not the act of a just man, but of the opposite, who is the unjust?

I think that what you say is quite true, Socrates.

Then if a man says that justice consists in the repayment of debts, and that good is the debt which a just man owes to his friends, and evil the debt which he owes to his enemies – to say this is not wise; for it is not true, if, as has been clearly shown, the injuring of another can be in no case just.

I agree with you, said Polemarchus.

Then you and I are prepared to take up arms against any one who attributes such a saying to Simonides or Bias or Pittacus, or any other wise man or seer?

I am quite ready to do battle at your side, he said.

Shall I tell you whose I believe the saying to be?

Whose?

I believe that Periander or Perdiccas or Xerxes or Ismenias the Theban, or some other rich and mighty man, who had a great opinion of his own power, was the first to say that justice is 'doing good to your friends and harm to your enemies'.

Most true, he said.

Yes, I said; but if this definition of justice and just action also breaks down, what other can be offered?

Several times in the course of the discussion

Thrasymachus had made an attempt to get the argument into his own hands, and had been put down by the rest of the company, who wanted to hear the end. But when Polemarchus and I had done speaking and there was a pause, he could no longer hold his peace; and, gathering himself up, he came at us like a wild beast, seeking to devour us. We were quite panic-stricken at the sight of him.

He roared out to the whole company: What folly, Socrates, has taken possession of you all? And why this absurd politeness and deference to one another? I say that if you want really to know what justice is, you should not only ask the questions, and because you are well aware that questioning is much easier, seek honour to yourself from the refutation of an opponent. No! Come forward and give your own answer to the question what justice is. And I will not have you say that is it duty or advantage or profit or gain or interest, for this sort of nonsense will not do for me; I must have clearness and accuracy.

I was panic-stricken at his words, and could not look at him without trembling. Indeed I believe that if I had not fixed my eye upon him first, I should have been struck dumb: but when his fury at the discussion began to rise, I looked at him first, and was therefore able to reply to him.

Thrasymachus, I said, with a quiver, don't be hard upon us. Polemarchus and I may have been guilty of a little mistake in the argument, but I can assure you that the error was not intentional. If we were seeking for a piece of gold, you would not imagine that we were 'deferring to one another', and so losing our chance of finding it. And why, when we are seeking for justice, a thing more precious than many pieces of gold, do you say that we are weakly yielding to one another and not doing our utmost to get at the truth? Believe me, my good friend, we are most anxious to do so, but the fact is that we cannot. And if so, you clever people should pity us and not be angry with us.

How characteristic of Socrates! he replied, with a bitter laugh; that's your ironical style! Did I not foresee – have I not already told you, that whatever he was asked he would refuse to answer, and try irony or any other shuffle, in order that he might avoid answering?

You have an acute mind, Thrasymachus, I replied, and well know that if you ask a person what numbers make up twelve, taking care to prohibit him whom you ask from answering twice six, or three times four, or six times two, or four times three, 'for this sort of nonsense will not do for me' – then obviously, if that is your way of putting the question, no one can answer you. But suppose that he were to retort, 'Thrasymachus, what do you mean? If one of these numbers which you interdict be the true answer to the question, am I falsely to say some other number which is not the right one? Is that your meaning?' – how would you answer him?

Just as if the two cases were at all alike! he said.

Why should they not be? I replied; and even if they are not, but only appear to be so to the person who is asked, ought he not to say what he thinks, whether you and I forbid him or not?

I presume then that you are going to make one of the interdicted answers?

I dare say that I may, if upon reflection I approve of any of them.

But what if I give you an answer about justice other

and better, he said, than any of these? What do you deserve to have done to you?

Done to me! As becomes the ignorant, I must learn from the wise – that is what I deserve to have done to me.

What, and no payment for what you learn! A pleasant notion!

I will pay when I have the money, I replied.

But you have, Socrates, said Glaucon: and you, Thrasymachus, need be under no anxiety about money, for we will all make a contribution for Socrates.

Yes indeed, he replied, and then Socrates will do as he always does – refuse to answer himself, but take and pull to pieces the answer of someone else.

Why, my good friend, I said, how can anyone answer who knows, and says that he knows, just nothing; and who, even if he has some faint notions of his own, is told by a man of authority not to utter them? The natural thing is, that the speaker should be someone like yourself who professes to know and can tell what he knows. Will you then kindly answer as a favour to me, for the edification of Glaucon and the rest of us?

Glaucon and the rest of the company joined in my request, and Thrasymachus, as anyone might see, was in reality eager to speak; for he thought that he had an excellent answer, and would distinguish himself. But at first he affected to insist on my answering; at length he consented to begin. Behold, he said, the wisdom of Socrates; he refuses to be the teacher, and goes about learning of others, to whom he never even says thank you.

That I learn of others, I replied, is quite true; but that I am ungrateful I wholly deny. Money I have none, and therefore I pay in praise, which is all I have; and how ready I am to praise anyone who appears to me to speak well, you will very soon find out when you answer; for I expect that you will answer well.

Listen, then, he said; I proclaim that justice is nothing else than the interest of the stronger. And now why do you not praise me? But of course you won't.

Let me first understand you, I replied; for I am not yet clear. Justice, as you say, is the interest of the stronger. What, Thrasymachus, is the meaning of this? You cannot mean to say that because Polydamas the pancratiast is stronger than we are, and finds the eating of beef conducive to his bodily strength, that to eat beef is therefore equally for our good who are weaker than he is, and right and just for us?

That's abominable of you, Socrates; you take the words in the sense which is most damaging to the argument.

Not at all, my good sir, I said; but tell us your meaning more clearly.

Well, he said, have you never heard that forms of government differ; there are tyrannies, and there are democracies, and there are aristocracies?

Yes, I know.

And the government is the ruling power in each state?

Certainly.

And the different forms of government make laws democratical, aristocratical, tyrannical, with a view to their several interests; and thereby proclaim that what is advantageous to themselves is justice for those ruled; and him who transgresses this principle they punish as a breaker of the law, and unjust. And that is what I mean, sir, when I say that in all states there is the same principle of justice, which is the interest of the established government; and as the government must be supposed to have power, the only reasonable conclusion is that everywhere there is one principle of justice, which is the interest of the stronger.

Now I understand you, I said; and whether you are right or not I will try to discover. But let me remark, that in defining justice you have yourself used the word 'interest' which you forbade me to use. It is true, however, that in your definition the words 'of the stronger' are added.

A small addition, of course, he said.

Whether great or small is not yet plain, but it is plain that we must first inquire whether what you are saying is the truth. Now we are both agreed that justice is interest of some sort, but you go on to say 'of the stronger'; about this addition I am not so sure, and must therefore consider further.

Proceed.

I will; and first tell me, do you not likewise admit that it is just for subjects to obey their rulers?

I do.

But are the rulers of the various states infallible, or are they sometimes liable to err?

To be sure, he replied, they are liable to err.

Then in making their laws they may sometimes make them rightly, and sometimes not?

I think so.

When they make them rightly, they make them agreeably to their interest; when they are mistaken, contrary to their interest; you admit that?

Yes.

And whatever laws they make must be obeyed by their subjects – and that is what you call justice?

Doubtless.

Then justice, according to your argument, is not only observance of the interest of the stronger but the reverse?

What is that you are saying? he asked.

I am only repeating what you are saying, I believe. But let us consider: have we not agreed that the rulers, in commanding some actions, may be mistaken about their own interest but that it is just for the subjects to do whatever their rulers command? Has not that been agreed?

I think so.

Then think that you have acknowledged that it is just to do actions which are contrary to the interest of the government or the stronger, when the governors unintentionally command things to be done which are to their own injury, assuming with you that the obedience which the subject renders to their commands, is just. In that case, O wisest of men, is there any escape from the conclusion that the weaker are commanded to do, not what is for the interest, but what is for the injury of the stronger?

Nothing can be clearer, Socrates, said Polemarchus.

Yes, said Cleitophon, interposing, if you are allowed to be his witness.

But there is no need of any witness, said Polemarchus, for Thrasymachus himself acknowledges that rulers may sometimes command what is harmful to themselves, and that for subjects to obey them is justice.

Yes, Polemarchus – Thrasymachus said that for subjects to do what was commanded by their rulers is just.

Yes, Cleitophon, but he also laid down that justice

is the interest of the stronger, and, while admitting both these propositions, he further acknowledged that the stronger may command the weaker who are his subjects to do what is not for his own interest; whence it follows that justice is the injury quite as much as the interest of the stronger.

But, said Cleitophon, he meant by the interest of the stronger what the stronger thought to be his interest – this was what the weaker had to do; and this was affirmed by him to be justice.

Those were not his words, rejoined Polemarchus.

Never mind, I replied, if he now says that they are, let us understand him in that way. Tell me, Thrasymachus, I said, did you mean to define justice as that which the stronger thought to be his interest, whether really so or not?

Certainly not, he said. Do you suppose that I call him who is mistaken the stronger at the time when he is mistaken?

Yes, I said, my impression was that you did so, when you admitted that the ruler was not infallible but might be sometimes mistaken.

You argue like an informer, Socrates. Do you mean, for example, that he who is mistaken about the sick is a physician in respect of this mistaken judgement? or that he who errs in arithmetic is an arithmetician at the time when he is making the mistake, in respect of the mistake? True, we say that the physician or arithmetician or grammarian has made a mistake, but this is only a way of speaking; for the fact is that none of these persons ever makes a mistake in so far as he is what his name implies. You are a lover of accuracy; well, it is not accurate to say that craftsmen can make mistakes; they none of them err unless their skill fails them, and then they cease to be skilled craftsmen. No craftsman or sage or ruler errs at the time when he is what his name implies; though a doctor or ruler is commonly said to err, and you must suppose that in my answer just now I adopted the common mode of speaking. But to be perfectly accurate, we should say that the ruler, in so far as he is a ruler, is unerring, and, being unerring, always commands that which is for his own interest; and the subject is required to execute his commands; and therefore, as I said at first and now repeat, justice is action in the interest of the stronger.

Indeed, Thrasymachus, and do I really appear to you to argue like an informer?

Certainly, he replied.

And do you suppose that I ask these questions with any design of injuring you in the argument?

Nay, he replied, I know it; but you will not take me by surprise, and by sheer force of argument you will never prevail.

I shall not make the attempt, my dear man; but to avoid any misunderstanding occurring between us in future, let me ask, in what sense do you speak of a ruler or stronger whose interest, as you were saying, he being the superior, it is just that the inferior should execute – is he a ruler in the popular or in the strict sense of the term?

In the strictest of all senses, he said. And now cheat and play the informer if you can; I ask no quarter at your hands. But you never will be able, never.

And do you imagine, I said, that I am such a madman as to try and cheat Thrasymachus? I might as well shave a lion.

Why, he said, you made the attempt a minute ago, and you failed.

PLATO

Enough, I said, of these civilities. But tell me: is the physician, taken in that strict sense of which you are speaking, a healer of the sick or a maker of money? And remember that I am now speaking of the true physician.

A healer of the sick, he replied.

And the pilot – that is to say, the true pilot – is he a captain of sailors or a mere sailor?

A captain of sailors.

The circumstance that he sails in the ship is not to be taken into account, neither is he to be called a sailor; the name pilot by which he is distinguished has nothing to do with sailing, but is significant of his skill and of his authority over the sailors.

Very true, he said.

Now, I said, has not each of these craftsmen an interest?

Certainly.

For which the art has to consider and provide, that being its origin and purpose?

Yes.

And the interest of any art consists in its being, as far as possible, perfect – this and nothing else?

What do you mean?

I mean what I may illustrate negatively by the example of the body. Suppose you were to ask me whether the body is self-sufficing or wants assistance, I should reply: 'Certainly it does so; that is why the science which we call medicine was invented, because the body is unsound and cannot survive by itself. The art has been established in order to provide it with things which are beneficial to it.' Should I not be right if I gave this answer?

Quite right, he replied.

But is the art of medicine or any other art faulty or

deficient in any quality in the same way that the eye may be deficient in sight or the ear fail of hearing, and therefore require another art to provide for the interests of seeing and hearing – has art in itself, I say, any similar liability to fault or defect, and does every art require another supplementary art to provide for its interests, and that another and another without end? Or is each of them able to look after its own interests? Or have they no need either of themselves or of another to provide the remedy for their own unsoundness – for there is no such thing as a fault or unsoundness in any art, and the only benefit which an art need consider is that of its subject? For every art remains pure and faultless while remaining true – that is to say, while perfect and unimpaired. Take the words in your precise sense, and tell me whether I am not right.

Yes, clearly.

Then medicine does not consider the interest of medicine, but the interest of the body?

True, he said.

Nor does the art of horsemanship consider the interests of the art of horsemanship, but the interests of the horse; neither do any other arts care for themselves, for they have no needs; they care only for that which is the subject of their art?

So it seems, he said.

But surely, Thrasymachus, the arts are the superiors and rulers of their own subjects?

To this he assented with a good deal of reluctance.

Then, I said, no science or art considers or enjoins the interest of the stronger [or superior], but only the interest of the subject and weaker?

He made an attempt to contest this proposition also, but finally acquiesced.

Then, I continued, no physician, in so far as he is a physician, considers his own good in what he prescribes, but the good of his patient; for the true physician is also a ruler having the human body as a subject, and is not a mere money-maker; that has been admitted?

Yes.

And the pilot likewise, in the strict sense of the term, is a ruler of sailors and not a mere sailor?

That has been admitted.

And such a pilot and ruler will provide and prescribe for the interest of the sailor who is under him, and not for his own interest?

He gave a reluctant 'Yes'.

Then, I said, Thrasymachus, there is no one in any rule who, in so far as he is ruler, considers or enjoins what is for his own interest. On the contrary, a ruler attends to the subject which he has undertaken to direct; to that he looks, and in everything which he says and does, considers what is suitable or advantageous to it.

When we had got to this point in the argument, and everyone saw that the definition of justice had been completely turned round, Thrasymachus, instead of replying to me, said: Tell me, Socrates, have you got a nurse?

Why do you ask such a question, I said, when you ought rather to be answering?

Because she leaves you to snivel, and never wipes your nose: she has not even taught you to know the shepherd from the sheep.

What makes you say that? I replied.

Because you fancy that the shepherd or neatherd fattens and tends the sheep or oxen with a view to something other than the good of himself or his master; and you further imagine that the rulers of states, if they are true rulers, never think of their subjects as sheep, and that they are not studying their own advantage day and night. Oh, no; and so entirely astray are you in your ideas about the just and unjust as not even to know that justice and the just are in reality another's good, that is to say, the interest of the ruler and stronger, and the loss of the subject and servant; and injustice the opposite, for the unjust is lord over the truly simple and just: he is the stronger, and his subjects do what is for his interest, and minister to his happiness, which is very far from being their own. Consider further, most foolish Socrates, that the just is always a loser in comparison with the unjust. First of all, in private contracts: wherever the unjust is the partner of the just you will never find that, when the partnership is dissolved, the just man has secured more than the unjust. Secondly, in their dealings with the state: when there is an income-tax, the just man will pay more and the unjust less on the same amount of income; and when there is anything to be received, the one gains nothing and the other much. Observe also what happens when they hold an office; there is the just man neglecting his private affairs, even if he suffers no worse losses, and getting nothing out of the public, because he is just; moreover he is hated by his friends and acquaintance for refusing to serve them in unlawful ways. But all this is reversed in the case of the unjust man. I am speaking, as before, of one who can achieve gain on a large scale, for there the unjust man's private advantage is most apparent. Most clearly of all will the truth be seen if we turn to that highest form of injustice in which the criminal is the happiest of men, and the sufferers or those who would refuse to do injustice are the most miserable – that is to say tyranny, which by fraud and force takes away the property of others, not little by little but wholesale; confiscating things sacred as well as profane, private and public; for which acts of wrong, if he were detected perpetrating any one of them singly, he would be punished and incur the greatest disgrace – they who do such wrong in particular cases are called temple-robbers and man-stealers and burglars and swindlers and thieves. But when a man besides taking away the money of the citizens has seized their persons and made slaves of them, then, instead of these names of reproach, he is termed happy and blessed, not only by the citizens but by all who hear of his having achieved the consummation of injustice. For mankind censure injustice, fearing that they may be the victims of it and not because they shrink from committing it. And thus, as I have shown, Socrates, injustice, when on a sufficient scale, has more strength and freedom and mastery than justice; and, as I said at first, justice is in fact the interest of the stronger, whereas injustice is a man's own profit and interest.

Thrasymachus, when he had thus spoken, having, like a bath-man, deluged our ears with his words, had a mind to go away. But the company would not let him; they insisted that he should remain and defend his position; and I myself added my own urgent request that he should not leave us. Thrasymachus, I said to him, excellent man, how provocative are your remarks! And are you going to run away before you have fairly taught or learned whether they are true or not? Is the attempt to determine the way of man's life so small a matter in your eyes – to determine how life may be passed by each one of us to the greatest advantage?

And do I differ from you, he said, as to the importance of the inquiry?

Either that, I replied, or you seem to have no care or thought about us, Thrasymachus – whether we live better or worse from not knowing what you say you know, is to you a matter of indifference. Prithee, friend, do not keep your knowledge to yourself; we are a large party; and any benefit which you confer upon us will be amply rewarded. For my own part I openly declare that I am not convinced, and that I do not believe injustice to be more gainful than justice, even if uncontrolled and allowed to have free play. For, granting that there may be an unjust man who is able to commit injustice either by fraud or force, still this does not convince me of the superior advantage of injustice, and there may be others who are in the same predicament with myself. Perhaps we may be wrong; if so, you in your wisdom should convince us that we are mistaken in preferring justice to injustice.

And how am I to convince you, he said, if you are not already convinced by what I have just said; what more can I do for you? Would you have me put the proof bodily into your souls?

Heaven forbid! I said; I would only ask you to be consistent; or, if you change, change openly and let there be no deception. For I must remark, Thrasymachus, if you will recall what was previously said, that although you began by defining the true physician in an exact sense, you did not observe a like exactness when speaking of the shepherd; you thought that the shepherd as a shepherd tends the sheep not with a view to their own good, but like a mere diner or banqueter with a view to the pleasures of the table; or, again, as a trader, for sale in the market, and not as a shepherd. Yet surely the art of the shepherd is concerned only with the good of his subjects; he has only to provide the best for them, since the perfection of the art itself is already ensured whenever the shepherd's work is perfectly performed. And that was what I was saying just now about the ruler. I conceived that the art of the ruler, considered as ruler, whether in a state or in private life, could only have regard to the maximum good of his flock or subjects; whereas you seem to think that the rulers in states, that is to say, the true rulers, like being in authority.

Think! Nay, I am sure of it.

Then why in the case of lesser offices do men never take them willingly without payment, unless because they assume that their rule is to be advantageous not to themselves but to the governed? Let me ask you a question: are not the several arts different, by reason of their each having a separate function? And, my dear illustrious friend, do say what you think, that we may make a little progress.

Yes, that is the difference, he replied.

And each art gives us a particular good and not merely a general one – medicine, for example, gives us health; navigation, safety at sea; and so on?

Yes, he said.

And the art of earning has the special function of giving pay: but we do not confuse this with other arts, any more than the art of the pilot is to be confused with the art of medicine, because the health of the pilot may be improved by a sea voyage. You would not be inclined to say, would you, that navigation is the art of medicine, at least if we are to adopt your exact use of language?

Certainly not.

Or because a man is in good health when he receives pay, you would not say that the art of earning is medicine?

I should not.

Nor would you say that medicine is the art of receiving pay, because a man takes fees when he is engaged in healing?

No.

And we have admitted, I said, that the good of each art is specially confined to the art?

Let us take it for granted.

Then, if there be any good which all craftsmen have in common, that is to be attributed to something of which they all make common use?

True, he replied.

Moreover, we say that if the craftsman is benefited by receiving pay, that comes from his use of the art of earning in addition to his own?

He gave a reluctant assent to this.

Then the benefit, or receipt of pay, is not derived by the several craftsmen from their respective crafts. But it is more accurate to say that while the art of medicine gives health, and the art of the builder builds a house, another art attends them which is the art of earning. The various arts may be doing their own business and benefiting that over which they preside, but would the craftsman receive any benefit from his art unless he were paid as well?

I suppose not.

But does he therefore confer no benefit when he works for nothing?

Certainly, he confers a benefit.

Then now, Thrasymachus, there is no longer any doubt that neither arts nor governments provide for their own interests; but, as we were before saying, they rule and provide for the interests of their subjects who are the weaker and not the stronger – to their good they attend and not to the good of the superior. And this is the reason, my dear Thrasymachus, why, as I was just now saying, no one is willing to govern, because no one likes to take in hand the reformation of evils which are not his concern without remuneration. For in the execution of his work, and in giving his orders to another, the true artist does not regard his own interest, but always that of his subjects; and therefore in order that rulers may be willing to rule, they must be paid in one of three modes of payment – money, or honour, or a penalty for refusing.

What do you mean, Socrates? said Glaucon. The first two modes of payment are intelligible enough, but what the penalty is I do not understand, or how a penalty can be a payment.

You mean that you do not understand the nature of this payment which to the best men is the sole inducement to rule? Of course you know that ambition and avarice are held to be, as indeed they are, a disgrace?

Very true.

And for this reason, I said, they will not consent to rule for the sake of money and honour; good men do not wish to be openly demanding payment for governing and so to get the name of hirelings, nor by secretly helping themselves out of the public revenues to get the name of thieves. And not being ambitious they do not care about honour. Wherefore necessity must be laid upon them, and they must be induced to serve from the fear of punishment. And this, as I imagine, is the reason why the forwardness to take office, instead of waiting to be compelled, has been deemed dishonourable. Now the worst part of the punishment is that he who refuses to rule is liable to be ruled by one who is worse than himself. And the fear of this, as I conceive, induces the good to take office, not because they would, but because they cannot help – not under the idea that they are going to have any benefit or enjoyment themselves, but as a necessity, and because they are not able to commit the task of ruling to anyone who is better than themselves, or indeed as good. For there is reason to think that if a city were composed entirely of good men, then to avoid office would be as much an object of contention as to obtain office is at present; then we should have plain proof that the true ruler is not meant by nature to regard his own interest, but that of his subjects; and everyone who knew this would choose rather to receive a benefit from another than to have the trouble of conferring one. So far am I from agreeing with Thrasymachus that justice is the interest of the stronger. This latter question we can discuss on a future occasion; but when Thrasymachus says that the life of the unjust is superior to that of the just, his new statement appears to me to be of a far more serious character. Which of us has spoken truly? And which sort of life, Glaucon, do you prefer.

I for my part deem the life of the just to be the more advantageous, he answered.

Did you hear all the advantages of the unjust which Thrasymachus was rehearsing?

Yes, I heard him, he replied, but he has not convinced me.

Then shall we try to find some way of convincing him, if we can, that he is saying what is not true?

Most certainly, he replied.

If, I said, we make an earnest set speech in opposition to his, recounting all the advantages of being just, and he answers and we rejoin, there must be a numbering and measuring of the goods which are claimed on either side, and in the end we shall want judges to decide; but if we proceed in our inquiry as we lately did, by making admissions to one another, we shall unite the offices of judge and advocate in our own persons.

Very good, he said.

Let us take whichever method you prefer, I said.

I prefer the second.

Well, then, Thrasymachus, I said, suppose you begin at the beginning and answer me. You say that perfect injustice is more gainful than perfect justice?

Yes, that is what I say, and I have given you my reasons.

And what is your view about them? Would you call one of them virtue and the other vice?

Certainly.

I suppose that you would call justice virtue and injustice vice?

What a charming notion! So likely too, seeing that I affirm injustice to be profitable and justice not.

What else then would you say?

The opposite, he replied.

And would you call justice vice?

No, I would rather say sublime simplicity.

Then would you call injustice malignity?

No; I would rather say good counsel.

And do the unjust appear to you to be wise and good?

Yes, he said; at any rate those of them who are able to be perfectly unjust, and who have the power of subduing cities and nations; but perhaps you imagine me to be talking of cut-purses. Even this profession if undetected has advantages, though they are not to be compared with those of which I was just now speaking.

I do not think that I misapprehend your meaning, Thrasymachus, I replied; but still I cannot hear without amazement that you class injustice with wisdom and virtue, and justice with the opposite.

Certainly, I do so class them.

Now, I said, you are on more substantial and almost unanswerable ground; for if the injustice which you were maintaining to be profitable had been admitted by you as by others to be vice and deformity, an answer might have been given to you on received principles; but now I perceive that you will call injustice honourable and strong, and to the unjust you will attribute all the qualities which were attributed by us before to the just, seeing that you have not hesitated to rank injustice as wisdom and virtue.

You have prophesied most infallibly, he replied.

Then I certainly ought not to shrink from going through with the argument so long as I have reason to think that you, Thrasymachus, are speaking your real mind; for I do believe that you are now saying what you believe and are not amusing yourself at our expense.

I may believe it or not, but what is that to you? To refute the argument is your business.

Very true, I said. But will you please try to answer yet one more question? Would the just man try to gain any advantage over the just?

Far otherwise; if he did he would not be the simple well-bred creature which he is.

And would he try to go beyond just action?

He would not.

And how would he regard the attempt to gain an advantage over the unjust? Would that be considered by him as just or unjust?

He would think it just, and would try to gain the advantage; but he would not be able.

Whether he would or would not be able, I said, is not to the point. My question is only whether the just man, while refusing to have more than another just man, would wish and claim to have more than the unjust?

Yes, he would.

And what of the unjust – does he claim to have more than the just man and to do more than is just?

Of course, he said, for he claims to have more than all men.

And the unjust man will strive and struggle to obtain more than the unjust man or action, in order that he may have more than all?

True.

We may put the matter thus, I said – the just does not desire more than his like but more than his unlike, whereas the unjust desires more than both his like and his unlike?

Nothing, he said, can be better than that statement.

And the unjust is good and wise, and the just is neither?

Good again, he said.

And is not the unjust like the wise and good and the just unlike them?

Of course, he said, he who is of a certain nature, is like those who are of a certain nature; he who is not, not.

Each of them, I said, is such as his like is?

Certainly, he replied.

Very good, Thrasymachus, I said; and now to take the case of the arts: you would admit that one man is a musician and another not a musician?

Yes.

And which is wise and which is foolish?

Clearly the musician is wise, and he who is not a musician is foolish.

And he is good in as far as he is wise, and bad in as far as he is foolish?

Yes.

And you would say the same thing of the physician?

Yes.

And do you think, my excellent friend, that a musician when he tunes the lyre would desire or claim to exceed or go beyond a musician in the tightening and loosening the strings?

I do not think that he would.

But he would claim to exceed the non-musician?

Of course.

And what would you say of the physician? In prescribing meats and drinks would he wish to go beyond another physician or surpass what medicine prescribes?

He would not.

But he would wish to surpass the non-physician?

Yes.

And about knowledge and ignorance in general; see whether you think that any man who has knowledge would ever deliberately choose to say or do more than another man who has knowledge. Would he not rather say or do the same as his like in the same case?

That, I suppose, can hardly be denied.

And what of the ignorant? Would he not desire to have more than either the knowing or the ignorant?

I dare say.

And the possessor of knowledge is wise?

Yes.

And the wise is good?

True.

Then the wise and good will not desire to gain more than his like, but more than his unlike and opposite?

I suppose so.

Whereas the bad and ignorant will desire to gain more than both?

Apparently.

But did we not say, Thrasymachus, that the unjust goes beyond both his like and unlike? Were not these your words?

They were.

And you also said that the just will not go beyond his like but his unlike?

Yes.

Then the just is like the wise and good, and the unjust like the evil and ignorant?

That is the inference.

And each of them, as we previously admitted, is such as his like is?

That was admitted.

Then the just has turned out to be wise and good and the unjust evil and ignorant.

Thrasymachus made all these admissions, not fluently, as I repeat them, but with extreme reluctance; it was a hot summer's day, and the perspiration poured from him in torrents; and then I saw what I had never seen before, Thrasymachus blushing. As we were now agreed that justice was virtue and wisdom, and injustice vice and ignorance, I proceeded to another point:

Well, I said, Thrasymachus, let us take this as settled; but were we not also saying that injustice had strength; do you remember?

Yes, I remember, he said, but do not suppose that I approve of what you are saying or have no answer; if however I were to answer, you would be quite certain to accuse me of haranguing; therefore either permit me to have my say out, or if you would rather ask, do so, and I will answer 'Very good', as they say to story-telling old women, and will nod 'Yes' and 'No'.

Certainly not, I said, if it is contrary to your real opinion.

Yes, he said, I will, to please you, since you will not let me speak. What else would you have?

Nothing in the world, I said; and if that is your intention I will ask and you shall answer.

Proceed.

Then I will repeat the question which I asked before, in order that our examination of the relative nature of justice and injustice may proceed in due order. A statement was made that injustice is stronger and more powerful than justice, but now justice, having been identified with wisdom and virtue, will, I hope, easily be shown to be stronger than injustice, if injustice is ignorance; this should now be obvious to anyone. But I want to view the matter, Thrasymachus, in a somewhat less simple way: You would not deny that a state may be unjust and may be unjustly attempting to enslave other states, or may have already enslaved them, and may be holding many of them in subjection?

True, he replied; and I will add that the best and

most perfectly unjust state will be most likely to do so.

I know, I said, that such was your position; but what I would further consider is whether this power which is possessed by the superior [or stronger] state can exist or be exercised without justice, or cannot be divorced from justice.

If you are right in your view, and justice is wisdom, then only with justice; but if I am right, then rather with injustice.

I am delighted, Thrasymachus, to see you not only nodding assent and dissent, but making answers which are quite excellent.

That is out of civility to you, he replied.

You are very kind, I said; and would you have the goodness also to inform me, whether you think that a state, or an army, or a band of robbers and thieves, or any other gang of evil-doers could act at all if they injured one another?

No indeed, he said, they could not.

But if they abstained from injuring one another, then they might act together better?

Yes.

And this is because injustice creates divisions and hatreds and fighting, and justice imparts harmony and friendship; is not that true, Thrasymachus?

I agree, he said, because I do not wish to quarrel with you.

How good of you, I said; but I should like to know also whether injustice, having this tendency to arouse hatred, wherever it be found, among slaves or among freemen, will not make them hate one another and set them at variance and render them incapable of common action?

Certainly.

And even if injustice be found in two only, will they not quarrel and fight, and become enemies to one another and to the just?

They will.

And suppose injustice abiding in a single person, would your wisdom say that she loses her natural power, or retains it still?

Let us assume that she retains her power.

Then is not the power which injustice exercises of such a nature that wherever she takes up her abode, whether in a city, in an army, in a family, or in any other body, that body is, to begin with, rendered incapable of united action by reason of sedition and distraction; and does it not become the enemy not merely of itself, but of the just and all else that is opposed to it? Is not this the case?

Yes, certainly.

And is not injustice equally fatal when existing in a single person; in the first place rendering him incapable of action because he is not at unity with himself, and in the second place making him an enemy to himself and the just? Is not that true, Thrasymachus?

Yes.

And O my friend, I said, surely the gods are just?

Granted that they are.

But if so, the unjust will be the enemy of the gods, and the just will be their friend?

Feast away in triumph, and take your fill of the argument; I will not oppose you, lest I should displease the company.

Well then, proceed with your answers, and let me have the remainder of my repast. For we have already shown that the just are clearly wiser and better and abler than the unjust, and that the unjust are incapable of common action; nay more, that to speak as we did of men who are unjust acting at any time vigorously together, is not strictly true, for if they had been perfectly evil they would have laid hands upon one another; but it is evident that there must have been some remnant of justice in them, which hindered them from doing wrong to one another as well as to their victims; they were but half-villains in their enterprises; for had they been whole villains and utterly unjust, they would have been utterly incapable of action. That, as I understand, is the truth of the matter, and not what you said at first. But whether the just have a better and happier life than the unjust is a further question which we also proposed to consider. I think that they have, and for the reasons which I have given; but still I should like to examine further, for no light matter is at stake, nothing less than the rule of human life.

Proceed.

I will proceed by asking a question: would you not say that a horse has some function, or end?

I should.

And the end or use of a horse, or of anything else, would be that which could not be accomplished, or not so well accomplished, by any other thing?

I do not understand, he said.

Let me explain: can you see, except with the eye?

Certainly not.

Or hear, except with the ear?

No.

These then may be truly said to be the ends of these organs?

They may.

But you can cut off a vine-branch with a dagger or with a chisel, and in many other ways?

Of course.

And yet not so well as with a pruning-hook made for the purpose?

True.

May we not say that this is the end of a pruning-hook?

We may.

Then now I think you will have no difficulty in understanding my meaning when I asked the question whether the end of anything would be that which could not be accomplished, or not so well accomplished, by any other thing?

I understand your meaning, he said, and agree in this account of the end.

And everything to which an end is appointed has also an excellence? Let us return to the same examples; we say that the eyes have an end?

Yes.

And have they not also an excellence?

Yes.

And the ears have an end and, in consequence, an excellence also?

True.

And the same is true of all other things; they have each of them an end and a special excellence?

That is so.

Well, and can the eyes fulfil their end, if they are wanting in their own proper excellence and have a defect instead?

How can they, he said, if they are blind and cannot see?

You mean to say, if they have lost their proper excellence, which is sight; but I have not arrived at that point yet. I only inquire whether the things which fulfil their ends fulfil them by their own proper excellence, and fail of fulfilling them by their own defect?

Certainly, he replied.

I might say the same of the ears; when deprived of their own proper excellence they cannot fulfil their end?

True.

And the same observation will apply to all other things?

I agree.

Well; and has not the soul an end which nothing else can fulfil? For example, to superintend and command and deliberate and the like. Are not these functions proper to the soul, and can they rightly be assigned to any other?

To no other.

What of living – is not that a function of the soul?

Assuredly, he said.

And we say that there is an excellence or virtue of the soul?

Yes.

And can she or can she not fulfil her own ends, Thrasymachus, when deprived of her proper excellence?

She cannot.

Then an evil soul must necessarily be an evil ruler and superintendent, and the good soul a fortunate and successful one.

Yes, necessarily.

And we have admitted that justice is the excellence of the soul, and injustice the defect of the soul?

That has been admitted.

Then the just soul and the just man will live well, and the unjust man will live ill?

That is what your argument proves.

And he who lives well is blessed and happy, and he who lives ill the reverse of happy?

Certainly.

Then the just is happy, and the unjust miserable?

So be it.

But happiness and not misery is profitable.

Of course.

Then, my blessed Thrasymachus, injustice can never be more profitable than justice.

Let this, Socrates, he said, be your entertainment at the Bendidea.

For which I am indebted to you, I said, now that you have grown gentle towards me and left off scolding. Nevertheless, I have not been well entertained; but that was my own fault and not yours. As a gourmand snatches a taste of every dish which is successively brought to table, without having allowed himself time to enjoy the one before, so have I gone from one subject to another without having discovered what I sought at first, the nature of justice. I left that inquiry and turned away to consider whether justice is virtue and wisdom or evil and folly; and when there arose a further question about the comparative advantages of justice and injustice, I could not refrain from passing on to that. And the result of the whole discussion has been that I know nothing at all. For I know not what justice is, and therefore I am not likely to know whether it is or is not a virtue, nor can I say whether the just man is happy or unhappy.

BOOK TWO

With these words I was thinking that I had made an end of the discussion; but the end, in truth, proved to be only a beginning. For Glaucon, who is always the most pugnacious of men, would not submit quietly to the retirement of Thrasymachus. So he said to me: Socrates, do you wish really to persuade us, or only to seem to have persuaded us, that to be just is in every way better than to be unjust?

I should wish really to persuade you, I replied, if I could.

Then you certainly have not succeeded. Let me ask you now: how would you arrange goods – are there not some which we welcome for their own sakes, and not from any desire for their consequences, as, for example, the enjoyment and the harmless pleasures which delight us at the time, although nothing follows from them?

I agree in thinking that there is such a class, I replied.

Is there not also a second class of goods, such as knowledge, sight, health, which are desirable not only in themselves, but also for their results?

Certainly, I said.

And would you not recognise a third class, such as gymnastic exercise and medical treatment; also the medical art and all those occupations by which money is made – these do us good but we regard them as disagreeable; and no one would choose them for their own sakes, but only for the sake of some reward or result which flows from them?

There is, I said, this third class also. But why do you ask?

Because I want to know in which of the three classes you would place justice.

In the highest class, I replied – among those goods which he who would be happy desires both for their own sake and for the sake of their results.

Then the many are of another mind; they think that justice is to be reckoned in the troublesome class, among goods which are to be pursued for the sake of rewards and of reputation, but in themselves are disagreeable and rather to be avoided.

I know, I said, that this is their manner of thinking, and that this was the thesis which Thrasymachus has all along been maintaining when he censured justice and praised injustice. But I seem to be a slow learner.

Please listen to me as well, he said, and perhaps I shall persuade you to change your opinion. For Thrasymachus seems to me, like a snake, to have been charmed by your voice sooner than he ought to have been; but to my mind the nature of justice and injustice has not yet been made clear. Setting aside their rewards and results, I want to know what they are in themselves, and how they inwardly work in the soul. If you please, then, I will revive the argument of Thrasymachus. And first I will speak of the nature and origin of justice according to the common view of them. Secondly, I will show that all men who practise justice do so against their will, of necessity, but not as a good. And thirdly, I will argue that there is reason in this view, for the life of the unjust is after all better far than the life of the just – if what they say is true, Socrates, since I myself am not of their opinion. But still I acknowledge that I am perplexed when I hear the voices of Thrasymachus and myriads of others dinning in my ears; and, on the other hand, I have never yet heard the superiority of justice to injustice maintained by anyone in a satisfactory way. I want to hear justice praised in respect of itself; then I shall be satisfied, and you are the person from whom I think that I am most likely to hear this; and therefore I will praise the unjust life to the utmost of my power, and my manner of speaking will indicate the manner in which I desire to hear you too praising justice and censuring injustice. Will you say whether you approve of my proposal?

Indeed I do; nor can I imagine any theme about which a man of sense would oftener wish to converse.

I am delighted, he replied, to hear you say so, and shall begin by speaking, as I proposed, of the nature and origin of justice.

They say that to do injustice is, by nature, good; to suffer injustice, evil; but that there is more evil in the latter than good in the former. And so when men have both done and suffered injustice and have had experience of both, any who are not able to avoid the one and obtain the other, think that they had better agree among themselves to have neither; hence they began to establish laws and mutual covenants; and that which was ordained by law was termed by them lawful and just. This, it is claimed, is the origin and nature of justice; it is a mean or compromise, between the best of all, which is to do injustice and not be punished, and the worst of all, which is to suffer injustice without the power of retaliation; and justice, being at a middle point between the two, is tolerated not as a good, but as the lesser evil, and honoured where men are too feeble to do injustice.

For no man who is worthy to be called a man would ever submit to such an agreement with another if he had the power to be unjust; he would be mad if he did. Such is the received account, Socrates, of the nature of justice, and the circumstances which bring it into being.

Now that those who practise justice do so involuntarily and because they have not the power to be unjust will best appear if we imagine something of this kind: having given to both the just and the unjust power to do what they will, let us watch and see whither desire will lead them; then we shall discover in the very act the just and unjust man to be proceeding along the same road, following their interest, which all creatures instinctively pursue as their good; the force of law is required to compel them to pay respect to equality. The liberty which we are supposing may be most completely given to them in the form of such a power as is said to have been possessed by Gyges, the ancestor of Croesus the Lydian. According to the tradition, Gyges was a shepherd in the service of the reigning king of Lydia; there was a great storm, and an earthquake made an opening in the earth at the place where he was feeding his flock. Amazed at the sight, he descended into the opening, where, among other marvels which form part of the story, he beheld a hollow brazen horse, having doors, at which he stooping and looking in saw a dead body of stature, as appeared to him, more than human; he took from the corpse a gold ring that was on the hand, but nothing else, and so reascended. Now the shepherds met together, according to custom, that they might send their monthly report about the flocks to the king; into their assembly he came having the ring on his finger, and as he was sitting among them he chanced to turn the collet of the ring to the inside of his hand, when instantly he became invisible to the rest of the company and they began to speak of him as if he were no longer present. He was astonished at this, and again touching the ring he turned the collet outwards and reappeared; when he perceived this, he made several trials of the ring, and always with the same result – when he turned the collet inwards he became invisible, when outwards he was visible. Whereupon he contrived to be chosen one of the messengers who were sent to the court; where as soon as he arrived he seduced the queen, and with her help conspired against the king and slew him, and took the kingdom. Suppose now that there were two such magic rings, and the just put on one of them and the unjust the other; no man can be imagined to be of such an iron nature that he would stand fast in justice. No man would keep his hands off what was not his own when he could safely take what he liked out of the market, or go into houses and lie with any one at his pleasure, or kill or release from prison whom he would, and in all respects be like a god among men. Then the actions of the just would be as the actions of the unjust; they would both tend to the same goal. And this we may truly affirm to be a great proof that a man is just, not willingly or because he thinks that justice is any good to him individually, but of necessity; for wherever anyone thinks that he can safely be unjust, there he is unjust. For all men believe in their hearts that injustice is far more profitable to the individual than justice, and he who argues as I have been supposing will say that they are right. If you could imagine anyone obtaining this power of becoming invisible, and never doing any wrong or touching what was another's, he would be thought by the lookers-on to be an unhappy man and a fool, although they would praise him to one another's faces, and keep up appearances with one another from a fear that they too might suffer injustice. Enough of this.

Now, if we are to form a real judgment of the two lives in these respects, we must set apart the extremes of justice and injustice; there is no other way. And how is the contrast to be effected? I answer: let the unjust man be entirely unjust, and the just man entirely just; nothing is to be taken away from either of them, and both are to be perfectly furnished for the work of their respective lives. First, let the unjust be like other distinguished masters of craft; like the skilful pilot or physician, who knows intuitively what is possible or impossible in his art and keeps within those limits, and who, if he fails at any point, is able to recover himself. So let the unjust man attempt to do the right sort of wrongs, and let him escape detection if he is to be pronounced a master of injustice. To be found out is a sign of incompetence; for the height of injustice is to be deemed just when you are not. Therefore I say that in the perfectly unjust man we must assume the most perfect injustice; there is to be no deduction, but we must allow him, while doing the most unjust acts, to have acquired the greatest reputation for justice. If he has taken a false step he must be able to recover himself; he must be one who can speak with effect, if any of his deeds come to light, and who can force his way where force is required, by his courage and strength and command of wealth and friends. And at his side let us place the just man in his nobleness and simplicity, wishing, as Aeschylus says, to be and not to seem good. There must be no seeming, for if he seems to be just he will be honoured and rewarded, and then we shall not know whether he is just for the sake of justice or for the sake of honours and rewards; therefore, let him be clothed in justice only, and have no other covering; and he must be imagined in a state of life the opposite of the former. Let him be the best of men, and let him be reputed the worst; then he will have been put to the test and we shall see whether his justice is proof against evil reputation and its consequences. And let him continue thus to the hour of death; being just and seeming to be unjust. When both have reached the uttermost extreme, the one of justice and the other of injustice, let judgment be given which of them is the happier of the two.

Heavens! My dear Glaucon, I said, how energetically you polish them up for the decision, first one and then the other, as if they were two statues.

I do my best, he said. And now that we know what they are like, there is no difficulty in tracing out the sort of life which awaits either of them. This I will proceed to describe; but as you may think the description a little too coarse, I ask you to suppose, Socrates, that the words which follow are not mine, but those of the eulogists of injustice: They will tell you that the just man who is thought unjust will be scourged, racked, bound – will have his eyes burnt out; and, at last, after suffering every kind of evil, he will be impaled: then he will understand that he ought to seem only, and not to be, just; the words of Aeschylus may be more truly spoken of the unjust than of the just. For the unjust, they will say, is in fact pursuing a reality; he does not live with a view to appearances – he wants to be really unjust and not to seem only:

'His mind has a soil deep and fertile,
Out of which spring his prudent counsels.'

In the first place, he is thought just, and therefore
bears rule in the city; he can marry whom he will, and
give in marriage to whom he will; also he can trade and
deal where he likes, and always to his own advantage,
because he has no misgivings about injustice; and at
every contest, whether in public or in private, he gets
the better of his antagonists, and gains at their expense,
and is rich, and out of his gains he can benefit his
friends, and harm his enemies; moreover, he can offer
sacrifices, and dedicate gifts to the gods abundantly
and magnificently, and can honour the gods or any
man whom he wants to honour in a far better style than
the just, and therefore he is likely to be dearer than they
are to the gods. And thus, Socrates, they say that a
better life is provided, by gods and men alike, for the
unjust than for the just.

I was going to say something in answer to Glaucon,
when Adeimantus, his brother, interposed: Socrates,
he said, you do not suppose that there is nothing more
to be urged?

Why, what else is there? I answered.

The strongest point of all has not been even
mentioned, he replied.

Well, then, according to the proverb, 'Let brother
help brother' – if he fails in any part do you assist him;
although I must confess that Glaucon has already said
quite enough to lay me in the dust, and take from me
the power of helping justice.

Nonsense, he replied. But let me add something
more: in order to bring out what I believe to be
Glaucon's meaning, it is equally necessary to consider

exhortations of an opposite sort, in which justice is praised and injustice censured. Parents and tutors are always telling their sons and their wards that they are to be just; but why? Not for the sake of justice, but for the sake of character and reputation; in the hope of obtaining for him who is reputed just some of those offices, marriages, and the like which Glaucon has enumerated among the advantages accruing to a just man from his reputation of justice. More, however, is made of appearances by this class of persons than by the others; for they throw in the good opinion of the gods, and will tell you of a shower of benefits which the heavens, as they say, rain upon the pious; and this accords with the testimony of the noble Hesiod and Homer, the first of whom says, that the gods make the oaks of the just –

'To bear acorns at their summit, and bees
                                          in the middle;
And the sheep are bowed down with the
                                          weight of their fleeces,'

and many other blessings of a like kind are provided for them. And Homer has a very similar strain; for he speaks of one whose fame is –

'As the fame of some blameless king who, like a god,
Maintains justice; to whom the black earth
                                          brings forth
Wheat and barley, whose trees are bowed
                                          with fruit,
And his sheep never fail to bear, and the sea
                                          gives him fish.'

Still grander are the gifts of heaven which Musaeus and his son vouchsafe to the just; they take them down into the world below, where they have the saints lying on couches at a feast, everlastingly drunk, crowned with garlands; their idea seems to be that an immortality of drunkenness is the highest meed of virtue. Some extend the rewards promised on behalf of the gods yet further; the posterity, as they say, of the faithful and just shall survive to the third and fourth generation. This is the style in which they praise justice. But about the impious and unjust there is another strain; they bury them in a slough in Hades, and make them carry water in a sieve; also while they are yet living they bring them to infamy, and inflict upon them the punishments which Glaucon described as the portion of the just who are reputed to be unjust; nothing else does their invention supply. Such is their manner of praising the one and censuring the other.

Once more, Socrates, I will ask you to consider another way of speaking about justice and injustice, which is not confined to the poets but is heard in daily life. The universal voice of mankind is always declaring that justice and virtue are honourable, but grievous and toilsome; and that the pleasures of vice and injustice are easy of attainment, and are only censured by law and opinion. They say also that honesty is for the most part less profitable than dishonesty; and they are quite ready to call wicked men happy, and to honour them both in public and private when they are rich or in any other way influential, while they despise and overlook those who may be weak and poor, even though acknowledging them to be better than the others. But most extraordinary of all is their mode of speaking about virtue and the gods: they say that even the gods have apportioned calamity and misery to many good men, and an opposite destiny to the wicked. And mendicant prophets go to rich men's doors and persuade them that they have a power committed to them by the gods of making an atonement for a man's own or his ancestor's sins by sacrifices or charms, with rejoicings and feasts; and they offer their services in harming an enemy, whether just or unjust, at a small cost; with magic arts and incantations binding heaven, as they say, to execute their will. And the poets are the authorities to whom they appeal for all this, now smoothing the path of vice with the words of Hesiod:

'Vice may be had in abundance without trouble; the way is smooth and her dwelling-place is near. But before virtue the gods have set toil,'

and a tedious and rough and uphill road: then citing Homer as a witness that the gods may be influenced by men; for he also says:

'The gods, too, may be turned from their purpose; and men pray to them and avert their wrath by sacrifices and soothing entreaties, and by libations and the odour of fat, when they have sinned and transgressed.'

And they produce a host of books written by Musaeus and Orpheus, who were children of the Moon and the Muses – that is what they say – according to which they perform their ritual, and persuade not only individuals, but whole cities, that expiations and atonements for sin may be made by sacrifices and amusements, which fill a vacant hour and are equally at the service of the living and dead; the latter sort they call initiations, and they redeem us from the pains of hell, but if we neglect them no one knows what awaits us.

He proceeded: And now when the young hear all this said about virtue and vice, and the way in which gods and men regard them, how are their minds likely to be affected, my dear Socrates? Those of them, I mean, who are quick-witted, and, like bees on the wing, lighting on every flower, are not slow to draw conclusions as to what manner of persons they should be and in what way they should walk if they would make the best of life. Probably the youth will say to himself in the words of Pindar:

'Can I by justice or by crooked ways of deceit ascend a loftier tower which may be a fortress to me all my days?'

For what men say is that, if I am really just and am not also thought just, profit there is none, but the pain and loss on the other hand are unmistakable. But if, though unjust, I acquire the reputation of justice, a heavenly life is promised to me. Since then, as philosophers prove, appearance tyrannises over truth and is lord of happiness, to appearance I must devote myself. I will surround myself with an illusory screen of virtue to be the vestibule and exterior of my house; behind I will trail the subtle and crafty fox, as Archilochus, greatest of sages, recommends. But I hear someone exclaiming that the concealment of wickedness on all occasions is difficult; to which I answer, 'Nothing great is easy.' Nevertheless, the argument indicates this, if we would be happy, to be the the path along which we should proceed. With a view to concealment we will establish secret brotherhoods and political clubs. And there are professors of rhetoric who teach the art of persuading courts and assemblies; and so, partly by persuasion and partly by force, I shall make unlawful gains and not be punished. Still I hear a voice saying that the gods cannot be deceived, neither can they be compelled. But what if there are no gods? Or, suppose them to have no care of human things – why in either case should we mind about concealment? And even if there are gods and they do care about us, yet we know of them only from tradition and the genealogies of the poets; and these are the very persons who say that they may be influenced and turned by 'sacrifices and soothing entreaties' and by offerings. Let us be consistent then, and believe both or neither. If the poets speak truly, why then we had better be unjust, and offer in sacrifice some of the fruits of injustice; for if we are just, although we may escape the vengeance of heaven we shall lose the gains of injustice; but if we are unjust, we shall secure the gains, and by atoning in prayer for our sins and transgressions, shall propitiate the gods, and shall escape all harm or loss. 'But there is a world below in which either we or our posterity will suffer for our unjust deeds.' Yes, my friend, will be the reflection, but there are initiations and absolving deities, and these have great power. That is what mighty cities declare; and the children of the gods, who were their poets and prophets, bear a like testimony.

On what principle, then, shall we any longer choose justice rather than the worst injustice, when, if we only unite the latter with a deceitful regard to appearances, we shall fare to our mind both with gods and men, in life and after death, as the most numerous and the highest authorities tell us. Knowing all this, Socrates, how can a man who has any superiority of mind or person or rank or wealth, be willing to honour justice? How indeed can he refrain from laughing when he hears justice praised? And even if there should be someone who is able to disprove the truth of my words, and who knows beyond doubt that justice is best, still he can hardly be angry with the unjust but is very ready to forgive them, because he also knows that men are not just of their own free will; unless peradventure there be someone whom the divinity within him has inspired with a hatred of injustice, or who shuns it because he has attained knowledge of the truth – but no other man. He only blames injustice who, owing to cowardice or age or some weakness, has not the power of being unjust. And this is proved by the fact that when he obtains the power, any such man is the first to become unjust as far as he can be.

The cause of all this, Socrates, was indicated by us at the beginning of the argument, when my brother and I told you how astonished we were to find that of all the professing panegyrists of justice – beginning with the ancient heroes of whom any memorial has been preserved to us, and ending with the men of our own time – no one has ever blamed injustice or praised justice except with a view to the glories, honours, and privileges which flow from them. No one has ever adequately described either in verse or in prose the power and effect of either of them abiding in the soul, though it be invisible to any human or divine eye; or shown that of all intrinsic qualities of the soul, justice is the greatest good, and injustice the greatest evil. Had this been the universal strain, had you sought to persuade us of this from our youth upwards, we should not have been on the watch to keep one another from doing wrong, but everyone would have been his own watchman, because afraid, if he did wrong, of harbouring in himself the greatest of evils.

I dare say that Thrasymachus and others would seriously use the language which I have been repeating, and words even stronger than these, about justice and injustice, crudely, as I conceive, perverting their true nature. But I speak in this vehement manner, as I must frankly confess to you, because I want to hear from you the opposite side; and I would ask you to show not only the superiority which justice has over injustice, but what effect, inseparable from their nature, they have on the possessor of them which makes the one to be a good and the other an evil to him. And please, as Glaucon requested of you, to exclude reputations; for unless you take away from each of them his true reputation and add on the false, we shall say that you do not praise justice, but the appearance of it; we shall think that you are only exhorting us to keep injustice dark, and that you really agree with Thrasymachus in thinking that justice is another's good and the interest of the stronger, and that injustice is a man's own profit and interest, though injurious to the weaker. Now as you have admitted that justice is one of that highest class of goods which are desired indeed for their results, but in a far greater degree for their own sakes – like sight or hearing or knowledge or health, yes, or any good which is fertile by nature, and not merely esteemed so – I would ask you in your praise of justice to regard one point only: I mean the essential good and evil which justice and injustice work in the possessors of them. Let others praise justice and censure injustice, magnifying the rewards and honours of the one and abusing the other; that is a manner of arguing which, coming from them, I am ready to tolerate, but from you who have spent your whole life in the consideration of this question, unless I hear the contrary from your own

lips, I expect something better. And therefore, I say, not only prove to us that justice is better than injustice, but show what they either of them do to the possessor of them, which makes the one to be a good and the other an evil, whether seen or unseen by gods and men.

I had always admired the genius of Glaucon and Adeimantus, but on hearing these words I was quite delighted, and said: Sons of an illustrious father, that was not a bad beginning of the elegiac verses which the admirer of Glaucon made in honour of you after you had distinguished yourselves at the battle of Megara: 'Sons of Ariston,' he sang, 'divine offspring of an illustrious hero.'

The epithet is very appropriate, for there is something truly divine in being able to argue as you have done for the superiority of injustice, and remaining unconvinced by your own arguments. And I do believe that you are not convinced – this I infer from your general character, for had I judged only from your speeches I should have mistrusted you. But now, the greater my confidence in you, the greater is my difficulty in knowing what to say. For on the one hand I cannot offer any help, because I feel that I am unequal to the task; and my inability is brought home to me by the fact that you were not satisfied with the answer which I made to Thrasymachus, proving, as I thought, the superiority which justice has over injustice. And yet I cannot refuse to help, while breath and speech remain to me; I am afraid that there would be an impiety in being present when justice is evil spoken of and not lifting up a hand in her defence. And therefore I had best give such help as I can.

Glaucon and the rest entreated me by all means not to let the question drop, but, in the first place, to inquire thoroughly into the nature of justice and injustice, and secondly, to discover the truth about their relative advantages. I told them, what I really thought, that the inquiry would be of a serious nature, and would require very good eyes. Seeing then, I said, that we are no great wits, I think that we had better adopt a method which I may illustrate thus: suppose that a short-sighted person had been asked to read small letters from a distance; and someone observed that the same inscription was written elsewhere on a larger scale – if they were the same, and he could read the larger letters first and then proceed to the lesser, this would have been thought a rare piece of good fortune.

Very true, said Adeimantus; but how does the illustration apply to our inquiry about justice?

I will tell you, I replied; justice is, as you know, sometimes spoken of as the virtue of an individual, and sometimes as the virtue of a state.

True, he replied.

And is not a state larger than an individual?

It is.

Then in the larger, justice is likely to be more abundant and more easily discernible. I propose therefore that we inquire into the nature of justice and injustice, first as they appear in the state, and secondly in the individual, proceeding from the greater to the lesser and comparing them.

That, he said, is an excellent proposal.

And if we imagine the state in process of creation, we shall see the justice and injustice of the state in process of creation also.

I dare say.

When the state is completed there may be a hope

that the object of our search will be more easily discovered.

Yes, far more easily.

But ought we to attempt to construct one? I said; for to do so, as I am inclined to think, will be a very serious task. Reflect therefore.

I have reflected, said Adeimantus, and am anxious that you should proceed.

A state, I said, arises, as I conceive, out of the needs of mankind; no one is self-sufficing, but all of us have many wants. Can any other origin of a state be imagined?

There can be no other.

Then, as we have many wants, and many persons are needed to supply them, one takes a helper for one purpose and another for another; and when these partners and helpers are gathered together in one habitation, the body of inhabitants is termed a state.

True, he said.

And it is in the belief that it is for his own good, that one man gives to another or receives from him in exchange.

Very true.

Then, I said, let us construct a state in theory from the beginning; and yet the true creator, it seems, will be necessity.

Of course, he replied.

Now the first and greatest of necessities is food, which is the condition of life and existence.

Certainly.

The second is a dwelling, and the third clothing and the like.

True.

And now let us see what must be the size of a city

able to supply such a demand: We may suppose that one man is a husbandman, another a builder, someone else a weaver – shall we add to them a shoemaker, or perhaps some other purveyor to our bodily wants?

By all means.

The simplest possible state must include four or five men.

Clearly.

And how will they proceed? Will each bring the result of his labours into a common stock – the individual husbandman, for example, producing for four, and labouring four times as long and as much as he need in the provision of food with which he supplies others as well as himself; or will he have nothing to do with others and not be at the trouble of producing for them, but provide for himself alone a fourth of the food in a fourth of the time, and in the remaining three fourths of his time be employed in making a house or a coat or a pair of shoes, not bothering to form a partnership with others, but supplying himself all his own wants?

Adeimantus thought that he should aim at producing food only and not at producing everything.

Probably, I replied, that would be the better way; and when I hear you say this, I am myself reminded that we are not all alike; there are diversities of natures among us which are adapted to different occupations.

Very true.

And will you have a work better done when every workman tries his hand at many occupations, or when each has only one?

When he has only one.

Further, there can be no doubt that a work is spoilt when not done at the right time?

No doubt.

For business is not disposed to wait until the doer of the business is at leisure; but the doer must follow up his opportunity, and make the business his first object.

He must.

And if so, we must infer that all things are produced more plentifully and easily and of a better quality when one man does one thing which is natural to him and does it at the right time, leaving other crafts alone.

Undoubtedly.

Then more than four citizens will be required to furnish all that has been mentioned; for the husband-man will not make his own plough or mattock, or other implements of agriculture, if they are to be good for anything. Neither will the builder make his tools – and he too needs many; and in like manner the weaver and shoemaker.

True.

Then carpenters, and smiths, and many other artisans, will be sharers in our little state, which is already beginning to grow?

True.

Yet even if we add neatherds, shepherds, and other herdsmen, in order that our husbandmen may have oxen to plough with, and builders as well as hus-bandmen may have draught cattle, and curriers and weavers fleeces and hides – still our state will not be very large.

That is true; yet neither will it be a very small state which contains all these.

Then, again, there is the situation of the city – to find a place where nothing need be imported is wellnigh impossible.

Impossible.

Then there must be another class of citizens who will bring the required supply from another city?

There must.

But if the trader goes empty-handed, having nothing which they require who would supply his need, he will come back empty-handed.

That is probable.

And therefore what they produce at home must be not only enough for themselves, but such both in quantity and quality as to accommodate those from whom their wants are supplied.

Very true.

Then more husbandmen and more artisans will be required?

They will.

Not to mention those who serve as importers and exporters of goods, who are called, I believe, merchants?

Yes.

Then we shall want merchants?

We shall.

And if merchandise is to be carried over the sea, we shall also require men who have been bred to various nautical occupations.

Yes, a large class.

Then, again, within the city, how will they exchange their productions? To secure such an exchange was, as you will remember, one of our principal objects when we formed them into a society and constituted a state.

Clearly they will buy and sell.

Then they will need a marketplace, and a money-token for purposes of exchange.

Certainly.

Suppose now that a husbandman, or an artisan,

brings some production to market, and comes at a time when there is no one to exchange with him – is he to sit idle in the marketplace, taking a holiday from his work?

Not at all; he will find people there who, seeing the want, undertake the office of salesmen. In well-ordered states they are commonly those who are weakest in bodily strength, and therefore of little use for any other purpose; their duty is to be in the market, and to give money in exchange for goods to those who desire to sell and to take money from those who desire to buy.

This want, then, creates a class of retail-traders in our state. Is not 'retailer' the term which is applied to those who sit in the marketplace engaged in buying and selling, while those who wander from one city to another are called merchants?

Yes, he said.

And there is another class of servants, who are intellectually hardly on the level of association; still they have plenty of bodily strength for labour, which accordingly they sell, and are called, if I do not mistake, hirelings, hire being the name which is given to the price of their labour.

True.

Then hirelings will help to make up our population?

Yes.

And now, Adeimantus, is our state matured and perfected?

I think so.

Where, then, is justice within it, and where is injustice, and at what stage did they make their entrance?

Probably in the dealings of these citizens with one

another. I cannot suggest where else they may be found.

I dare say that you are right in your suggestion, I said; we had better think the matter out, and not shrink from the inquiry.

Let us then consider, first of all, what will be their way of life, now that we have thus established them. Will they not work at the production of corn, and wine, and clothes, and shoes? And when they are housed, in summer they will commonly work stripped and barefoot, but in winter substantially clothed and shod. They will feed on barley-meal and flour of wheat, baking the one and kneading the other, making noble cakes and loaves; these they will serve up on a mat of reeds or on clean leaves, themselves reclining the while upon beds strewn with yew or myrtle. And they and their children will feast, drinking of the wine which they have made, wearing garlands on their heads, and hymning the praises of the gods, in happy converse with one another. And they will take care that their families do not exceed their means; having an eye to poverty or war.

But, said Glaucon, interposing, you have not given them a relish to their meal.

True, I replied, I had forgotten; of course they must have a relish – salt, and olives, and cheese, and they will boil roots and herbs such as country people prepare; for a dessert we shall give them figs, and peas, and beans; and they will roast myrtle-berries and acorns at the fire, sipping their wine in moderation. And with such a diet they may be expected to live in peace and health to a good old age, and bequeath a similar life to their children after them.

Yes, Socrates, he said, and if you were providing for a city of pigs, how else would you feed the beasts?

But what would you have, Glaucon? I replied.

Why, he said, you should give them the ordinary conveniences of life. People who are to be comfortable are accustomed to lie on sofas, and dine off tables, and they should have sauces and sweets in the modern style.

Yes, I said, now I understand: the question which you would have me consider is, not only how a state, but how a luxurious state is created; and possibly there is no harm in this, for by extending our inquiry to such a state we shall be more likely to see how political justice and injustice originate. In my opinion the true and healthy constitution of the state is the one which I have described. But if you wish also to see a state at fever-heat, I have no objection. For I suspect that many will not be satisfied with the simpler way of life. They will be for adding sofas, and tables, and other furniture; also dainties, and perfumes, and incense, and courtesans, and cakes, all these not of one sort only, but in every variety; we must go beyond the necessaries of which I was at first speaking, such as houses, and clothes, and shoes: the arts of the painter and the embroiderer will have to be set in motion, and gold and ivory and all sorts of materials must be procured.

True, he said.

Then we must enlarge our borders; for the original healthy state is no longer sufficient. Now will the city have to fill and swell with a multitude of callings which are not required by any natural want; such as the tribe of hunters, and again imitators, of whom one large class have to do with forms and colours; another will be the votaries of music – poets and their attendant train of rhapsodists, players, dancers, contractors; also

makers of divers kinds of articles, including those
which serve for the adornment of women. And we
shall want more servants. Will not tutors be also in
request, and nurses wet and dry, tirewomen and
barbers, as well as confectioners and cooks? Then we
shall also now need swineherds, who were not needed
and therefore had no place in our former state. They
must not be forgotten: also a vast number of cattle will
be required, if meat is to be eaten.

Certainly.

And living in this way we shall have much greater
need of physicians than before?

Much greater.

And the country which was once enough to support
the original inhabitants will now have become too
small?

Quite true.

Then a slice of our neighbours' land will be wanted
by us for pasture and tillage, and they will want a slice
of ours, if, like ourselves, they exceed the limit of
necessity, and give themselves up to the unlimited
accumulation of wealth?

That, Socrates, will be inevitable.

And so we shall go to war, Glaucon. Shall we not?

Most certainly, he replied.

Then, without determining as yet whether war does
good or harm, thus much we may affirm, that now we
have discovered war to be derived from causes which
are also the causes of almost all the evils in states,
private as well as public.

Undoubtedly.

And our state must once more enlarge; and this time
the enlargement will be nothing short of a whole army,
which will have to go out and fight with the invaders

for all that we have, as well as for the things and persons whom we were describing above.

Why? he said; are they not capable of defending themselves?

No, I said; not if we were right in the principle which was acknowledged by all of us when we were framing the state: the principle, as you will remember, was that one man cannot practise many arts with success.

Very true, he said.

But is not armed combat in war an art?

Certainly.

And an art requiring as much attention as shoe-making?

Quite true.

And the shoemaker was not allowed by us to be a husbandman, or a weaver, or a builder – in order that we might have our shoes well made; but to him and to every other worker was assigned one work for which he was by nature fitted, and at that he was to continue working all his life long and at no other; he was not to let opportunities slip, and then he would become a good workman. Now can anything be more important than that the work of a soldier should be well done? Or is war an art so easily acquired that a man may be a warrior who is also a husbandman, or shoemaker, or other artisan; although no one in the world would be a good dice- or chess-player who merely took up the game as a recreation, and had not from his earliest years devoted himself to this and nothing else? No equipment will make a man a skilled workman, or athlete, nor be of any use to him who has not learned how to handle it, and has never bestowed sufficient attention upon it. How then will he who takes up a shield or other implement of war become a good fighter all in a day, whether with heavy-armed or any other kind of troops?

Yes, he said, the tools which would teach men their own use would be beyond price.

And just as the duties of the guardian surpass all others in importance, I said, so does his business require the most skill and practice, as well as undivided attention.

No doubt, he replied.

Will he not also require natural aptitude for his calling?

Certainly.

Then it will be our duty to select, if we can, natures which are fitted for the task of guarding the city?

It will.

It is no light task, then, that we have undertaken, I said; but we must be brave and do our best.

We must.

[*a discussion of the character required in the guardians leads to some reflections on the stories they should read and be told as part of their education*]

BOOK THREE

[the moral education – poetry and music – and physical education of the guardians is described in detail]

Such, then, are our principles of nurture and education: Where would be the use of going into further details about the dances of our citizens, or about their hunting and coursing, their gymnastic and equestrian contests? For these all follow the general principle, and having found that, we shall have no difficulty in discovering them.

I dare say that there will be no difficulty.

Very good, I said; then what is the next question? Must we not ask who are to be rulers and who subjects?

Certainly.

There can be no doubt that the elder must rule the younger.

Clearly.

And that the best of these must rule.

That is also clear.

Now, are the best husbandmen those who are most devoted to husbandry?

Yes.

And as we are to have the best of guardians for our city, must they not be those who have most the character of guardians?

Yes.

And to this end they ought to be wise and efficient, and to have a special care of the state?

True.

And a man will be most likely to care about that which he loves?

To be sure.

And he will be most likely to love that which he regards as having the same interests with himself, and that of which the good or evil fortune is supposed by him at any time most to affect his own?

Very true, he replied.

Then there must be a selection. Let us note among the guardians those who in their whole life show the greatest eagerness to do what they suppose to be for the good of their country, and the greatest repugnance to do what is against her interests.

Those are the right men.

And they will have to be watched at every age, in order that we may see whether they preserve their resolution, and never yield either to force or to enchantment, so as to forget or cast off their sense of duty to the state.

How cast off? he said.

I will explain to you, I replied. A resolution may go out of a man's mind either with his will or against his will: with his will when he gets rid of a falsehood and learns better, against his will whenever he is deprived of a truth.

I understand, he said, the willing loss of a resolution; the meaning of the unwilling I have yet to learn.

Why, I said, do you not see that men are unwillingly deprived of good, and willingly of evil? Is not to have lost the truth an evil, and to possess the truth a good? And you would agree that to conceive things as they are is to possess the truth?

Yes, he replied; I agree with you in thinking that mankind are deprived of truth against their will.

And is not this involuntary deprivation caused either by theft, or force, or enchantment?

Still, he replied, I do not understand you.

I must have been talking darkly, like the tragedians. As for theft, I only mean that some men are changed by persuasion and that others forget; argument steals away the beliefs of one class, and time of the other. Now you understand me?

Yes.

Those again who are forced, are those whom the violence of some pain or grief compels to change their opinion.

I understand, he said, and you are quite right.

And you would also acknowledge that the enchanted are those who change their minds either under the softer influence of pleasure, or the sterner shock of fear?

Yes, he said; everything that deceives may be said to enchant.

Therefore, as I was just now saying, we must inquire who are the best guardians of their own conviction that they should always do what they judge most advantageous to the state. We must watch them from their youth upwards, and make them perform actions in which they are most likely to forget or to be deceived, and he who remembers and is not deceived is to be selected, and he who fails in the trial is to be rejected. That will be the way?

Yes.

And there should also be toils and pains and conflicts prescribed for them, in which they will be made to give further proof of the same qualities.

Very right, he replied.

And then, I said, we must try them with enchantments – that is the third sort of test – and see what will

be their behaviour: like those who take colts amid
noise and tumult to see if they are of a timid nature, so
must we take our youth amid terrors of some kind, and
thence pass them into pleasures, and prove them more
thoroughly than gold is proved in the furnace, that
we may discover whether they are armed against all
enchantments, and of a noble bearing always, good
guardians of themselves and of the music which they
have learned, and retaining under all circumstances a
rhythmical and harmonious nature, such as will be
most serviceable to themselves and to the state. And
he who at every age, as boy and youth and in mature
life, has come out of the trial victorious and pure, shall
be appointed a ruler and guardian of the state; he shall
be honoured in life and death, and shall receive
sepulture and other memorials of honour, the greatest
that we have to give. But him who fails, we must reject.
I am inclined to think that this is the sort of way in
which our rulers and guardians should be chosen and
appointed. I speak generally, and not with any pretension to exactness.

And, speaking generally, I agree with you, he said.

And perhaps the word 'guardian' in the fullest sense
ought to be applied to this higher class only who both
preserve us against foreign enemies and maintain
peace among our citizens at home, that the one may
not have the will, or the others the power, to harm us.
The young men whom we before called guardians
may be more properly designated auxiliaries and
supporters of the principles of the rulers.

I agree with you, he said.

How then may we devise one of those needful
falsehoods of which we lately spoke – just one royal lie
which may deceive the rulers, if that be possible, and at

any rate the rest of the city?

What sort of lie? he said.

Nothing new, I replied; only an old Phoenician tale of what has often occurred before now in other places (as the poets say, and have made the world believe), though not in our time, and I do not know whether such an event could ever happen again, or could now even be made to seem probable.

How your words seem to hesitate on your lips!

You will not wonder, I replied, at my hesitation when you have heard.

Speak, he said, and fear not.

Well then, I will speak, although I really know not how to look you in the face, or in what words to utter the audacious fiction, which I propose to communicate gradually, first to the rulers, then to the soldiers, and lastly to the people. They are to be told that the education and training which they seemed to receive from us in youth was but a dream; in reality during all that time they were being formed and fed in the womb of the earth, where they themselves and their arms and appurtenances were manufactured; when they were completed, the earth, their mother, sent them up; and so, their country being their mother and also their nurse, they are bound to advise for her good, and to defend her against attacks; and the other citizens they are to regard as children of the earth and their own brothers.

You had good reason, he said, to be ashamed of the lie which you were going to tell.

No doubt, I replied, but listen to the continuation of the tale. Citizens, we shall say to them in our tale, you are brothers, yet god has framed you differently. Some of you have the power of command, and in the composition of these he has mingled gold, wherefore also they have the greatest honour; others he has made of silver, to be auxiliaries; others again who are to be husbandmen and craftsmen he has composed of brass and iron; and the species will generally be preserved in the children. But as all are of the same original stock, a golden parent will sometimes have a silver son, a silver parent a golden son, and so forth. And god proclaims as a first principle to the rulers, and above all else, that there is nothing which they should so anxiously guard, or of which they are to be such good guardians, as of the mixture of elements in the soul. First, if one of their own offspring has an admixture of brass or iron, they shall in no wise have pity on it, but give it the rank which is its due and send it down to the husbandmen or artisans. On the other hand, if there are sons of artisans who have an admixture of gold or silver in them, they will be raised to honour, and become guardians or auxiliaries. For an oracle says that when a man of brass or iron guards the state, it will be destroyed. Such is the tale; is there any possibility of making our citizens believe in it?

Not in the first generation, he replied; but their sons may be made to believe in the tale, and their sons' sons, and posterity after them.

I see the difficulty, I replied; yet the fostering of such a belief will make them care more for the city and for one another. Enough, however, of the fiction, which may now fly abroad upon the wings of rumour, while we arm our earth-born heroes, and lead them forth under the command of their rulers. Let them look round and select a spot whence they can best suppress insurrection, if any prove refractory within, and also defend themselves against enemies, who like wolves may come down on the fold from without; there let them encamp, and when they have encamped, let them sacrifice to the proper gods and prepare their lodging.

Just so, he said.

And this must be such as will shield them against the cold of winter and the heat of summer.

I suppose that you mean houses, he replied.

Yes, I said; but they must be the houses of soldiers, and not of shopkeepers.

What is the difference? he said.

That I will endeavour to explain, I replied. To keep watchdogs, who, from want of discipline or hunger, or some evil habit or other, would turn upon the sheep and worry them, and behave not like dogs but wolves, would be a foul and monstrous thing in a shepherd?

Truly monstrous, he said.

And therefore every care must be taken that our auxiliaries, being stronger than our citizens, may not behave in this fashion and become like savage tyrants instead of friends and allies?

Yes, great care should be taken.

And if they have really received a good education, will not that furnish the best safeguard?

But they have received it, he replied.

I cannot be so confident, my dear Glaucon, I said; but I believe the truth is as I said, that a sound education, whatever that may be, will have the greatest tendency to civilise and humanise them in their relations to one another, and to those who are under their protection.

Very true, he replied.

And not only their education, but their habitations, and all that belongs to them, should be such as will neither impair their virtue as guardians, nor tempt them to prey upon the other citizens. Any man of sense must acknowledge that.

He must.

Then now let us consider what will be their way of life, if they are to realise our idea of them. In the first place, none of them should have any property of his own beyond what is absolutely necessary; neither should they have a private house or store closed against anyone who has a mind to enter; their provisions should be only such as are required by trained warriors, who are men of temperance and courage; they should agree to receive from the citizens a fixed rate of pay, enough to meet the expenses of the year and no more; and they will go to mess and live together like soldiers in a camp. Gold and silver we will tell them that they have from god; the diviner metal is within them, and they have therefore no need of the dross which is current among men, and ought not to pollute the divine by any such earthly admixture; for that commoner metal has been the sources of many unholy deeds, but their own is undefiled. And they alone of all the citizens may not touch or handle silver or gold, or be under the same roof with them, or wear them, or drink from them. And this will be their salvation, and they will be the saviours of the state. But should they ever acquire homes or lands or moneys of their own, they will become householders and husbandmen instead of guardians, enemies and tyrants instead of allies of the other citizens; hating and being hated, plotting and being plotted against, they will pass their whole life in much greater terror of internal than of external enemies, and the hour of ruin, both to themselves and to the rest of the state, will be at hand. For all which reasons may we not say that thus shall our state be ordered, and that these shall be the regulations appointed by us for our guardians concerning their lodging and all other matters?

Yes, said Glaucon.

BOOK FOUR

Here Adeimantus interposed a question: How would you answer, Socrates, said he, if a person were to say that you are not making these men very happy, and that they are themselves to blame; the city in fact belongs to them, but they reap no advantage from it; whereas other men acquire lands, and build large and handsome houses, and have everything handsome about them, offering sacrifices to the gods on their own account, and practising hospitality? Moreover, they have the gold and silver which you have just mentioned, and all that is usual among the favourites of fortune; but our poor citizens are no better than mercenaries who are quartered in the city and are always mounting guard.

Yes, I said; and you may add that they are only fed, and not paid in addition to their food like other men; and therefore they cannot, if they would, take a private journey abroad; they have no money to spend on a mistress or any other luxurious fancy, which, as the world goes, is thought to be happiness; and many other accusations of the same nature might be added.

But, said he, let us suppose all this to be included in the charge.

You mean to ask, I said, what will be our answer?

Yes.

If we proceed along the old path, my belief, I said, is that we shall find the answer. And our answer will be that, even as they are, our guardians may very likely be the happiest of men; but that our aim in founding the state was not the disproportionate happiness of any one class, but the greatest happiness of the whole; we thought that in a state which is ordered with a view to the good of the whole we should be most likely to find justice, and in the worst-ordered state injustice: and, having found them, we might then decide upon the answer to our first question. At present, I take it, we are fashioning the happy state, not piecemeal, or with a view of making a few happy citizens, but as a whole; and by-and-by we will proceed to view the opposite kind of state. Suppose that we were painting a statue, and someone came up to us and said 'Why do you not put the most beautiful colours on the most beautiful parts of the body – the eyes ought to be purple, but you have made them black' – to him we might fairly answer 'Sir, you would not surely have us beautify the eyes to such a degree that they are no longer eyes; consider rather whether, by giving this and the other features their due proportion, we make the whole beautiful.' And so I say to you, do not compel us to assign to the guardians a sort of happiness which will make them no guardians at all; for we too can clothe our husbandmen in royal apparel, and set crowns of gold on their heads, and bid them till the ground as much as they like, and no more. Our potters also might be allowed to repose on couches, and feast by the fireside, passing round the winecup, while their wheel is conveniently at hand, so that they may make a few pots when they feel inclined; in this way we might make every class happy – and then, as you imagine, the whole state would be happy. But do not put this idea into our heads; for, if we listen to you, the husbandman will be no longer a husbandman, the potter will cease to be a potter, and no one will have the character of any distinct class in the state. Now this is not of much consequence where the corruption of society, and pretension to be what you are not, is confined to cobblers; but when the guardians of the laws and of the government are only seeming and not real guardians, then see how they turn the state upside down; and on the other hand they alone have the power of giving order and happiness to the state. We mean our guardians to be true saviours and not the destroyers of the state, whereas our opponent is thinking of peasants at a festival, who are enjoying a life of revelry, not of citizens who are doing their duty to the state. But, if so, we mean different things, and he is speaking of something which is not a state. And therefore we must consider whether in appointing our guardians we look to their greatest happiness individually, or whether our aim is not to ensure that happiness appears in the state as a whole. What these guardians or auxiliaries must be compelled or induced to do (and the same may be said of every other trade), is to become as expert as possible in their professional work. And thus the whole state will grow up in a noble order, and the several classes will receive the proportion of happiness which nature assigns to them.

I think that you are quite right.

I wonder whether you will agree with another remark which occurs to me.

What may that be?

There seem to be two causes of the deterioration of the arts.

What are they?

Wealth, I said, and poverty.

How do they act?

The process is as follows: when a potter becomes rich, will he, think you, any longer take the same pains with his art?

Certainly not.

He will grow more and more indolent and careless?

Very true.

And the result will be that he becomes a worse potter?

Yes; he greatly deteriorates.

But, on the other hand, if he has no money and cannot provide himself with tools or other requirements of his craft, his own work will not be equally good, and he will not teach his sons or apprentices to work equally well.

Certainly not.

Then, under the influence either of poverty or of wealth, workmen and their work are equally liable to degenerate?

That is evident.

Here then is a discovery of new evils, I said, against which the guardians will have to watch, or they will creep into the city unobserved.

What evils?

Wealth, I said, and poverty; the one is the parent of luxury and indolence, and the other of meanness and viciousness, and both of a revolutionary spirit.

That is very true, he replied; but still I should like to know, Socrates, how our city will be able to go to war, especially against an enemy who is rich and powerful, if deprived of the sinews of war.

Evidently it would be difficult, I replied, to wage war with one such enemy; but it will be easier where there are two of them.

How so? he asked.

In the first place, I said, if we have to fight, our side will be trained warriors fighting against an army of rich men.

That is true, he said.

And do you not suppose, Adeimantus, that a single boxer who was perfect in his art would easily be a match for two stout and well-to-do gentlemen who were not boxers?

Hardly, if they came upon him at once.

What, not, I said, if he were able to run away and then turn and strike at the one who first came up? And supposing he were to do this several times under the heat of a scorching sun, might he not, being an expert, overturn more than one stout personage?

Certainly, he said, there would be nothing wonderful in that.

And yet rich men probably have more instruction in the science and practise of boxing than they have in military science.

Likely enough.

Then we may assume that our athletes will be able to fight with two or three times their own number?

I will accept that, for I think you right.

And suppose that, before engaging, our citizens send an embassy to one of the two cities, telling them what is the truth: 'Silver and gold we neither have nor are permitted to have, but you may; do you therefore come and help us in war, and take the spoils of the other city.' Who, on hearing these words, would choose to fight against lean wiry dogs, rather than, with the dogs on their side, against fat and tender sheep?

That is not likely; and yet there might be a danger to the poor state if the wealth of many states were to be gathered into one.

But how simple of you to think that the term state is applicable at all to any but our own!

Why so?

You ought to speak of other states in the plural number; not one of them is a city, but many cities, as they say in the game. Each will contain not less than two divisions, one the city of the poor, the other of the rich, which are at war with one another; and within each there are many smaller divisions. You would be altogether beside the mark if you treated these as a single state; but if you deal with them as many, and give the wealth or power or persons of the one to the others, you will always have a great many friends and not many enemies. And your state, while the wise order which has now been prescribed continues to prevail in her, will be the greatest of states, I do not mean to say in reputation or appearance, but in deed and truth, though she number not more than a thousand defenders. A single state of that size you will hardly find, either among Hellenes or barbarians, though many that appear to be as great and many times greater.

That is most true, he said.

Hence, I said, it can be seen what will be the best limit for our rulers to fix when they are considering the size of the state and the amount of territory which they are to include, and beyond which they will not go.

What limit would you propose?

I would allow the state to increase so far as is consistent with unity; that, I think, is the proper limit.

Very good, he said.

Here then, I said, is another order which will have to be conveyed to our guardians: let them guard against our city becoming small, or great only in appearance. It must attain an adequate size, but it must remain one.

And perhaps, said he, you do not think this is a very severe order?

And here is another, said I, which is lighter still – I mean the duty, of which some mention was made before, of degrading the offspring of the guardians when inferior, and of elevating into the rank of guardians the offspring of the lower classes, when naturally superior. The intention was that, in the case of the citizens generally, each individual should be put to the use for which nature intended him, one to one work, and then every man would do his own business, and become one and not many; and so the whole city would be one and not many.

Yes, he said; that is not so difficult.

The regulations which we are prescribing, my good Adeimantus, are not, as might be supposed, a number of great principles, but trifles all, if care be taken, as the saying is, of the one great thing – a thing, however, which I would rather call, not great, but sufficient for our purpose.

What may that be? he asked.

Education, I said, and nurture: if our citizens are well educated, and grow into sensible men, they will easily see their way through all these, as well as other matters which I omit; such, for example, as marriage, the possession of women and the procreation of children, which will all follow the general principle that friends have all things in common, as the proverb says.

That will be the best way of settling them.

Also, I said, the state, if once started well, moves with accumulating force like a wheel. For where good nurture and education are maintained, they implant good constitutions, and these good constitutions taking root in a good education improve more and more, and this improvement affects the breed in man as in other animals.

Very possibly, he said.

Then to sum up: this is the principle to which our rulers should cling throughout, taking care that neglect does not creep in – that music and gymnastic be preserved in their original form, and no innovation made. They must do their utmost to maintain them intact. And when anyone says that

'Mankind most regard the newest song which the singers have',

they will be afraid that he may be praising, not new songs, but a new kind of song; and this ought not to be praised, or conceived to be the meaning of the poet; for any musical innovation is to be shunned, as likely to bring danger to the whole state. So Damon tells me, and I can quite believe him; he says that when modes of music change, the fundamental laws of the state always change with them.

Yes, said Adeimantus; and you may add my suffrage to Damon's and your own.

Then, I said, our guardians must lay the foundations of their fortress in music?

Yes, he said; the lawlessness of which you speak too easily steals in.

Yes, I replied, in the form of amusement, and as though it were harmless.

Why, yes, he said, and harmless it would be; were it not that little by little this spirit of licence, finding a home, imperceptibly penetrates into manners and customs; whence issuing with greater force it invades contracts between man and man, and from contracts goes on to laws and constitutions, in utter recklessness, ending at last, Socrates, in an overthrow of all rights, private as well as public.

Is that true? I said.

That is my belief, he replied.

Then, as I was saying, our boys should be trained from the first in a stricter system, for if childish amusement becomes lawless, it will produce lawless children, who can never grow up into well-conducted and virtuous citizens.

Very true, he said.

And when boys who have made a good beginning in play, have later gained the habit of good order through music, then this habit accompanies them in all their actions and is a principle of growth to them, and is able to correct anything in the state which had been allowed to lapse. It is the reverse of the picture I have just drawn.

Very true, he said.

Thus educated, they will discover for themselves any lesser rules which their predecessors have altogether neglected.

What do you mean?

I mean such things as these: when the young are to be silent before their elders; how they are to show respect to them by standing and making them sit; what honour is due to parents; what garments or shoes are to be worn; the mode of dressing the hair; deportment and manners in general. You would agree with me?

Yes.

But there is, I think, small wisdom in legislating about such matters – precise written enactments cannot create these observances, and are not likely to make them lasting.

Impossible.

It would seem, Adeimantus, that the direction in which education starts a man will determine his future life. Does not like always attract like?

To be sure.

Until some one grand result is reached which may be good, and may be the reverse of good?

That is not to be denied.

And for this reason, I said, I for my part should not attempt to extend legislation to such details.

Naturally enough, he replied.

Well, and about the business of the agora, and the ordinary dealings between man and man, or again about agreements with artisans; about insult and injury, or the commencement of actions, and the appointment of juries, what would you say? There may also arise questions about any impositions and exactions of market and harbour dues which may be required, and in general about the regulations of markets, police, harbours, and the like. But, oh heavens! shall we condescend to legislate on any of these particulars?

No, he said, it is unseemly to impose laws about them on good men; what regulations are necessary they will find out soon enough for themselves.

Yes, I said, my friend, if god will only preserve to them the laws which we have given them.

And without divine help, said Adeimantus, they will go on for ever making and mending their laws and their lives in the hope of attaining perfection.

You would compare them, I said, to those invalids who, having no self-restraint, will not leave off their habits of intemperance?

Exactly.

Yes, I said; and what a delightful life they lead! They

are always doctoring their disorders, with no result except to increase and complicate them, and always fancying that they will be cured by any nostrum which anybody advises them to try.

Such cases are very common, he said, with invalids of this sort.

Yes, I replied; and the charming thing is that they deem him their worst enemy who tells them the truth, which is simply that, unless they give up gorging and drinking and wenching and idling, neither drug nor cautery nor amputation nor spell nor amulet nor any other remedy will avail.

Charming? he replied. I see nothing charming in going into a passion with a man who tells you what is right.

These gentlemen, I said, do not seem to be in your good graces.

Assuredly not.

Nor would you approve if a whole state behaves in this way, and that brings me back to my point. For when, in certain ill-ordered states, the citizens are forbidden under pain of death to alter the constitution; and yet he who most sweetly courts those who live under this régime and indulges them and fawns upon them and is skilful in anticipating and gratifying their humours is honoured as a great and good statesman – do not these states resemble the persons whom I was describing?

Yes, he said; the fault is the same; and I am very far from approving it.

But what of these ready and eager ministers of political corruption? I said. Do you not admire their coolness and dexterity?

Yes, he said, I do; but not of all of them, for there are

some whom the applause of the multitude has deluded into the belief that they are really statesmen.

What do you mean? I said; you should have more feeling for them. When a man cannot measure, and a great many others who cannot measure declare that he is four cubits high, can he help believing what they say?

Nay, he said, certainly not in that case.

Well, then, do not be angry with them; for are they not as good as a play, trying their hand at paltry reforms such as I was describing; they are always fancying that by legislation they will make an end of frauds in contracts, and the other rascalities which I was mentioning, not knowing that they are in reality cutting off the heads of a hydra?

Yes, he said; that is just what they are doing.

I conceive, I said, that the true legislator will not trouble himself with this class of enactments whether concerning laws or the constitution either in an ill-ordered or in a well-ordered state; for in the former they are quite useless, and in the latter they will either be of a kind which anyone can devise, or will naturally flow out of our previous regulations.

What, then, he said, is still remaining to us of the work of legislation?

Nothing to us, I replied; but to Apollo, the god of Delphi, there remains the ordering of the greatest and noblest and chiefest things of all.

Which are they? he said.

The institution of temples and sacrifices, and the entire service of gods, demigods, and heroes; also the ordering of the repositories of the dead, and the rites which have to be observed by him who would propitiate the inhabitants of the world below. These are matters of which we are ignorant ourselves, and as founders of a city we should be unwise in trusting them to any interpreter but the ancestral one. For it is Apollo who, sitting at the navel of the earth, is the ancestral interpreter of such observances to all mankind.

You are right, and we will do as you propose.

So now the foundation of your city, son of Ariston, is finished. What comes next? Provide yourself with a bright light and search, and get your brother and Polemarchus and the rest of our friends to help, and let us see where in it we can discover justice and where injustice, and in what they differ from one another, and which of them the man who would be happy should have for his portion, whether seen or unseen by gods and men.

Nonsense, said Glaucon: did you not promise to search yourself, saying that for you not to help justice in her need would be an impiety?

Your reminder is true, and I will be as good as my word; but you must join.

We will, he replied.

Well, then, I hope to make the discovery in this way: I mean to begin with the assumption that our state, if rightly ordered, is perfect.

That is most certain.

And being perfect, is therefore wise and valiant and temperate and just.

That is likewise clear.

And whichever of these qualities we first find in the state, the one which is not yet found will be the residue?

Very good.

If in some other instance there were four things, in one of which we were most interested, the one sought for might come to light first, and there would be no further trouble; or if we came to know the other three first, we should thereby attain the object of our search, for it must clearly be the part remaining.

Very true, he said.

And is not a similar method to be pursued about the virtues, which are also four in number?

Clearly.

First among the virtues found in the state, wisdom comes into view, and in this I detect a certain peculiarity.

What is that?

The state which we have been describing has, I think, true wisdom. You would agree that it is good in counsel?

Yes.

And this good counsel is clearly a kind of knowledge, for not by ignorance, but by knowledge, do men counsel well?

Clearly.

And the kinds of knowledge in a state are many and diverse?

Of course.

There is the knowledge of the carpenter; but is that the sort of knowledge which gives a city the title of wise and good in counsel?

Certainly not; that would only give a city the reputation of skill in carpentering.

Then a city is not to be called wise because possessing a knowledge which counsels for the best about wooden implements?

Certainly not.

Nor by reason of a knowledge which advises about brazen pots, he said, nor as possessing any other similar knowledge?

Not by reason of any of them, he said.

Nor yet by reason of a knowledge which cultivates the earth; that would give the city the name of agricultural?

Yes.

Well, I said, and is there any knowledge in our recently founded state among any of the citizens which advises not about any particular thing in the state, but about the whole, and considers how it can best conduct itself in relation with itself and with other states?

There certainly is.

And what is this knowledge, and among whom is it found? I asked.

It is the knowledge of guarding, he replied, and is found in those rulers whom we were just now describing as perfect guardians.

And what is the name which the city derives from the possession of this sort of knowledge?

The name of good in counsel and truly wise.

And will there be in our city more of these true guardians or more smiths?

The smiths, he replied, will be far more numerous.

Will not the guardians probably be the smallest of all the classes who receive a name from the profession of some kind of knowledge?

Much the smallest.

And so by reason of the smallest part or class, and of the knowledge which resides in this presiding and ruling part of itself, the whole state, being thus constituted according to nature, will be wise; and this, which can claim a share in the only knowledge worthy to be called wisdom, has been ordained by nature to be of all classes the smallest.

Most true.

Thus, then, I said, the nature and place in the state of one of the four virtues has somehow or other been discovered.

And, in my humble opinion, very satisfactorily discovered, he replied.

Again, I said, there is no difficulty in seeing the nature of courage, and in what part that quality resides which gives the name of courageous to the state.

How do you mean?

Why, I said, everyone who calls any state courageous or cowardly, will be thinking of the part which fights and goes out to war on the state's behalf.

No one, he replied, would ever think of any other.

The rest of the citizens may be courageous or may be cowardly, but their courage or cowardice will not, as I conceive, have the effect of making the city either the one or the other.

No.

The city will be courageous also by one part of herself, in which resides the power to preserve under all circumstances that opinion about the nature and description of things to be feared in which our legislator educated them; and this is what you term courage.

I should like to hear what you are saying once more, for I do not think that I perfectly understand you.

I mean that courage is a kind of preservation.

Preservation of what kind?

Of the opinion respecting things to be feared, what they are and of what nature, which the law implants through education; and I mean by the words 'under all circumstances' to intimate that in pleasure or in pain, or under the influence of desire or fear, a man preserves and does not lose this opinion. Shall I give you an illustration?

If you please.

You know, I said, that dyers, when they want to dye wool for making the true sea-purple, begin by choosing the white from among all the colours available; this they prepare and dress with much care and pains, in order that the white ground may take the purple hue in full perfection. The dyeing then proceeds; and whatever is dyed in this manner becomes a fast colour, and no washing either with lyes or without them can take away the bloom. But, when the ground has not been duly prepared, you will have noticed how poor is the look either of purple or of any other colour.

Yes, he said; I know that they have a washed-out and ridiculous appearance.

Then now, I said, you will understand that our object in selecting our soldiers, and educating them in music and gymnastic, was very similar; we were contriving influences which would prepare them to take the dye of the laws in perfection, and the colour of their opinion about dangers and of every other opinion was to be indelibly fixed by their nurture and training, not to be washed away by such potent lyes as pleasure – mightier agent far in washing the soul than any soda or lye – or by sorrow, fear, and desire, the mightiest of all other solvents. And this sort of universal saving power of true opinion in conformity with law about real and false dangers I call and maintain to be courage, unless you disagree.

But I agree, he replied; for I suppose that you mean to exclude mere right belief about dangers when it has grown up without instruction, such as that of a wild beast or of a slave – this, in your opinion, is something not quite in accordance with law, which in any case should have another name than courage.

Most certainly.

Then I concede courage to be such as you describe.

Excellent, said I, and if you add the words 'of a citizen', you will not be far wrong; hereafter, if you agree, we will carry the examination of courage further, but at present we are seeking not for courage but justice; and for the purpose of our inquiry we have said enough.

You are right, he replied.

Two virtues remain to be discovered in the state – first, temperance, and then justice which is the end of our search.

Very true.

Now, can we find justice without troubling ourselves about temperance?

I do not know how that can be accomplished, he said, nor do I desire that justice should be brought to light and temperance lost sight of; and therefore I wish that you would do me the favour of considering temperance first.

Certainly, I replied, I should not be justified in refusing your request.

Then consider, he said.

Yes, I replied; I will; and as far as I can at present see, temperance has more of the nature of harmony and symphony than have the preceding virtues.

How so? he asked.

Temperance, I replied, is the ordering or controlling of certain pleasures and desires; this is curiously enough implied in the saying of 'a man being his own master'; and other traces of the same notion may be found in language, may they not?

No doubt, he said.

There is something ridiculous in the expression 'master of himself'; for the master must also be the servant and the servant the master, since in all these modes of speaking the same person is denoted.

Certainly.

The meaning of this expression is, I believe, that there is within the man's own soul a better and also a worse principle; and when the better has the worse under control, then he is said to be master of himself; and this is a term of praise: but when, owing to evil education or association, the better principle, which is also the smaller, is overwhelmed by the greater mass of the worse – in this case he is blamed and is called the slave of self and dissolute.

Yes, there is reason in that.

And now, I said, look at our newly created state, and there you will find one of these two conditions realised; for the state, as you will acknowledge, may be justly called master of itself, if the words 'temperance' and 'self-mastery' truly express the rule of the better part over the worse.

On looking, he said, I see that what you say is true.

Let me further note that the manifold and complex pleasures and desires and pains are generally found in children and women and servants, and in the freemen so called who are of the lowest and more numerous class.

Certainly, he said.

Whereas the simple and moderate desires, which follow reason and are under the guidance of mind and true opinion, are to be found only in a few, and those the best born and best educated.

Very true.

These too, as you may perceive, have a place in your

state; and the meaner desires of the many are held down by the desires and wisdom of the more virtuous few.

That I perceive, he said.

Then if there be any city which may be described as master of its own pleasures and desires, and master of itself, ours may claim such a designation?

Certainly, he replied.

It may also for all these reasons be called temperate?

Yes.

And if there be any state in which rulers and subjects will be agreed as to the question who are to rule, that again will be our state? Do you think so?

I do, emphatically.

And the citizens being thus agreed among themselves, in which class will temperance be found – in the rulers or in the subjects?

In both, as I should imagine, he replied.

Do you observe that we were not badly inspired in our guess that temperance bore some resemblance to harmony?

Why so?

Why, because temperance is unlike courage and wisdom, each of which resides in a part only, the one making the state wise and the other valiant; not so temperance, which extends to the whole, and runs through all the notes of the scale, and produces a unison of the weaker and the stronger and the middle class, whether you suppose them to be stronger or weaker in wisdom or power or numbers or wealth, or anything else you please. Most truly then may we deem this unity of mind to be temperance, an agreement of the naturally superior and inferior as to the right to rule of either both in states and individuals.

I entirely agree with you.

And so, I said, we may consider three out of the four virtues to have been discovered in our state. What remainder is there of qualities which make a state virtuous? For this, it is evident, must be justice.

The inference is obvious.

The time then has arrived, Glaucon, when, like huntsmen, we should surround the cover, and look sharp that justice does not steal away, and pass out of sight and escape us; for beyond a doubt she is somewhere in this country: watch therefore and strive to catch a sight of her, and if you see her first, let me know.

Would that I could! But you will do right to regard me rather as a follower who has just eyes enough to see what you show him.

Offer up a prayer with me and follow.

I will, but you must show me the way.

Here is no path, I said, and the wood is dark and perplexing; still we must push on.

Let us push on.

Here I saw something: Halloo! I said, I begin to perceive a track, and I believe that the quarry will not escape.

Good news, he said.

Truly, I said, we are stupid fellows.

Why so?

Why, my dear friend, far back from the beginning of our inquiry, justice has been lying at our feet, and we never saw her; nothing could be more ridiculous. Like people who go about looking for what they have in their hands, we looked not at what we were seeking, but at what was far off in the distance; and that, I suppose, was how we missed her.

What do you mean?

I mean to say that for a long time past we have been talking or hearing of justice, and yet have failed to recognise that we were in some sense actually describing it.

I grow impatient at the length of your exordium.

Well then, tell me, I said, whether I am right or not: You remember the original principle which we laid down at the foundation of the state; we decided, and more than once insisted, that one man should practise one occupation only, that to which his nature was best adapted; now justice, in my view, either is this principle or is some form of it.

Yes, we did.

Further, we affirmed that justice was doing one's own business, and not being a busybody; we said so again and again, and many others have said the same to us.

Yes, we said so.

Then to attend to one's own business, in some form or another, may be assumed to be justice. Do you know my evidence for this?

No, but I should like to be told.

Because I think that this is the virtuous quality which remains in the state when the other virtues of temperance and courage and wisdom are abstracted; and that this not only made it possible for them to appear, but is also their preservative as long as they remain; and we were saying that if the three were discovered by us, justice would be the fourth or remaining one.

That follows of necessity.

If we are asked to determine which of these four qualities by its presence will contribute most to the

excellence of our state, whether the agreement of
rulers and subjects, or the preservation in the soldiers
of the opinion which the law ordains about the true
nature of dangers, or wisdom and watchfulness in the
rulers, or this other which is found in children and
women, slave and freeman, artisan, ruler, subject (I
mean the quality of every one doing his own work, and
not being a busybody), the decision is not so easy.

Certainly, he replied, there would be a difficulty in
saying which.

Then the attention of each individual to his own work
appears to be a quality rivalling wisdom, temperance,
and courage, with reference to the excellence of the
state.

Yes, he said.

And the only virtue which, from that point of view,
is of equal importance with them, is justice?

Exactly.

Let us look at the question also in this way: are not
the rulers in a state those to whom you would entrust
the office of determining suits at law?

Certainly.

In the decision of such suits will any principle be
prior to this, that a man may neither take what is
another's nor be deprived of what is his own?

No.

Because it is a just principle?

Yes.

Then on this view also justice will be admitted to be
the having and doing what is a man's own, and
belongs to him?

Very true.

Think, now, and say whether you agree with me or
not. Suppose a carpenter sets out to do the business of

a cobbler, or a cobbler that of a carpenter; and suppose them to exchange their implements or social position, or the same person to try to undertake the work of both, or whatever be the change; do you think that any great harm would result to the state?

Not much.

But when the cobbler or any other man whom nature designed to be a trader, having his heart lifted up by wealth or strength or the number of his followers or any like advantage, attempts to force his way into the class of warriors, or a warrior into that of legislators and guardians, to which he ought not to aspire, and when these exchange their implements and their social position with those above them; or when one man would be trader, legislator, and warrior all in one, then I think you will agree with me in saying that this interchange and this meddling of one with another is the ruin of the state.

Most true.

Seeing then, I said, that there are three distinct classes, any meddling of one with another, or the change of one into another, is the greatest harm to the state, and may be most justly termed evil-doing?

Precisely.

And the greatest degree of evil-doing to one's own city would be termed by you injustice?

Certainly.

This then is injustice; and on the other hand when the three main classes, traders, auxiliaries, and guardians, each do their own business, that is justice, and will make the city just.

I agree with you.

We will not, I said, be over-positive as yet; but if, on trial, this conception of justice be verified in the individual as well as in the state, there will be no longer any room for doubt; if it be not verified, we must have a fresh inquiry. First let us complete the old investigation, which we began, as you remember, under the impression that, if we could previously examine justice on the larger scale, there would be less difficulty in discerning her in the individual. That larger example appeared to be the state, and accordingly we constructed as good a one as we could, knowing well that in the good state justice would be found. Let the discovery which we made be now applied to the individual – if they agree, we shall be satisfied; or, if there be a difference in the individual, we will come back to the state and have another trial of the theory. The friction of the two when rubbed together may possibly strike the light of justice, from which we can kindle a steady flame in our souls.

That will be in regular course; let us do as you say.

I proceeded to ask: When two things, a greater and less, are called by the same name, are they like or unlike in so far as they are called the same?

Like, he replied.

The just man then, if we regard the idea of justice only, will be like the just state?

He will.

And a state was thought by us to be just when the three classes in the state severally did their own business; and also thought to be temperate and valiant and wise by reason of certain other affections and qualities of these same classes?

True, he said.

And so of the individual: we may assume that he has the same three principles in his own soul which are found in the state; and he may be rightly described in the same terms, because he is affected in the same manner?

Certainly, he said.

Once more then, O my friend, we have alighted upon an easy question – whether the soul has these three principles or not?

An easy question? Nay, rather, Socrates, the proverb holds that hard is the good.

Very true, I said; and I must impress upon you, Glaucon, that in my opinion our present methods of argument are not at all adequate to the accurate solution of this question; the true method is another and a longer one. Still we may arrive at a solution not below the level of the previous inquiry.

May we not be satisfied with that? he said; under the circumstances, I am quite content.

I too, I replied, shall be extremely well satisfied.

Then faint not in pursuing the speculation, he said.

Must we not perforce acknowledge, I said, that in each of us there are the same principles and habits which there are in the state; for it is from the individual that the state derives them. Take the quality of passion or spirit; it would be ridiculous to imagine that this quality, when found in states, is not derived from the individuals who are supposed to possess it, e.g. the Thracians, Scythians, and in general the northern nations; and the same may be said of the love of knowledge, which may be claimed as the special characteristic of our part of the world, or of the love of money, which may, with equal truth, be attributed to the Phoenicians and Egyptians.

Exactly so, he said.

This is a fact, and there is no difficulty in perceiving it.

None whatever.

But the question is not quite so easy when we proceed to ask whether these principles are three or one; whether, that is to say, we learn with one part of our nature, are angry with another, and with a third part desire the satisfaction of our natural appetites; or whether the whole soul comes into play in each sort of action – to determine that is the difficulty.

Yes, he said; there lies the difficulty.

Then let us now try and determine whether they are the same or different.

How?

Clearly the same thing cannot act or be acted upon in the same part or in relation to the same thing at the same time, in contrary ways; and therefore whenever this contradiction occurs in things apparently the same, we know that they are really not the same, but different.

Good.

For example, I said, can the same thing be at rest and in motion at the same time in the same part?

Impossible.

Now, I said, let us have still more precise understanding, lest we should hereafter fall out by the way. Imagine the case of a man who is standing and also moving his hands and his head, and suppose a person to say that one and the same person is in motion and at rest at the same moment – to such a mode of speech we should object, and should rather say that one part of him is in motion while another is at rest.

Very true.

And suppose the objector to refine still further, and to draw the nice distinction that not only parts of tops, but whole tops, when they spin round with their pegs fixed on the spot, are at rest and in motion at the same time (and he may say the same of anything which revolves in the same spot), his objection would not be admitted by us, because in such cases things are not at rest and in motion in the same parts of themselves; we should rather say that they have both an axis and a circumference; and that the axis stands still, for there is no deviation from the perpendicular; and that the circumference goes round. But if, while revolving, the axis inclines either to the right or left, forwards or backwards, then in no point of view can they be at rest.

That is the correct mode of describing them, he replied.

Then none of these objections will confuse us, or incline us to believe that the same thing at the same time, in the same part or in relation to the same thing, can be contrary or act or be acted upon in contrary ways.

Certainly not, according to my way of thinking.

Yet, I said, that we may not be compelled to examine all such objections, and prove at length that they are untrue, let us assume their absurdity, and go forward on the understanding that hereafter, if this assumption turn out to be untrue, all the consequences which follow from it shall be withdrawn.

Yes, he said, that will be the best way.

Well, I said, would you not allow that assent and dissent, desire and aversion, attraction and repulsion, are all of them opposites, whether they are regarded as active or passive (for that makes no difference in the fact of their opposition)?

Yes, he said, they are opposites.

Well, I said, and hunger and thirst, and the desires in general, and again willing and wishing – all these you would refer to the classes already mentioned. You would say – would you not? – that the soul of him who desires is either seeking after the object of desire; or is drawing towards herself the thing which she wishes to possess: or again – for she may merely consent that something should be offered to her – intimates her wish to have it by a nod of assent, as if she had been asked a question?

Very true.

And what would you say of unwillingness and dislike and the absence of desire; should not these be referred to the opposite class of repulsion and rejection?

Certainly.

Admitting this to be true of desire generally, let us suppose a particular class of desires, and out of these we will select hunger and thirst, as they are termed, which are the most obvious of them?

Let us take that class, he said.

The object of one is food, and of the other drink?

Yes.

And here comes the point: is not thirst the desire which the soul has of drink, and of drink only, not of drink qualified by anything else; for example, warm or cold, or much or little, or, in a word, drink of any particular sort? But if there is heat additional to the thirst, it will bring with it the desire of cold drink; or, if cold, then that of warm drink. And again, if the thirst is qualified by abundance or by smallness, it will become a desire for much or little drink, as the case may be: but thirst pure and simple will desire drink pure and simple, which is the natural satisfaction of thirst, as food is of hunger?

Yes, he said; the simple desire is, as you say, in every case of the simple object, and the qualified desire of the qualified object.

But here a confusion may arise; and I should wish to

guard against an opponent starting up and saying that no man desires drink only, but good drink, or food only, but good food; for good is the universal object of desire, and if thirst be a desire, it will necessarily be thirst after good drink (or whatever its object is); and the same is true of every other desire.

Yes, he replied, the opponent might seem to be talking sense.

Nevertheless I should still maintain that of relatives some have a quality attached to either term of the relation; others are simple and have their correlatives simple.

I do not know what you mean.

Well, you know of course that the greater is relative to the less?

Certainly.

And the much greater to the much less?

Yes.

And the sometime greater to the sometime less, and the greater that is to be to the less that is to be?

Certainly, he said.

And so of more and less, and of other correlative terms, such as the double and the half, or again, the heavier and the lighter, the swifter and the slower; and of hot and cold, and of any other relatives; is not this true of all of them?

Yes.

And does not the same principle hold in the sciences? The object of science is knowledge (assuming that to be the true definition), but the object of a particular science is a particular kind of knowledge; I mean, for example, that the science of house-building is a kind of knowledge which is defined and distinguished from other kinds and is therefore termed architecture.

Certainly.

Because it has a particular quality which no other has?

Yes.

And it has this particular quality because it has an object of a particular kind; and this is true of the other arts and sciences?

Yes.

Now, then, if I have made myself clear, you will understand my original meaning in what I said about relatives. My meaning was, that if one term of a relation is taken alone, the other is taken alone; if one term is qualified, the other is also qualified. I do not mean to say that relative terms must possess all the same qualities as their correlates; that the science of health is healthy, or that of disease necessarily diseased, or that the sciences of good and evil are therefore good and evil; but only that, when the term science is no longer used absolutely, but has a qualified object which in this case is the nature of health and disease, it becomes defined, and is hence called not merely science, but the science of medicine.

I quite understand, and I think as you do.

Would you not say that thirst is one of these essentially relative terms, having clearly a relation –

Yes, thirst is relative to drink.

And a certain kind of thirst is relative to a certain kind of drink; but thirst taken alone is neither of much nor little, nor of good nor bad, nor of any particular kind of drink, but of drink only?

Certainly.

Then the soul of the thirsty one, in so far as he is thirsty, desires only drink; for this she yearns, and for this she strives?

That is plain.

And if you suppose something which pulls a thirsty soul away from drink, that must be different from the thirsty principle which draws him like a beast to drink; for, as we were saying, the same thing cannot at the same time with the same part of itself act in contrary ways about the same.

Impossible.

No more than you can say that the hands of the archer push and pull the bow at the same time, but what you say is that one hand pushes and the other pulls.

Exactly so, he replied.

Now are there times when men are thirsty, and yet unwilling to drink?

Yes, he said, it constantly happens.

And in such a case what is one to say? Would you not say that there was something in the soul bidding a man to drink, and something else forbidding him, which is other and stronger than the principle which bids him?

I should say so.

And the prohibition in such cases is derived from reasoning, whereas the motives which lead and attract proceed from passions and diseases?

Clearly.

Then we may fairly assume that they are two, and that they differ from one another; the one with which a man reasons, we may call the rational principle of the soul, the other, with which he loves and hungers and thirsts and feels the flutterings of any other desire, may be termed the irrational or appetitive, the ally of sundry pleasures and satisfactions?

Yes, he said, we may fairly assume them to be different.

So much, then, for the definition of two of the principles existing in the soul. And what now of passion, or spirit? Is it a third, or akin to one of the preceding?

I should be inclined to say – akin to desire.

Well, I said, there is a story which I remember to have heard, and in which I put faith. The story is, that Leontius, the son of Aglaion, coming up one day from the Piraeus, under the north wall on the outside, observed some dead bodies lying on the ground at the place of execution. He felt a desire to see them, and also a dread and abhorrence of them; for a time he struggled and covered his eyes, but at length the desire got the better of him; and forcing them open, he ran up to the dead bodies, saying, Look, ye wretches, take your fill of the fair sight.

I have heard the story myself, he said.

The moral of the tale is that anger at times goes to war with desire, as though they were two distinct things.

Yes, that is the meaning, he said.

And are there not many other cases in which we observe that when a man's desires violently prevail over his reason, he reviles himself, and is angry at the violence within him, and that in this struggle, which is like the struggle of factions in a state, his spirit is on the side of his reason; but for the passionate or spirited element to take part with the desires when reason decides that she should not be opposed, is a sort of thing which I believe that you never observed occurring in yourself, nor, as I should imagine, in anyone else?

Certainly not.

Suppose that a man thinks he has done a wrong to another, the nobler he is the less able is he to feel indignant at any suffering, such as hunger, or cold, or any other pain which the injured person may inflict upon him – these he deems to be just, and, as I say, his spirit refuses to be excited by them.

True, he said.

But when a man thinks that he is the sufferer of the wrong, then the spirit within him boils and chafes, and is on the side of what it believes to be justice; and though it suffers hunger or cold or other pain, it is only the more determined to persevere and conquer. Such a noble spirit will not be quelled until it has achieved its object or been slain, or until it has been recalled by the reason within, like a dog by the shepherd?

The illustration is perfect, he replied; and in our state, as we were saying, the auxiliaries were to be dogs, and to hear the voice of the rulers, who are their shepherds.

Yes, I said, you understand me admirably; there is, however, a further point which I wish you to consider.

What point?

You remember that passion or spirit appeared at first sight to be a kind of desire, but now we should say quite the contrary; for in the conflict of the soul spirit is arrayed on the side of the rational principle.

Most assuredly.

But a further question arises: is passion different from reason also, or only a kind of reason; in which latter case, instead of three principles in the soul, there will only be two, the rational and the concupiscent? Or rather, as the state was composed of three classes, traders, auxiliaries, counsellors, so may there not be in the individual soul a third element which is passion or spirit, and when not corrupted by bad education is the natural auxiliary of reason?

Yes, he said, there must be a third.

Yes, I replied, if passion, which has already been shown to be different from desire, turn out also to be different from reason.

But that is easily proved: we may observe even in young children that they are full of spirit almost as soon as they are born, whereas some of them never seem to attain to the use of reason, and most of them late enough.

Excellent, I said, and you may see passion equally in brute animals, which is a further proof of the truth of what you are saying. And we may once more appeal to the words of Homer, which have been already quoted by us,

'He smote his breast, and thus rebuked his heart;' for in this verse Homer has clearly supposed the power which reasons about the better and worse to be different from the unreasoning anger which is rebuked by it.

Very true, he said.

And so, after much tossing, we have reached land, and are fairly agreed that the same principles which exist in the state exist also in the individual, and that they are three in number.

Exactly.

Must we not then infer that the individual is wise in the same way and in virtue of the same quality which makes the state wise?

Certainly.

Also that the state is brave in the same way and by the same quality as an individual is brave, and that there is the same correspondence in regard to the other virtues?

Assuredly.

Therefore the individual will be acknowledged by us to be just in the same way in which the state has been found just?

That follows of course.

We cannot but remember that the justice of the state consisted in each of the three classes doing the work of its own class?

I do not think we have forgotten, he said.

We must now record in our memory that the individual in whom the several components of his nature do their own work will be just, and will do his own work?

Yes, he said, we must record that important fact.

First, it is proper for the rational principle, which is wise, and has the care of the whole soul, to rule, and for the spirit to be the subject and ally?

Certainly.

And, as we were saying, the blending of music and gymnastic will bring them into accord, nerving and sustaining the reason with noble words and lessons, and moderating and soothing and civilising the wildness of passion by harmony and rhythm?

Quite true, he said.

And these two, thus nurtured and educated, and having learned truly to know their own functions, will rule over the concupiscent, which in each of us is the largest part of the soul and by nature most insatiable of gain; over this they will keep guard, lest, waxing great and strong with the fullness of bodily pleasures, as they are termed, the concupiscent soul, no longer confined to her own sphere, should attempt to enslave and rule those who are not her natural-born subjects, and overturn the whole life of man?

Very true, he said.

Both together will they not be the best defenders of the whole soul and the whole body against attacks from without; the one counselling, and the other going out to fight as the leader directs, and courageously executing his commands and counsels?

True.

Likewise it is by reference to spirit that an individual man is deemed courageous, because his spirit retains in pleasure and in pain the commands of reason about what he ought or ought not to fear?

Right, he replied.

And we call him wise on account of that little part which rules, and which proclaims these commands; the part in which is situated the knowledge of what is for the interest of each of the three parts and of the whole?

Assuredly.

And would you not say that he is temperate who has these same elements in friendly harmony, in whom the one ruling principle of reason, and the two subject ones of spirit and desire, are equally agreed that reason ought to rule, and do not rebel?

Certainly, he said, that is a precise account of temperance whether in the state or individual.

And, finally, I said, a man will be just in that way and by that quality which we have often mentioned.

That is very certain

And is justice dimmer in the individual, and is her form different, or is she the same which we found her to be in the state?

There is no difference in my opinion, he said.

Because, if any doubt is still lingering in our minds, a few commonplace instances will satisfy us of the truth of what I am saying.

What sort of instances do you mean?

If the case is put to us, must we not admit that the just state, or the man of similar nature who has been trained in the principles of such a state, will be less likely than the unjust to make away with a deposit of gold or silver? Would any one deny this?

No one, he replied.

Will such a man ever be involved in sacrilege or theft, or treachery either to his friends or to his country?

Never.

Neither will he ever, for any reason, break faith where there have been oaths or agreements?

Impossible.

No one will be less likely to commit adultery, neglect his father and mother, or fail in his religious duties?

No one.

And the reason for all this is that each part of him is doing its own business, whether in ruling or being ruled?

Exactly so.

Are you satisfied then that the quality which makes such men and such states is justice, or do you hope to discover some other?

Not I, indeed.

Then our dream has been realised, and the suspicion which we expressed that, at the beginning of our work of construction, some divine power must have conducted us to a primary form of justice, has now been verified?

Yes, certainly.

And the division of labour which required the carpenter and the shoemaker and the rest of them to devote himself to the work for which he is naturally fitted, and to do nothing else, was a shadow of justice, and for that reason it was of use?

Clearly.

And in reality justice was such as we were describing, being concerned however, not with a man's external affairs, but with an inner relationship in which he himself is more truly concerned; for the just man does not permit the several elements within him to interfere with one another, or any of them to do the work of others – he sets in order his own inner life, and is his own master and his own law, and at peace with himself; and when he has bound together the three principles within him, which may be compared to the higher, lower, and middle notes of the scale, and any that are intermediate between them – when he has bound all these together, and is no longer many, but has become one entirely temperate and perfectly adjusted nature, then he proceeds to act, if he has to act, whether in a matter of property, or in the treatment of the body, or in some affair of politics or private business; always thinking and calling that which preserves and co-operates with this harmonious condition, just and good action, and the knowledge which presides over it, wisdom, and that which at any time impairs this condition, he will call unjust action, and the opinion which presides over it ignorance.

You have said the exact truth, Socrates.

Very good; and if we were to affirm that we had discovered the just man and the just state, and the nature of justice in each of them, we should not be far from the truth?

Most certainly not.

May we say so, then?

Let us say so.

And now, I said, injustice has to be considered.

Clearly.

Must not injustice be a strife which arises among the same three principles – a meddlesomeness, and interference, and rising up of a part of the soul against the whole, an assertion of unlawful authority, which is made by a rebellious subject against a true prince, of whom he is the natural vassal – what is all this confusion and delusion but injustice and intemperance and cowardice and ignorance, and, in short, every form of vice?

Exactly so.

And if the nature of justice and injustice is known, then the meaning of acting unjustly and being unjust, or again of acting justly, is now also perfectly clear?

How so? he said.

Why, I said, they are like disease and health; being in the soul just what disease and health are in the body.

How so? he said.

Why, I said, that which is healthy causes health, and that which is unhealthy causes disease.

Yes.

And just actions cause justice, and unjust actions cause injustice?

That is certain.

And the creation of health is the institution of a natural order and government of one by another in the parts of the body; and the creation of disease is the production of a state of things at variance with this natural order?

True.

And is not the creation of justice the institution of a natural order and government of one by another in the parts of the soul, and the creation of injustice the production of a state of things at variance with the natural order?

Exactly so, he said.

Then virtue is the health and beauty and well-being of the soul, and vice the disease and weakness and deformity of the same?

True.

And how are virtue and vice acquired – is it not by good and evil practices?

Assuredly.

The time has come, then, to answer the final question of the comparative advantage of justice and injustice: which is the more profitable, to be just and act justly and honourably, whether one's character is or is not known, or to be unjust and act unjustly, if one is unpunished, that is to say unreformed?

In my judgement, Socrates, the question has now become ridiculous. We know that, when the bodily constitution is gone, life is no longer endurable, though pampered with all kinds of meats and drinks, and having all wealth and all power; and shall we be told that when the natural health of our vital principle is undermined and corrupted, life is still worth having to a man, if only he be allowed to do whatever he likes, except to take steps to acquire justice and virtue and escape from injustice and vice; assuming them both to be such as we have described?

Yes, I said, the question is, as you say, ridiculous. Still, as we are near the spot at which we may see the truth in the clearest manner with our own eyes, let us not faint by the way.

Certainly not, he replied.

Come here, then, I said, and behold the various

forms of vice, those of them, I mean, which are worth looking at.

I am following you, he replied: proceed.

I said, The argument seems to have reached a height from which, as from some tower of speculation, a man may look down and see that virtue is one, but that the forms of vice are innumerable; there being four special ones which are deserving of note.

What do you mean? he said.

I mean, I replied, that there appear to be as many forms of the soul as there are distinct forms of the state.

How many?

There are five of the state, and five of the soul, I said.

What are they?

The first, I said, is that which we have been describing, and which may be given either of two names, monarchy or aristocracy, according as rule is exercised by one man distinguished among the ruling class or by more.

True, he replied.

But I regard the two names as describing one form only; for whether the government is in the hands of one or many, if the governors have been bred and trained in the manner which we have supposed, the fundamental laws of the state will not be disturbed.

Probably not, he replied.

BOOK FIVE

Such is the city and constitution which I call good and true, and the good and true man is of the same pattern; and if this is true, every other is faulty and wrong; and whether we have regard to the ordering of states, or to the regulation of the individual soul, four kinds of wrongness are to be observed.

What are they? he said.

I was proceeding to tell the order in which the four wrong forms appeared to me to succeed one another, when Polemarchus, who was sitting a little way off, just beyond Adeimantus, stretched forth his hand, and took hold of the upper part of his coat by the shoulder, and drew him towards him, leaning forward himself and saying something in his ear, of which I only caught the words, 'Shall we let it go, or what shall we do?'

Certainly not, said Adeimantus, raising his voice.

What is it, I said, that you are refusing to let go?

You, he said.

Why am I especially not to be let go? I said.

Why, he said, we think that you are lazy, and mean to cheat us out of a whole chapter which is a very important part of the story; and you fancy that we shall not notice your airy way of proceeding; as if it were self-evident to everybody, that in the matter of women and children 'friends have all things in common'.

And was I not right, Adeimantus?

Yes, he said; but what is right in this particular case, as in any other, requires to be explained; for there are various ways in which things may be held in common, and you should not omit to say which you have in mind.

We have been long expecting that you would tell us something about the family life of your citizens – how they will bring children into the world, and rear them when they have arrived, and, in general, what is the nature of this community of women and children – for we are of opinion that the right or wrong management of such matters will have a great and indeed paramount influence on the state. And now, since you are taking in hand another state before this question has been sufficiently determined, we have resolved, as you heard, not to let you go until you supply an account of all this.

To that resolution, said Glaucon, you may regard me as saying 'Agreed'.

And without more ado, said Thrasymachus, you may consider us all to be equally agreed.

I said, You know not what you are doing in thus assailing me. What an argument are you raising about the state! Just as I thought with satisfaction that I had finished, and was reflecting how fortunate I was in your acceptance of what I then said, you ask me to begin again at the very foundation, ignorant of what a hornet's nest of words you are stirring. I meant to omit this discussion because I foresaw how troublesome it might be.

For what purpose do you conceive that we have come here, said Thrasymachus – to look for gold, or to hear discourse?

Yes, but discourse should have a limit.

Yes, Socrates, said Glaucon, and the whole of life is the only limit which wise men assign to the hearing of such discourses. But never mind about us; take heart yourself and answer the question in your own way: What sort of community of women and children is this which is to prevail among our guardians? And what of the common nurture of infants in the period between birth and education? This seems the most troublesome part of the plan, and you ought to try to explain how it is to be managed.

Yes, my simple friend, but the answer is the reverse of easy; many more doubts arise about this than about our previous conclusions. For the practicability of what is said may be doubted; and another kind of doubt may be felt, whether the scheme, if ever so practicable, would be for the best. Hence I feel a reluctance to approach the subject, lest our aspiration, my dear friend, should turn out to be a dream only.

Fear not, he replied, for your audience will not be hard upon you; they are not sceptical or hostile.

I said: My good friend, I suppose that you mean to encourage me by these words.

Yes, he said.

Then let me tell you that you are doing just the reverse; the encouragement which you offer would have been all very well had I myself been confident that I knew what I was talking about: to declare the truth about matters of high interest, which a man honours and loves, among wise men who love him, need occasion no fear or faltering in his mind; but to carry on an argument when you are yourself only a hesitating inquirer, which is my condition, is a dangerous and slippery thing; and the danger is not that I shall be laughed at (of which the fear would be childish), but that I shall miss the truth where I have most need to be sure of my footing, and drag my friends after me in my fall. And I pray Nemesis not to visit upon me the words which I am going to utter. For I do indeed believe that to be an involuntary homicide is a less crime than to be a deceiver about noble or good or just institutions. And that is a risk which I would rather run among enemies than among friends, so that yours is a fine sort of encouragement.

Glaucon laughed and said: Well then, Socrates, in case you and your argument do us any serious injury you are acquitted beforehand of the homicide, and shall not be held to be a deceiver; take courage then and speak.

Well, I said, the law says that when a man is absolved by the person injured he is free from guilt, and what holds at law may hold in argument.

Then why should you mind?

Well, I replied, I suppose that I must retrace my steps and say what I perhaps ought to have said before in the proper place. The drama of the men has been played out, and now properly enough comes the turn of the women, especially in view of your challenge.

For men born and educated like our citizens there can, in my opinion, be no right possession and use of women and children unless they follow the path on which we sent them forth. We proposed, as you know, to treat them as watchdogs of the herd.

True.

Let us abide by that comparison in our account of their birth and breeding, and let us see whether the result accords with our design.

What do you mean?

What I mean may be put into the form of a question, I said: are female sheepdogs expected to keep watch together with the males, and to go hunting with them and share in their other activities? Or do we entrust to the males the entire and exclusive care of the flocks, while we leave the females at home, because we think

213

that the bearing and suckling their puppies is labour enough for them?

No, he said, they share alike; the only difference between them is that the males are regarded as stronger and the females as weaker.

But can you use different animals for the same purpose, unless they are bred and fed in the same way?

You cannot.

Then if women are to have the same duties as men, they must have the same education?

Yes.

The education which was assigned to the men was music and gymnastic.

Yes.

Then women also must be taught music and gymnastic and military exercises, and they must be treated like the men?

That is the inference, I suppose.

I fully expect, I said, that our proposals, if they are carried out, being unusual, may in many respects appear ridiculous.

No doubt of it.

Yes, and the most ridiculous thing of all will be the sight of women naked in the palaestra, exercising with the men, even when they are no longer young; they certainly will not be a vision of beauty, any more than the enthusiastic old men who in spite of wrinkles and ugliness continue to frequent the gymnasia.

Yes, indeed, he said: according to present notions the proposal would be thought ridiculous.

But then, I said, as we have determined to speak our minds, we must not fear the jests of the wits which will be directed against this sort of innovation; how they will talk of women's attainments both in music and gymnastic, and above all about their wearing armour and riding upon horseback.

Very true, he replied.

Yet having begun we must go forward to the rough places of the law; at the same time begging of these gentlemen for once in their life to be serious. Not long ago, as we shall remind them, the Hellenes were of the opinion, which is still generally received among the barbarians, that the sight of a naked man was ridiculous and improper; and when first the Cretans and then the Lacedaemonians introduced the custom of stripping for exercise, the wits of that day might equally have ridiculed the innovation.

No doubt.

But no doubt when experience showed that to let all things be uncovered was far better than to cover them up, the ludicrous effect to the outward eye vanished before what reason had proved to be best, and the man was perceived to be a fool who directs the shafts of his ridicule at any other sight but that of folly and vice, or seriously inclines to weigh the beautiful by any other standard but that of the good.

Very true, he replied.

First, then, let us come to an understanding whether the course we propose is possible or not: let us admit any arguments put forward by comedians or persons more seriously inclined, and tending to show whether in the human race the female is able to take part in all the occupations of the male, or in some of them only, or in none; and to which class the art of war belongs. That will be the best way of commencing the inquiry, and will probably lead to the soundest conclusion.

That will be much the best way.

Shall we take the other side first and begin by arguing

against ourselves; in this manner the adversary's position will not be undefended.

Why not? he said.

Then let us put a speech into the mouths of our opponents. They will say: 'Socrates and Glaucon, no adversary is needed to convict you, for you yourselves, at the first foundation of the state, admitted the principle that everybody was to do the one work suited to his own nature.' And certainly, if I am not mistaken, such an admission was made by us. 'And do not the natures of men and women differ very much indeed?' And we shall reply: 'Of course they do.' Then we shall be asked, whether the tasks assigned to men and to women should not be different, and such as are agreeable to their different natures. 'Certainly they should.' 'But if so, have you not fallen into a serious inconsistency in saying that men and women, whose natures are so entirely different, ought to perform the same actions?' What defence will you make for us, my good sir, against these objections?

That is not an easy question to answer when asked suddenly; and I shall and I do beg of you to draw out the case on our side.

These are the objections, Glaucon, and there are many others of a like kind, which I foresaw long ago; they made me afraid and reluctant to take in hand any law about the possession and nurture of women and children.

By Zeus, he said, the problem to be solved is anything but easy.

Why yes, I said, but the fact is that when a man is out of his depth, whether he has fallen into a little swimming-bath or into mid ocean, he has to swim all the same.

Very true.

And must not we swim and try to reach the shore, while hoping that Arion's dolphin or some other miraculous help may save us?

I suppose so, he said.

Well then, let us see if any way of escape can be found. We acknowledged – did we not? – that different natures ought to have different pursuits, and that men's and women's natures are different. And now what are we saying? That different natures ought to have the same pursuits – this is the inconsistency which is charged upon us.

Precisely.

Verily, Glaucon, I said, glorious is the power of the art of disputation!

Why do you say so?

Because I think that many a man falls into the practice against his will. When he thinks that he is reasoning he is really disputing, just because he does not know how to inquire into a subject by distinguishing its various aspects, but pursues some verbal opposition in the statement which has been made. That is the difference between the spirit of contention and that of fair discussion.

Yes, he replied, that is a fairly common failing, but does it apply at present to us?

Yes, indeed; for there is a danger of our getting unintentionally into verbal contradiction.

In what way?

Why, we valiantly and pugnaciously insist upon the verbal truth that different natures ought to have different pursuits, but we never considered at all what was the meaning of sameness or difference of nature, or with what intention we distinguished them when we assigned different pursuits to different natures and the same to the same natures.

Why, no, he said, that was never considered by us.

I said: Yet it seems that we should be entitled to ask ourselves whether there is not an opposition in nature between bald men and hairy men; and if this is admitted by us, then, if bald men are cobblers, we should forbid the hairy men to be cobblers, and conversely?

That would be a jest, he said.

Yes, I said, a jest; and why? Because we were not previously speaking of sameness or difference in *any* sense; we were concerned with one *form* of difference or similarity, namely that which would affect the pursuit in which a man is engaged; we should have argued, for example, that a physician and one who is in mind a physician may be said to have the same nature.

True.

Whereas the physician and the carpenter have different natures?

Certainly.

And if, I said, the male and female sex appear to differ in their fitness for any art or pursuit, we should say that such pursuit or art ought to be assigned to one or the other of them; but if the difference consists only in women bearing and men begetting children, this does not amount to a proof that a woman differs from a man in respect of the sort of education she should receive; and we shall therefore continue to maintain that our guardians and their wives ought to have the same pursuits.

Quite rightly, he said.

Only then shall we ask our opponent to inform us with reference to which of the pursuits or arts of civic life the nature of a woman differs from that of a man?

That will be quite fair.

And perhaps he, like yourself a moment ago, will reply that to give a sufficient answer on the instant is not easy; but that given time for reflection there is no difficulty.

Yes, perhaps.

Suppose then that we invite such an objector to accompany us in the argument, in the hope of showing him that there is no occupation peculiar to women which need be considered in the administration of the state.

By all means.

Let us say to him: Come now, and we will ask you a question: when you spoke of a nature gifted or not gifted in any respect, did you mean to say that one man will acquire a thing easily, another with difficulty? The first, after brief instruction, is able to discover a great deal more for himself, whereas the other, after much teaching and application, cannot even preserve what he has learnt; or again, did you mean that the one has a body which is a good servant to his mind, while the body of the other is a hindrance to him? Would not these be the sort of differences which distinguish the man gifted by nature from the one who is ungifted?

No one will deny that.

And can you mention any pursuit of mankind in which the male sex has not all these gifts and qualities in a higher degree than the female? Need I waste time in speaking of the art of weaving, and the preparation of pancakes and preserves in which womankind is generally thought to have some skill, and in which for her to be beaten by a man is of all things the most absurd?

You are quite right, he replied, in maintaining that one sex greatly excels the other in almost every field. Although many woman are in many things superior to many men, yet on the whole what you say is true.

And if so, my friend, I said, there is no special faculty of administration in a state which a woman has because she is a woman, or which a man has by virtue of his sex, but the gifts of nature are alike diffused in both; all the pursuits of men can naturally be assigned to women also, but in all of them a woman is weaker than a man.

Very true.

Then are we to impose all our enactments on men and none of them on women?

That will never do.

Because we shall say that a woman too may, or may not, have the gift of healing; and that one is a musician, and another has no music in her nature?

Very true.

And it can hardly be denied that one woman has a turn for gymnastic and military exercises, and another is unwarlike and hates gymnastics?

I think not.

And one woman is a philosopher, and another is an enemy of philosophy; one has spirit, and another is without spirit?

That is also true.

Then one woman will have the temper of a guardian, and another not. For these, as you remember, were the natural gifts for which we looked in the selection of the male guardians.

Yes.

Men and women alike possess the qualities which make a guardian; they differ only in their comparative strength or weakness.

Obviously.

Therefore those women who have such qualities are to be selected as the companions and colleagues of men who also have them and whom they resemble in capacity and in character?

Very true.

But ought not the same natures to be trained in the same pursuits?

They ought.

Then we have come round to the previous point that there is nothing unnatural in assigning music and gymnastic to the guardian women.

Certainly not.

The law which we then enacted was agreeable to nature, and therefore not an impossibility or mere aspiration; it is rather the contrary practice, which prevails at present, that is a violation of nature.

That appears to be true.

We had to consider, first, whether our proposals were possible, and secondly whether they were the most beneficial?

Yes.

And the possibility has been acknowledged?

Yes.

The very great benefit has next to be established?

Quite so.

You will admit that the same education which makes a man a good guardian will make a woman a good guardian; especially if the original nature of both is the same?

Yes.

I should like to ask you a question.

What is it?

Is it your opinion that one man is better than

another? Or do you think them all equal?

Not at all.

And in the commonwealth which we were founding do you conceive the guardians who have been brought up on our model system to be more perfect men, or the cobblers whose education has been cobbling?

What a ridiculous question!

You have answered me, I replied: in fact, our guardians are the best of all our citizens?

By far the best.

And will not the guardian women be the best women?

Yes, by far the best.

And can there be anything better for the interests of the state than that the men and women of a state should be as good as possible?

There can be nothing better.

And this is what the arts of music and gymnastic, when present in such manner as we have described, will accomplish?

Certainly.

Then we have made an enactment not only possible but in the highest degree beneficial to the state?

True.

Then let the guardian women strip, for their virtue will be their robe, and let them share in the toils of war and the defence of their country; only in the distribution of labours the lighter are to be assigned to the women, who are the weaker natures, but in other respects their duties are to be the same. And as for the man who laughs at naked women exercising their bodies from the best of motives, in his laughter he is plucking 'a fruit of unripe wisdom', and he himself is ignorant of what he is laughing at, or what he is about; for that is, and ever will be, the best of sayings, that 'the useful is noble and the hurtful is base'.

Very true.

Here then is one difficulty in our law about women, which we may say that we have now escaped; the wave has not swallowed us up alive for enacting that the guardians of either sex should have all their pursuits in common; to the utility and also to the possibility of this arrangement the consistency of the argument with itself bears witness.

Yes, that was a mighty wave which you have escaped.

Yes, I said, but you may not think it so impressive when you see the next.

Go on; let me see.

The law, I said, which is the sequel of this and of all that has preceded, is to the following effect – that all these women are to be common to all the men of the same class, none living privately together; and moreover, that their children are to be common, and no parent is to know his own child, nor any child his parent.

Yes, he said, you will find it much harder to convince anyone either of the possibility or of the usefulness of such a law.

I do not think, I said, that there can be any dispute about the very great utility of having both women and children in common; the possibility is quite another matter, and will, no doubt, be very much disputed.

Both points are sure to be warmly disputed.

You imply that the two questions must be combined, I replied. I hoped that you would admit that the proposal was useful, and so I should escape from at least one of them, and then there would remain only the possibility.

But that attempt to escape is detected, and therefore you will please to give a defence of both.

Well, I said, I submit to my fate. Yet grant me a little favour: let me feast my mind with the dream as day-dreamers are in the habit of feasting themselves when they are walking alone; for before they have discovered any means of effecting their wishes – that is a matter which never troubles them; they would rather not tire themselves by thinking about possibilities – but assuming that what they desire is already granted to them, they proceed with their plan, and delight in detailing what they mean to do when their wish has come true – a recreation which tends to make an idle mind still idler. Now I myself am beginning to lose heart, and I should like, with your permission, to pass over the question of possibility at present. Assuming therefore the possibility of the proposal, I shall now proceed to inquire how the rulers will carry out these arrangements, and I shall demonstrate that our plan, if executed, will be of the greatest possible benefit both to the state and to the guardians. First of all, then, if you have no objection, I will endeavour with your help to consider the advantages of the measure; and hereafter the question of possibility.

I have no objection; proceed.

First, I think that if our rulers and their auxiliaries are to be worthy of the name which they bear, there must be the power of command in the one and willingness to obey in the other; the guardians must themselves obey the laws, and they must also imitate the spirit of them in any details which are entrusted to their care.

That is right, he said.

You, I said, who are their legislator, having selected the men, will now select the women and give them to them; they must be as far as possible of like natures with them; and they must live in common houses and meet at common meals. None of them will have anything specially his or her own; they will be together, and will be brought up together, and will associate at gymnastic exercises. And so they will be drawn by a necessity of their natures to have intercourse with each other – necessity is not too strong a word, I think?

Yes, he said; necessity, not geometrical, but another sort of necessity which lovers know, and which is far more convincing and constraining to the mass of mankind.

True, Glaucon, I said; but now we can hardly allow promiscuous unions, or any other kind of disorder; in a city of the blessed, licentiousness is an unholy thing which the rulers will forbid.

Yes, he said, and it ought not to be permitted.

Then clearly the next thing will be to arrange marriages that are sacred in the highest degree; and what is most beneficial will be deemed sacred?

Exactly.

And how can marriages be made most beneficial? That is a question which I put to you, because I see in your house dogs for hunting, and of the nobler sort of birds not a few. Now, I beseech you, do tell me, have you ever attended to their pairing and breeding?

In what particulars?

Why, in the first place, although they are all of good pedigree, do not some prove to be better than others?

True.

And do you breed from them all indifferently, or do you take care to breed from the best only?

From the best.

From the oldest or the youngest, or only those of ripe age?

From those of ripe age.

And if care was not taken in the breeding, your dogs and birds would greatly deteriorate?

Certainly.

What of horses and of animals in general? Is there any difference?

No, it would be strange if there were.

Good heavens! My dear friend, I said, what consummate skill will our rulers need if the same principle holds of the human species!

Certainly, the same principle holds; but why does this involve any particular skill?

Because, I said, our rulers will often have to practise upon the body corporate with medicines. Now you know that when patients do not require medicines but have only to be put under a regimen, the inferior sort of practitioner is deemed to be good enough; but when medicine has to be given, then the doctor should be more of a man.

That is quite true, he said; but to what are you alluding?

I mean, I replied, that our rulers will find a considerable dose of falsehood and deceit necessary for the good of their subjects: we said before that the use of all these things regarded as medicines might be of advantage.

And we were very right.

And this lawful use of them seems likely to be often needed in the regulations of marriages and births.

How so?

Why, I said, the principle has been already laid

down that the best of either sex should be united with the best as often, and the inferior with the inferior as seldom, as possible; and that they should rear the offspring of the one sort of union but not of the other, if the flock is to be maintained in first-rate condition. Now these goings-on must be a secret which the rulers only know, in order to keep our herd, as the guardians may be termed, as free as possible from dissension.

Very true.

Had we not better appoint certain festivals at which we will bring together the brides and bridegrooms, and sacrifices will be offered, and suitable hymeneal songs composed by our poets: the number of weddings is a matter which must be left to the discretion of the rulers, whose aim will be to preserve the same total number of guardians, having regard to wars, plagues, and any similar agencies, in order as far as this is possible to prevent the state from becoming either too large or too small.

Certainly, he replied.

We shall have to invent some ingenious kind of lottery, so that the less worthy may, on each occasion of our bringing them together, accuse their own ill luck and not the rulers.

To be sure, he said.

And I think that our braver and better youth, besides their other honours and rewards, might have greater facilities of intercourse with women given them; their bravery will be a reason, and such fathers ought to have as many sons as possible.

True.

And the proper officers, whether male or female or both, for offices are to be held by women as well as by men –

Yes.

The proper officers will take the offspring of the good parents to the pen or fold, and there they will deposit them with certain nurses who dwell in a separate quarter; but the offspring of the inferior, or of the better when they chance to be deformed, will be put away in some mysterious unknown place, as they should be.

Yes, he said, that must be done if the breed of the guardians is to be kept pure.

They will provide for their nurture, and will bring the mothers to the fold when they are full of milk, taking the greatest possible care that no mother recognises her own child; and other wet-nurses may be engaged if more are required. Care will also be taken that the process of suckling shall not be protracted too long; and the mothers will have no getting up at night or other trouble, but will hand over all this sort of thing to the nurses and attendants.

Maternity, according to you, will be an easy business for these guardian women.

Why, said I, and that is quite proper. Let us, however, proceed with our scheme. We were saying that the parents should be in the prime of life?

Very true.

And what is the prime of life? May it not be defined as a period of about twenty years in a woman's life, and thirty in a man's?

Which years do you mean to include?

A woman, I said, at twenty years of age may begin to bear children to the state, and continue to bear them until forty; a man may begin at five-and-twenty, when he has passed the point at which the pulse of life beats quickest, and continue to beget children until he be fifty-five.

Certainly, he said, both in men and women those years are the prime of physical as well as of intellectual vigour.

Anyone above or below the prescribed ages who presumes to beget children for the commonwealth shall be said to have done an unholy and unrighteous thing; the child of which he is the father, if it steals into life, will have been conceived under auspices very unlike the sacrifices and prayers which at each hymeneal priestesses and priests and the whole city will offer, that the new generation may be better and more useful than their good and useful parents; whereas his child will be the offspring of darkness and strange lust.

Very true, he replied.

And the same law will apply to any one of those within the prescribed age who forms a connection with any woman in the prime of life without the sanction of the rulers; for we shall say that he is raising up a bastard to the state, unsponsored and unconsecrated.

Very true, he replied.

This applies, however, only to men and women within the specified age: after that we shall probably allow them to range at will, except that a man may not marry his daughter or his daughter's daughter, or his mother or his mother's mother; and women, on the other hand, are prohibited from marrying their sons or fathers, or son's son or father's father, and so on in either direction. And we grant all this, accompanying the permission with strict orders to prevent any embryo which may come into being from seeing the light; and if any force a way to the birth, the parents must understand that the offspring of such a union cannot be maintained, and arrange accordingly.

That also, he said, is a reasonable proposition. But how will they know who are fathers and daughters, and so on?

They will never know. The way will be this: dating from the day of the hymeneal, the bridegroom who was then married will call all the male children who are born in the tenth month afterwards, and indeed in the seventh, his sons, and the female children his daughters, and they will call him father, and he will call their children his grandchildren, and they will call the elder generation grandfathers and grandmothers. All who were begotten at the time when their fathers and mothers came together will be called brothers and sisters, and these, as I was saying, will be forbidden to intermarry. This, however, is not an absolute prohibition of the marriage of brothers and sisters; if the lot favours them, and they receive the sanction of the Pythian oracle, the law will allow them.

Quite right, he replied.

Such is the scheme, Glaucon, according to which the guardians of our state are to have their wives and families in common. And now you would have it established by argument that this community is consistent with the rest of our polity, and also that nothing can be better – would you not?

Yes, certainly.

Shall we try to find a common basis by asking of ourselves what ought to be the chief aim of the legislator in making laws – what is the greatest good, and what is the greatest evil, in the organisation of a state; and then consider whether the manner of life we have just described has the stamp of the good and not that of the evil?

By all means.

Can we name anything more harmful for a state than a force, whatever it may be, which causes distraction and plurality where unity ought to reign? Or any greater good than the bond of unity?

We cannot.

And there is unity where there is community of pleasures and pains – where all the citizens are glad or grieved in the same degree on the same occasions of joy and sorrow?

No doubt.

But where there is no common but only private feeling a state is disorganised – when you have one half triumphing and the other plunged in grief at the same events happening to the city or the citizens?

Certainly.

Such differences commonly originate in a disagreement about the use of the terms 'mine' and 'not mine', 'his' and 'not his'.

Exactly so.

And is not that the best-ordered state in which the greatest number of persons apply the terms 'mine' and 'not mine' in the same way to the same thing?

Quite true.

Or that again which most nearly approaches to the condition of an individual? As in the body, when but a finger of one of us is hurt, the whole frame, drawn towards the soul as a centre and forming one kingdom under the ruling power therein, feels the hurt and sympathises all together with the part affected, and we say that the man has a pain in his finger; and the same expression is used about any other part of the body, which has a sensation of pain at suffering or of pleasure at the alleviation of suffering.

Very true, he replied; and I agree with you that in the

best-ordered state there is the nearest approach to this common feeling which you describe.

Then when any one of the citizens experiences any good or evil, such a state will make his case its own, and will either rejoice or sorrow with him?

Yes, he said, a well-ordered state must do so.

It will now be time, I said, for us to return to our state and see whether this or some other form is most in accordance with these fundamental principles.

Very good.

Well then, our state like every other has rulers and subjects?

True.

All of whom will call one another citizens?

Of course.

But is there not another name which people give to their rulers in other states?

Generally they call them masters, but in democratic states they simply call them rulers.

And in our state what other name besides that of citizens do the people give the rulers?

They are called saviours and helpers, he replied.

And what do the rulers call the people?

Their maintainers and foster-fathers.

And what do they call them in other states?

Slaves.

And what do the rulers call one another in other states?

Fellow rulers.

And what in ours?

Fellow guardians.

Did you ever know an example in any other state of a ruler who would speak of one of his colleagues as his friend and of another as not being his friend?

Yes, very often.

And the friend he regards and describes as one in whom he has an interest, and the other as a stranger in whom he has no interest?

Exactly.

But would any of your guardians think of, or address, any other guardian as a stranger?

Certainly he would not; for everyone whom they meet will be regarded by them either as a brother or sister, or father or mother, or son or daughter, or as the child or parent of those who are thus connected with him.

Capital, I said; but let me ask you once more: do you intend to make them a family in name only; or shall they in all their actions be true to the name? For example, in the use of the word 'father', would the care of a father be implied and the filial reverence and duty and obedience to him which the law commands; and is the violator of these duties to be regarded as an impious and unrighteous person who is not likely to receive much good either at the hands of god or of man? Are these to be or not to be the strains which the children will hear repeated in their ears by all the citizens, about those who are intimated to them to be their parents and the rest of their kinsfolk?

These, he said, and none other; for what can be more ridiculous than for them to utter the names of family ties with the lips only and not to act in the spirit of them?

Then in our city the language of harmony and concord will be more often heard than in any other. As I was describing before, when any one is faring well or ill, the universal word will be 'with me it is well' or 'it is ill'.

Most true.

And agreeably to this mode of thinking and speaking, were we not saying that they will have their pleasures and pains in common?

Yes, and so they will.

And they will have a common interest in the same thing which they will alike call 'my own', and having this common interest they will have a common feeling of pleasure and pain?

Yes, far more so than in other states.

And the reason of this, over and above the general constitution of the state, will be that the guardians will have a community of women and children?

That will be the chief reason.

And this unity of feeling we admitted to be the greatest good, as was implied in our own comparison of a well-ordered state to the relation of the body and the members, when affected by pleasure or pain?

That we acknowledged, and very rightly.

Then the community of women and children among our auxiliaries has now been shown to be the source of the greatest good to the state?

Certainly.

Moreover this agrees with the other principle which we were affirming – that the guardians were not to have houses or lands or any other property; their pay was to be their food, which they were to receive from the other citizens, and they were to have no private expenses; for we intended them to preserve their true character of guardians.

Right, he replied.

I mean, then, that our previous laws, and still more those of which we are now speaking, tend to make them true guardians; they will not tear the city in pieces by differing about 'mine' and 'not mine'; each man dragging any acquisition which he has made into a separate house of his own, where he has a separate wife and children who are the source of private pleasures and pains; but all will be affected as far as may be by the same pleasures and pains because they are all of one opinion about what is near and dear to them, and therefore they all tend towards a common end.

Certainly, he replied.

And as they have nothing but their persons which they can call their own, suits and complaints will practically disappear from among them; they will be delivered from all those quarrels of which money or children or relations are the occasion.

Of course they will.

Neither will trials for assault or insult ever be likely to occur among them. For that men should defend themselves against assailants of the same age we shall maintain to be honourable and right, thus forcing them to keep their bodies in training.

That is good, he said.

Yes; and there is a further good in the law; viz. that if a man has a quarrel with another he will satisfy his resentment then and there, and be less inclined to proceed to a lasting feud.

Certainly.

To the elder shall be assigned the duty of ruling and chastising the younger.

Clearly.

Nor can there be a doubt that the younger will not strike or do any other violence to an elder, unless the magistrates command him; nor will he slight him in any way. For there are two guardians, shame and fear, mighty to prevent him: shame, which makes men refrain from laying hands on those who are to them in the relation of parents; fear, that the injured one will be succoured by the others who are his brothers, sons, fathers.

Yes, that is natural, he replied.

Then in every way the laws will help the citizens to keep the peace with one another?

Yes, there will be no want of peace.

And as the guardians will never quarrel among themselves there will be no danger of the rest of the city being divided either against them or against one another.

None whatever.

I hardly like even to mention the little meannesses of which they will be rid, for they are beneath notice: such, for example, as the flattery of the rich by the poor, and all the pains and pangs which men experience in bringing up a family, and in finding money to buy necessaries for their household, borrowing and then repudiating, getting how they can, and giving the money into the hands of women and slaves to keep – the many evils of so many kinds which people suffer in this way are mean enough and obvious enough, and not worth speaking of.

Yes, he said, a man has no need of eyes in order to perceive that.

And from all these evils they will be delivered, and their life will be blessed as the life of Olympic victors and yet more blessed.

How so?

The Olympic victor, I said, is deemed happy in receiving a part only of the blessedness which is secured to our citizens, who have won a more glorious victory and have a more complete maintenance at the public cost. For the victory which they have won is the salvation of the whole state; and the crown with which they and their children are crowned is the fullness of all that life needs; they receive rewards from the hands of their country while living, and after death have an honourable burial.

Yes, he said, and glorious rewards they are.

Do you remember, I said, how in the course of the previous discussion, when some supposed critic accused us of failing to make our guardians happy, because they might have laid hands on all the wealth of the citizens but in fact possessed nothing, we replied that, if an occasion offered, we might perhaps hereafter consider this question; but that, as at present advised, we would make our guardians truly guardians, and that we were fashioning the state with a view to the greatest happiness, not of any particular class but of the whole?

Yes, I remember.

And what do you say, now that the life of our protectors is made out to be far better and nobler than that of Olympic victors – is the life of shoemakers, or any other artisans, or of husbandmen, to be compared with it?

Certainly not.

At the same time I ought here to repeat what I have said elsewhere, that if any of our guardians shall try to be happy in such a manner that he will utterly cease to be a guardian, and is not content with this safe and harmonious life, which in our judgment is of all lives the best, but infatuated by some youthful conceit of happiness which gets up into his head shall use his power to appropriate the whole wealth of the city to himself, then he will have to learn how wisely Hesiod spoke, when he said, 'half is more than the whole'.

My advice to him would be to remain content with his present life.

You agree then, I said, that men and women are to have a common way of life such as we have described – common education, common children; and they are to watch over the citizens in common whether abiding in the city or going out to war; they are to keep watch together, and to hunt together like dogs; and always and in all things, as far as they are able, women are to share with the men? And in so doing they will do what is best, and will not violate but preserve the natural relation of the sexes?

I agree with you, he replied.

The inquiry, I said, has yet to be made, whether such a community will be found possible – as among other animals, so also among men – and if possible, in what way possible?

You have anticipated the question which I was about to suggest.

There is presumably no difficulty, I said, in seeing how war will be carried on by them.

How?

Why, of course they will go on expeditions together; and will take with them any of their children who are strong enough, that, after the manner of the artisan's child, they may look on at the work which they will have to do when they are grown up; and besides looking on they will have to help and be of use in war, and to wait upon their fathers and mothers. Did you never observe in the arts how the potters' boys look on and help, long before they touch the wheel?

Yes, I have.

And shall potters be more careful in educating their children and in giving them the opportunity of seeing and practising their duties than our guardians will be?

The idea is ridiculous, he said.

Apart from this, all animals will fight most valiantly in the presence of their young ones.

That is quite true, Socrates; and yet if they are defeated, which may often happen in war, how great the danger is! The children will be lost as well as their parents, and the state will never recover.

True, I said; but, firstly, would you never allow them to run any risk?

I am far from saying that.

Well, but if they are ever to run a risk should they not do so on some occasion when, if they escape disaster, they will be the better for it?

Clearly.

Whether the future soldiers do or do not see war in the days of their youth is a very important matter, for the sake of which some risk may fairly be incurred.

Yes, very important.

This then is taken for granted, that we shall make our children spectators of war; but we must also contrive that they shall be secured against danger; then all will be well.

True.

Their parents may be supposed not to be blind to the risks of war, but to know, as far as human foresight can, what expeditions are safe and what dangerous?

That may be assumed.

And they will take them on the safe expeditions and be cautious about the dangerous ones?

True.

And they will place them under the command not of the weak and infirm, but of experienced veterans well qualified to be their guides and escort?

Very properly.

Still, we shall remind ourselves that the dangers and chances of war cannot be always foreseen.

True.

Then against such chances the children must be at once furnished with wings, in order that in the hour of need they may fly away and escape.

What do you mean? he said.

I mean that we must mount them on horses in their earliest youth, and when they have learnt to ride, take them on horseback to see war: the horses must not be spirited and warlike, but the most tractable and yet the swiftest that can be had. In this way they will get an excellent view of what is hereafter to be their own business; and if there is danger they have only to follow their elder leaders and escape.

I believe that you are right, he said.

Next, as to war; what are to be the relations of your soldiers to one another and to their enemies? I should be inclined to propose that the soldier who leaves his rank or throws away his arms, or is guilty of any other act of cowardice, should be degraded into the rank of a husbandman or artisan. What do you think?

By all means, I should say.

And he who allows himself to be taken prisoner may as well be made a present of to his enemies; he is their lawful prey, and let them do what they like with him.

Certainly.

But the hero who has distinguished himself, what shall be done to him? In the first place, he shall receive honour in the army from his youthful comrades; every one of them in succession shall crown him. What do you say?

I approve.

And what do you say to his receiving the right hand of fellowship?

To that too, I agree.

But you will hardly agree to my next proposal.

What is your proposal?

That he should kiss and be kissed by them.

Most certainly, and I should be disposed to go further, and say: 'Let no one whom he has a mind to kiss refuse to be kissed by him while the expedition lasts.' So that if there be a lover in the army, whether his love be youth or maiden, he may be more eager to win the prize of valour.

Capital, I said. That the brave man is to have readier access to marriage than others has been already determined: and he is to be chosen on these occasions more often than others, in order that such a parent may have as many children as possible?

Agreed.

Again, there is another manner in which, according to Homer, brave youths should be honoured; for he tells how Ajax, after he had distinguished himself in battle, was rewarded with long chines, which seems to be a compliment appropriate to a hero in the flower of his age, being not only a tribute of honour but also a very strengthening thing.

Most true, he said.

Then in this at least, I said, Homer shall be our teacher; and we too, at sacrifices and on the like occasions, will honour the brave according to the measure of their valour, with hymns and those other distinctions which we were mentioning; also with 'seats of precedence, and meats and full cups'; and in honouring them, we shall be at the same time training them, men and women alike.

That, he replied, is excellent.

Yes, I said; and when a man dies gloriously in war shall we not say, in the first place, that he is of the golden race?

To be sure.

Nay, have we not the authority of Hesiod for affirming that when men of this race are dead 'they are holy angels upon the earth, authors of good, averters of evil, the guardians of speech-gifted men'?

Yes; and we accept his authority.

We must inquire from the god how we are to order the sepulture of divine and heroic personages, and what is to be their special distinction; and we must do as he bids?

By all means.

And in ages to come we will reverence them and kneel before their sepulchres as at the graves of heroes. And not only they but any who are deemed pre-eminently good, whether they die from age, or in any other way, shall be admitted to the same honours.

That is very right, he said.

Next, how shall our soldiers treat their enemies? What about this?

In what respect do you mean?

First of all, in regard to slavery. Do you think it right that Hellenic states should enslave Hellenes? Should they not rather, if they have the power, prevent another city from doing so, and make it the general custom to spare them, considering the danger which there is that the whole race may one day fall under the yoke of the barbarians?

To spare them is infinitely better.

Then no Hellene should be owned by them as a slave; that is a rule which they will observe and advise the other Hellenes to observe.

Certainly, he said; they will in this way be united against the barbarians and will keep their hands off one another.

Next as to the slain; ought the conquerors, I said, to take anything but their armour? Does not the practice of despoiling an enemy afford an excuse for not facing the battle? Cowards skulk about the dead, pretending that they are fulfilling a duty, and many an army before now has been lost from this love of plunder.

Very true.

And is there not illiberality and avarice in robbing a corpse, and also a degree of meanness and woman-ishness in making an enemy of the dead body when the real enemy has flown away and left only his fighting gear behind him – is not this rather like a dog who cannot get at his assailant, quarrelling with the stones which strike him instead?

Very like a dog, he said.

Then we must abstain from spoiling the dead or hindering their burial?

Yes, he replied, we most certainly must.

Neither shall we offer up arms at the temples of the gods, least of all the arms of Hellenes, if we care to main-tain good feeling with other Hellenes; and, indeed, we have reason to fear that the offering of spoils taken from kinsmen may be a pollution unless commanded by the god himself?

Very true.

Again, as to the devastation of Hellenic territory or

the burning of houses, what is to be the practice of your soldiers?

May I have the pleasure, he said, of hearing your opinion?

Both should be forbidden, in my judgment; I would take the annual produce and no more. Shall I tell you why?

Pray do.

Why, you see, there is a difference in the names 'civil discord' and 'war', and I imagine that there is also a difference in the two sorts of quarrel; the one is expressive of what is internal and domestic, the other of what is external and foreign; and hostility to an internal enemy is termed discord, and hostility to a foreign one, war.

That is a very proper distinction, he replied.

And may I not observe with equal propriety that the Hellenic race is all united together by ties of blood and friendship, and alien and strange to the barbarians?

Very good, he said.

And therefore when Hellenes fight with barbarians and barbarians with Hellenes, they will be described by us as being at war when they fight, and by nature enemies, and this kind of antagonism should be called war; but should Hellenes ever fight with one another we shall say that Hellas is then in a state of fever and discord, they being by nature friends; and such enmity is to be called discord.

I agree.

Consider then, I said, when that which men already acknowledge to be discord occurs, and a city is divided, if both parties destroy the lands and burn the houses of one another, how wicked does the strife appear! There cannot be true patriots on either side, for no lover of his country would bring himself to tear in pieces his own nurse and mother. There might be reason in the conqueror depriving the conquered of their harvest, but still they would have the idea of peace in their hearts and would not mean to go on fighting for ever.

Yes, he said, that is a far more civilised temper than the other.

And will not the city which you are founding, be an Hellenic city?

It ought to be, he replied.

Then will not the citizens be good and civilised?

Yes, very civilised.

And will they not be lovers of Hellas, and think of Hellas as their own land, and share in the same temples as their foes?

Most certainly.

So that any difference which arises among them will be regarded by them as discord only – a quarrel among friends, which is not even to be named a war?

Certainly not.

Then they will quarrel as those who intend some day to be reconciled?

Certainly.

They will use friendly correction, but will not enslave or destroy their opponents; they will be correctors, not enemies?

Just so.

And as they are Hellenes themselves they will not devastate Hellas, nor will they burn houses, nor ever be persuaded that the whole population of a city – men, women, and children – are equally their enemies, for they know that the guilt of war is always confined to a few persons and that the many are their friends. And for all these reasons they will be unwilling to waste their lands and raze their houses; their enmity to them will only last until the many innocent sufferers have compelled the guilty few to give satisfaction?

I agree, he said, that our citizens should thus deal with their Hellenic enemies; and with barbarians as the Hellenes now deal with one another.

Then let us enact this law also for our guardians: that they are neither to devastate the lands of Hellenes nor to burn their houses.

Agreed; and we may agree also in thinking that these, like all our previous enactments, are very good. But still I must say, Socrates, that if you are allowed to go on in this way you will entirely forget the other question which at the commencement of this discussion you thrust aside: is such an order of things possible, and how, if at all? For I am quite ready to acknowledge that the plan which you propose, if only feasible, would do all sorts of good to the state. I will add, what you have omitted, that your citizens will be the bravest of warriors and will never leave their ranks, for they will all know one another, and each will call the other father, brother, son; and if you suppose the women to join their armies, whether in the same rank or in the rear, either as a terror to the enemy or as auxiliaries in case of need, I know that they will then be absolutely invincible; and there are, as I can see, many domestic advantages which might also be mentioned: but, as I admit all these advantages and as many more as you please, if only this state of yours were to come into existence, you need not proceed with your description of it. What we have next to do is to convince ourselves that it is possible, and show how it is so – the rest may be left.

If I loiter for a moment, you instantly make a raid upon me, I said, and have no mercy; I have hardly escaped the first and second waves, and you seem not to be aware that you are now bringing upon me the third, which is the greatest and heaviest. When you have seen and heard the third wave, I think you will be more considerate and will acknowledge that some fear and hesitation was natural respecting a proposal so extraordinary as that which I have now to state and investigate.

The more appeals of this sort which you make, he said, the more determined are we that you shall tell us how such a state is possible: speak out and at once.

Let me begin by reminding you that we found our way hither in the search after justice and injustice.

True, he replied; but what of that?

I was only going to ask whether, if we have discovered them, we are to require that the just man should in nothing fail of absolute justice; or may we be satisfied with an approximation, and the attainment in him of a higher degree of justice than is to be found in other men?

The approximation will be enough.

It was in order to have an ideal that we were inquiring into the nature of absolute justice and into the character of the supposed perfectly just man, and into injustice and the perfectly unjust man. We were to look at these two extremes in order that we might judge of our own happiness and unhappiness according to the standard of happiness and misery which they exhibited and the degree in which we resembled them, but not with any view of showing that they could exist in fact.

True, he said.

Would a painter, in your view, be less expert because, after having delineated with consummate art an ideal of a perfectly beautiful man, he was unable to show that any such man could ever have existed?

No, indeed.

Well, and were we not creating an ideal of a perfect state?

To be sure.

And is our theory a worse theory because we are unable to prove the possibility of a city being ordered in the manner described?

Surely not, he replied.

That is the truth, I said. But if, at your request, I am to try and show how and under what conditions the possibility is highest, I must ask you, having this in view, to repeat your former admissions.

What admissions?

I want to know whether a conception is ever fully realised in action? Must not action, whatever a man may think, always, in the nature of things, have less hold upon the truth than words? What do you say?

I agree.

Then you must not insist on my proving that the actual state will in every respect coincide with the ideal: if we are only able to discover how a city may be governed nearly as we proposed, you will admit that we have discovered the possibility which you demand; and will be contented. I am sure that I should be contented – will not you?

Yes, I will.

Let me next endeavour to show what is that fault in states which is the cause of their present malad-ministration, and what is the least change which will enable a state to pass into the truer form; and let the change, if possible, be of one thing only, or, if not, of two; at any rate, let the changes be as few and slight as possible.

Certainly, he replied.

I think, I said, that there might be a reform of the state if only one change were made, which is not a slight or easy though still a possible one.

What is it? he said.

Now then, I said, I am faced with that which I likened to the greatest of the waves; yet shall the word be spoken, even though the wave break and drown me in laughter and discredit; and do you mark my words.

Proceed.

I said: Until philosophers are kings in their cities, or the kings and princes of this world have the spirit and power of philosophy, and political greatness and wisdom meet in one, and those commoner natures who pursue either to the exclusion of the other are compelled to stand aside, cities will never have rest from their evils – no, nor the human race, as I believe – and then only will this our ideal state have a possibility of life and behold the light of day. Such was the thought, my dear Glaucon, which I would fain have uttered if it had not seemed too extravagant; for to be convinced that in no other state can there be happiness private or public is indeed a hard thing.

Socrates, what do you mean? I would have you consider that the word which you have uttered is one at which numerous persons, and very respectable persons too, in a figure pulling off their coats all in a moment and seizing any weapon that comes to hand, will run at you might and main before you know where you are, intending to do heaven knows what; and if you don't prepare an answer and make good your escape, you will be 'pared by their fine wits', and no mistake.

You got me into the scrape, I said.

And I was quite right; however, I will do all I can to protect you; but I can only give you goodwill and good advice, and, perhaps, I may be able to fit answers to your questions better than another – that is all. And now, having such an auxiliary, you must do your best to show the unbelievers that you are right.

I ought to try, I said, since you offer me such invaluable assistance. And I think that, if there is to be a chance of our escaping, we must explain to them whom we mean when we say that philosophers are to rule in the state; having brought them to light, our defence will be that there are some natures who ought to study philosophy and to be leaders in the state; and others who are not born to be philosophers, and are meant to be followers rather than leaders.

Then now for a definition, he said.

Follow me, I said, and I hope that I may in some way or other be able to give you a satisfactory explanation.

Proceed.

I dare say that you remember, and therefore I need not remind you, that a lover, if he is worthy of the name, ought to show his love, not to some one part of that which he loves, but to the whole.

Apparently you must remind me, for I have not fully understood.

Another person, I said, might fairly reply as you do; but a lover like yourself ought to be well aware that all who are in the flower of youth do somehow or other raise a pang or emotion in a lover's breast, and are thought by him to be worthy of his affectionate regards. Is not this a way which you have with the fair? One has a snub nose, and you praise his charming face; the hook-nose of another has, you say, a royal look; while he who is neither snub nor hooked has the grace of regularity: the dark visage is manly, the fair are children of the gods; and as to the sweet 'honey-pale', as they are called, what is the very name but the invention of a lover who talks in diminutives, and is not averse to paleness if appearing on the cheek of youth? In a word, there is no excuse which you will not make, and nothing which you will not say, in order not to lose a single flower that blooms in the springtime of youth.

If you make me an authority in matters of love, for the sake of the argument, I assent.

And what do you say of lovers of wine? Do you not see them doing the same? They are glad of any pretext of drinking any wine.

Very glad.

And the same is true, you must have noticed, of ambitious men; if they cannot command an army, they are willing to command a platoon; and if they cannot be honoured by really great and important persons, they are glad to be honoured by lesser and meaner people – for honour of some kind they must have.

Exactly.

Once more let me ask: does he who is said to desire something, desire the whole class to which it belongs, or a part only?

The whole.

Thus we shall say of the philosopher that he is a lover, not of a part of wisdom only, but of the whole?

True.

And he who dislikes learning, especially in youth, when he has no power of judging what is good and what is not, such a one we maintain not to be a philosopher or a lover of knowledge, just as he who refuses his food is not hungry, and may be said to have a bad appetite and not a good one?

Very true, he said.

Whereas he who has a taste for every sort of knowledge and who is curious to learn and is never satisfied, may be justly termed a philosopher? Am I not right?

Glaucon said: If curiosity makes a philosopher, you will find many a strange being will have a title to the name. All the lovers of sights have a delight in learning, and must therefore be included. Musical amateurs, too, are a folk strangely out of place among philosophers, for they are the last persons in the world who would come to anything like a philosophical discussion if they could help; while they run about at the Dionysiac festivals as if they had let out their ears for the season to hear every chorus, and miss no performance either in town or country. Now are we to maintain that all these and any who have similar tastes, as well as the professors of quite minor arts, are philosophers?

Certainly not, I replied; they are only an imitation.

He said: Who then are the true philosophers?

Those, I said, who are lovers of the vision of truth.

That is also good, he said; but I should like to know what you mean?

To another, I replied, I might have a difficulty in explaining; but I am sure that you will admit a proposition which I am about to make.

What is the proposition?

That since beauty is the opposite of ugliness, they are two?

Certainly.

And inasmuch as they are two, each of them is one?

True again.

And of just and unjust, good and evil, and of every other form, the same remark holds: taken singly, each of them is one; but from the various combinations of them with actions and bodies and with one another, they are seen in all sorts of lights and appear many?

Very true.

And this is the distinction which I draw between the sight-loving, art-loving, practical class which you have mentioned, and those of whom I am speaking, and who are alone worthy of the name of philosophers.

How do you distinguish them? he said.

The lovers of sounds and sights, I replied, are, as I conceive, fond of fine tones and colours and forms and all the artificial products that are made out of them, but their mind is incapable of seeing or loving absolute beauty.

The fact is plain, he replied.

Few are they who are able to attain to this ideal beauty and contemplate it.

Very true.

And he who, having a sense of beautiful things, has no sense of absolute beauty, or who, if another lead him to a knowledge of that beauty, is unable to follow – of such a one I ask, is he awake or in a dream only? Reflect: is not the dreamer, sleeping or waking, one who likens dissimilar things, who puts the copy in the place of the real object?

I should certainly say that such a one was dreaming.

But he who, on the contrary, recognises the existence

of absolute beauty and is able to contemplate both the idea and the objects which participate in it, neither putting the objects in the place of the idea nor the idea in the place of the objects – is he a dreamer, or is he awake?

He is wide awake.

And since he knows, it would be right to describe his state of mind as knowledge, and the state of mind of the other, who opines only, as opinion?

Certainly.

But suppose that the latter should quarrel with us and dispute our statement, can we administer any soothing cordial or advice to him, without revealing to him that there is sad disorder in his wits?

We must certainly offer him some good advice, he replied.

Come, then, and let us think of something to say to him. Shall we begin by assuring him that he is welcome to any knowledge which he may have, and that we are rejoiced at his having it? But we should like to ask him a question: does he who has knowledge know something or nothing? (You must answer for him.)

I answer that he knows something.

Something that is or is not?

Something that is; for how can that which is not ever be known?

And are we assured, after looking at the matter from many points of view, that the fully real is or may be fully known, but that the utterly unreal is utterly unknown?

Nothing can be more certain.

Good. But if there be anything which is of such a nature as to be and not to be, that will have a place intermediate between pure being and the absolute negation of being?

Yes, between them.

And, as knowledge corresponded to being and ignorance must obviously correspond to not-being, we have now to discover, for this intermediate between being and not-being, a corresponding intermediate between ignorance and knowledge, if there be such?

Certainly.

Do we admit the existence of opinion?

Undoubtedly.

As being the same faculty as knowledge, or another?

Another.

Then opinion and knowledge have to do with different things, each according to its faculty?

Yes.

And knowledge is relative to being and knows being as it is. But before I proceed further I shall have to make a division.

What division?

I will begin by placing faculties in a class by themselves: they are powers in us, and in all other things, by which we do as we do. Sight and hearing, for example, I should call faculties. Have I clearly explained the class which I mean?

Yes, I quite understand.

Then let me tell you my view about them. I do not perceive that a faculty has colour or figure, or any of those marks which enable me, in numerous cases, to differentiate one thing from another. In speaking of a faculty I think only of its sphere and its result; and that which has the same sphere and the same result I call the same faculty, but that which has another sphere and another result I call different. Would that be your way of speaking?

Yes.

And will you be so very good as to answer one more question? Would you say that knowledge is a faculty, or in what class would you place it?

Certainly knowledge is a faculty, and the mightiest of all faculties.

And is opinion also a faculty? Or is it to be ranked in another class?

No, he said; opinion is just that faculty whereby we are able to form an opinion.

But now you were acknowledging a little while ago that knowledge is not the same as opinion?

Why, yes, he said: how can any reasonable man ever identify that which is infallible with that which errs?

An excellent answer, proving, I said, that we are quite conscious of a distinction between them.

Yes.

Then knowledge and opinion, having distinct powers, are meant to operate in distinct spheres?

That is certain.

Being is the sphere of knowledge, and the function of knowledge is to know the nature of being?

Yes.

And that of opinion is to form an opinion?

Yes.

About the same object which is known to knowledge? And will the same thing be both known and opined? Or is that not possible?

Nay, he replied, that has been already disproven; if difference in faculty implies difference in the sphere, and if, as we say, opinion and knowledge are distinct faculties, then the sphere of knowledge and of opinion cannot be the same.

Then if being is the sphere of knowledge, something other than being must be the sphere of opinion?

Yes, something else.

Well then, is not-being the sphere of opinion? Or rather, how can there be even an opinion about that which is not? Reflect: when a man has an opinion, does he not refer it to something? Can he have an opinion which is an opinion about nothing?

Impossible.

He who has an opinion has an opinion about some one thing?

Yes.

And not-being is not one thing but, properly speaking, nothing?

True.

Of not-being, ignorance was assumed to be the necessary correlative; of being, knowledge?

And rightly, he said.

Then opinion is not concerned either with being or with not-being?

Not with either.

And can therefore neither be ignorance nor knowledge?

That seems to be true.

But is opinion to be sought without and beyond either of them, in a greater clearness than knowledge, or in a greater darkness than ignorance?

In neither.

Then I suppose that opinion appears to you to be darker than knowledge, but lighter than ignorance?

Both; and in no small degree.

And also to be within and between them?

Yes.

Then you would infer that opinion is intermediate?

No question.

But have we not said before, that if anything appeared to be of a sort which is and is not at the same time, that sort of thing would appear also to lie in the interval between pure being and absolute not-being; and that the corresponding faculty would be neither knowledge nor ignorance, but will be found in the interval between them?

True.

And in that interval there has now been discovered something which we call opinion?

There has.

Then what remains to be discovered is the object which partakes equally of the nature of being and not-being, and cannot rightly be termed either, pure and simple; this unknown term, when discovered, we may truly call the subject of opinion and assign each to their proper faculty – the extremes to the faculties of the extremes and the mean to the faculty of the mean.

True.

This being premised, I would ask the gentleman who is of opinion that there is no absolute or unchangeable idea of beauty, but only a number of beautiful things – he, I say, your lover of beautiful sights, who cannot bear to be told that the beautiful is one, and the just is one, or that anything is one – to him I would appeal, saying, 'Will you be so very kind, sir, as to tell us whether, of all these beautiful things, there is one which will not be found ugly; or of the just, which will not be found unjust; or of the holy, which will not also seem unholy?'

No, he replied; these things must, from different

points of view, be found both beautiful and ugly; and the same is true of the rest.

And do not the many which are doubles appear no less plainly to be halves?

Quite true.

And things great and small, heavy and light, will not be denoted by the names which we happen to use first any more than by the opposite names?

True; both names will always attach to all of them.

If so, can any one of those many things be said to be, rather than not to be, that which we happen to have termed it?

He replied: They are like the punning riddles which are asked at feasts or the children's puzzle about the eunuch aiming at the bat, with what he hit him, as they say in the puzzle, and upon what the bat was sitting. The individual objects of which I am speaking are also a riddle, and have a double sense: nor can you fix them in your mind, either as being or not-being, or both, or neither.

Then what will you do with them? I said. Can they have a better place than between being and not-being? For they are clearly not in greater darkness or negation than not-being, or more full of light and existence than being.

That is quite true, he said.

Thus then we seem to have discovered that the many notions which the multitude entertain about the beautiful and about all other things are tossing about in some region which is half-way between pure being and pure not-being?

We have.

Yes; and we had before agreed that anything of this kind which we might find was to be described as matter of opinion, and not as matter of knowledge, being the intermediate flux which is caught and detained by the intermediate faculty.

Quite true.

Then those who gaze on many beautiful things, and who yet neither see absolute beauty, nor can follow any guide who points the way thither; who see instances of justice, but not absolute justice, and the like – such persons may be said in all their pronouncements to have opinion but not knowledge?

That is certain.

But those who in everything look to the absolute and eternal and immutable may be said to know, and not to have opinion only?

Neither can that be denied.

The one love and embrace the subjects of knowledge, the other those of opinion? The latter are the same, as I dare say you will remember, who listened to sweet sounds and gazed upon fair colours, but would not tolerate the existence of absolute beauty.

Yes, I remember.

Shall we then be guilty of any impropriety in calling them lovers of opinion rather than lovers of wisdom, and will they be very angry with us for thus describing them?

Not if they will listen to me; no man should be angry at what is true.

But those who love the truth in each thing are to be called lovers of wisdom and not lovers of opinion.

Assuredly.

BOOK SIX

And thus, Glaucon, after the argument has gone a weary way, the true and the false philosophers have at length appeared in view.

I do not think, he said, that the way could have been shortened.

I suppose not, I said; and yet I believe that we might have had a better view of both of them if the discussion could have been confined to this one subject, and if there were not many other questions which must be resolved before we can see in what respect the life of the just differs from that of the unjust.

And what is the next question? he asked.

Surely, I said, the one which follows next in order. Inasmuch as philosophers only are able to grasp the eternal and unchangeable, and those who wander in the region of the many and variable are not philosophers, I must ask you which of the two classes should be the rulers of our state?

And how can we rightly answer that question?

Whichever of the two seem best able to guard the laws and institutions of our state – let them be appointed guardians.

Very good.

Neither, I said, can there be any question that the watcher who is to guard anything should have eyes rather than no eyes?

There can be no question of that.

And are not those who are verily and indeed wanting in the knowledge of the true being of each thing, and who have in their souls no clear pattern, and are unable to look like painters at the absolute truth and to that original to repair, and having perfect vision thereof to frame laws about beauty, goodness, and justice, if not already framed, or to guard and preserve order where it exists – are not such persons, I ask, simply blind?

Truly, he replied, they are much in that condition.

And shall they be our guardians when there are others who, besides being their equals in experience and falling short of them in no particular of virtue, also know the very truth of each thing?

There can be no reason, he said, for choosing others, if it is true that our men are not inferior in other ways; for they excel in what is probably the most important point of all.

Suppose then, I said, that we determine how this union of knowledge and experience in the same persons is to be achieved.

By all means.

In the first place, as we began by observing, the nature of the philosopher has to be ascertained. We must come to an understanding about him, and then we shall also, if I am not mistaken, acknowledge that such a union of qualities is possible, and that those in whom they are united, and those only, should be rulers in the state.

What do you mean?

Let us suppose it agreed that philosophical minds love any form of science which may give them a glimpse of an eternal reality not disturbed by generation and decay.

Agreed.

And further, I said, let us agree that they are lovers of all true being; there is no part whether greater or less, or more or less honourable, which they are willing to renounce, as we said before of the lover and the man of ambition.

True.

And if they are to be what we were describing, is there not another quality which they should also possess?

What quality?

Truthfulness: they will never intentionally receive into their mind falsehood, which is their detestation, and they will love the truth.

Yes, that may be safely affirmed of them.

'May be', my friend, I replied, is not the word; say rather, 'must be affirmed': for he whose nature is amorous of anything cannot help loving all that belongs or is akin to the object of his affections.

Right, he said.

And is there anything more akin to wisdom than truth?

How can there be?

Can the same nature be a lover of wisdom and a lover of falsehood?

Never.

The true lover of learning then must from his earliest youth, as far as in him lies, desire all truth?

Assuredly.

But then again, as we know by experience, he whose desires are strong in one direction will have them weaker in others; they will be like a stream which has been drawn off into another channel.

True.

He whose desires are drawn towards the sciences and other studies will be absorbed in the pleasures of the soul, and his eagerness for bodily pleasure will decline – I mean, if he be a true philosopher and not a sham one.

That is most certain.

Such a one is sure to be temperate and the reverse of covetous; for the motives which make another man desirous of wealth and lavish spending have no place in his character.

Very true.

Here is another criterion of the philosophical nature, which has also to be considered.

What is that?

There should be no secret corner of illiberality; nothing can be more antagonistic than meanness to a soul which is ever longing after the whole of things both divine and human.

Most true, he replied.

Then how can he who has magnificence of mind and is the spectator of all time and all existence, think human life to be a great thing?

He cannot.

Or can such a one account death fearful?

No indeed.

Then the cowardly and mean nature has no part in true philosophy?

Certainly not.

Or again: can he who is harmoniously constituted, who is not covetous or mean, or a boaster, or a coward – can he, I say, ever be unjust or hard in his dealings?

Impossible.

Then you have another sign which distinguishes even in youth the philosophical nature from the unphilosophical; you will observe whether a man is just and gentle, or rude and unsociable.

True.

There is another point which should be remarked.

What point?

Whether he has or has not facility in learning; for you must not expect him to find entire satisfaction in a study which gives him pain, and in which after much toil he makes little progress.

Certainly not.

And again, if he can retain nothing of what he learns, will he not be full of forgetfulness and devoid of knowledge?

That is certain.

Labouring in vain, he must end in hating himself and his fruitless occupation?

Yes.

Then a forgetful soul can never be ranked among genuine philosophic natures; we must insist that the philosopher should have a good memory?

Certainly.

And once more, the inharmonious and unseemly nature can only tend to disproportion?

Undoubtedly.

And do you consider truth to be akin to proportion or to disproportion?

To proportion.

Then, besides other qualities, we must try to find a naturally well-proportioned and gracious mind, which will be easily led to the vision of the true being of everything.

Certainly.

I hope you do not doubt that all these qualities, which we have been enumerating, go together, and are necessary to a soul which is to have a full and perfect participation in being.

They are absolutely necessary, he replied.

And must not that be a blameless occupation which he only can pursue who has the gift of a good memory, and is quick to learn – noble, gracious, the friend of truth, justice, courage, temperance, who are his kindred?

The god of jealousy himself, he said, could find no fault with such an occupation.

And to men like him, I said, when perfected by years and education, and to these only you will entrust the state.

Here Adeimantus interposed and said: To these statements, Socrates, no one can offer a reply; but whenever you talk in this way, a strange feeling passes over the minds of your hearers. They fancy that they are led astray a little at each step in the argument, owing to their own want of skill in asking and answering questions; these littles accumulate, and at the end of the discussion they are found to have sustained a mighty overthrow and their first opinion appears to be turned upside down. And as unskilful players of draughts are at last barred by their more skilful adversaries and have no piece to move, so they too find themselves barred at last; for they have nothing to say in this new game of which words are the pieces; and yet they are sure the truth is not on your side. I am speaking with reference to what is now occurring. For any one of us might say, that although in words he is not able to meet you at each step of the argument, he sees as a fact that the votaries of philosophy, when they carry on the study, not only in youth as a part of education, but as the pursuit of their maturer years, most of them become strange monsters, not to say utter rogues, and that those who may be considered the best of them are at least made useless to the world by this occupation which you extol.

Well, and do you think that those who say so are wrong?

I cannot tell, he replied; but I should like to know what is your opinion.

Hear my answer; I am of opinion that they are quite right.

Then how can we be justified in saying that cities will not cease from evil until philosophers rule in them, when we acknowledge that philosophers are useless to the state?

You ask a question, I said, to which a reply can only be given in a parable.

Yes, Socrates; and that is a way of speaking to which you are not at all accustomed, I suppose.

I perceive, I said, that you are vastly amused at having plunged me into such a hopeless discussion; but now hear the parable, and then you will be still more amused at the meagreness of my imagination: for the manner in which the best men are treated in their own states is so grievous that no single thing on earth is comparable to it; and therefore, if I am to plead their cause, I must have recourse to fiction, and put together a figure made up of many things, like the fabulous unions of goats and stags which are found in pictures. Imagine then a fleet or a ship in which the owner is sailing, and he is taller and stronger than any of the crew, but he is a little deaf and has a similar infirmity in sight, and his knowledge of navigation is not much better. The sailors are quarrelling with one another about the steering – everyone is of opinion that he has a right to steer, though he has never learned the art of navigation and cannot tell who taught him or when he learned, and will further assert that it cannot be taught at all, and they are ready to cut in pieces anyone who says the contrary. They throng about the owner, begging and praying him to commit the helm to them; and if at any time they do not prevail, but others are preferred to them, they kill the others or throw them overboard, and having first chained up the excellent shipowner's senses with drink or some narcotic drug, they assume control of the ship and make free with the stores; thus, feasting and drinking, they proceed on their voyage in such manner as might be expected of them. Him who is their partisan and cleverly aids them in their plot for getting the ship out of the owner's hands whether by force or persuasion, they compliment with the name of sailor, pilot, able seaman, and abuse the other sort of man, saying that he is unfit for any service; but that the true pilot must pay attention to the year and seasons and sky and stars and winds, and whatever else belongs to his art, if he intends to be really qualified for the command of a ship – this has never seriously entered into their thoughts; nor do they think it possible to learn some art, or obtain some experience, whereby a man will remain pilot whether the consent of other people has been granted or no. Yet such is the art of piloting. If all this should occur, how do you suppose that the true pilot will be regarded by the voyagers who sail in such an ill-regulated ship? Will he not be called by them a prater, a star-gazer, a good-for-nothing?

Of course, said Adeimantus.

Then you will hardly need, I said, to hear the interpretation of the figure, which describes the true philosopher in his relation to the state; for you understand already.

Certainly.

268

Then suppose you now take this parable to the gentleman who is surprised at finding that philosophers have no honour in their cities; explain it to him and try to convince him that their having honour would be far more extraordinary.

I will.

[*Socrates attempts to account for the low opnion in which philosophers are held in the Greek world, and introduces the idea of a higher knowledge which the rulers of his state must attain*]

What, he said, is there a knowledge still higher than this – higher than justice and the other virtues?

Yes, I said, there is. And of the virtues too we must behold not the outline merely, as at present – nothing short of the most finished picture should satisfy us. When things of little value are elaborated with an infinity of pains in order that they may appear in their full beauty and utmost clearness, how ridiculous that we should not think the highest truths worthy of the highest accuracy!

A right noble thought; but do you suppose that we shall refrain from asking you what you mean by this highest knowledge and what is its subject?

Nay, I said, ask if you will; but I am certain that you have heard the answer many times, and now you either do not understand me or, as I rather think, you are disposed to make trouble by holding me back; for you have often been told that the idea of good is the highest knowledge, and that all other things, justice among them, become useful and advantageous only by their use of this. You can hardly be ignorant that this is what I am about to say, and moreover that our knowledge of the idea of the good is inadequate. Yet you understand that without this knowledge, no other knowledge or possession of any kind will profit us at all. Do you think that the possession of all other things is of any value if it be not good? Or a sort of wisdom which includes all else, but has no thought of the honourable or good?

Assuredly not.

You are further aware that most people affirm pleasure to be the good, but the finer sort of wits say it is knowledge?

Yes.

You are aware too that the latter cannot explain what knowledge they mean, but are obliged after all to say knowledge of the good?

True, and very ridiculous it is.

Yes, I said, that they should begin by reproaching us with our ignorance of the good, and then presume our knowledge of it – for the good they define to be knowledge of the good, just as if we understood them when they use the term 'good' – this is of course ridiculous.

Most true, he said.

What of those who make pleasure their good? Are they not in equal perplexity? For they are compelled to admit that there are bad pleasures as well as good.

Certainly.

And therefore to acknowledge that the same things are both bad and good?

True.

Evidently, then, there are many great differences of opinion about the good.

Undoubtedly.

Is it not likewise evident that many are content to do or to have, or to seem to be, what is just and beautiful without the reality; but no one is satisfied with the appearance of good? The reality is what they seek; in the case of the good, appearance is despised by every one.

Very true, he said.

Of this then, which every soul of man pursues and makes the end of all his actions, having a presentiment that there is such an end, and yet hesitating because neither knowing the nature nor having the same assurance of this as of other things, and therefore losing whatever good there is in other things – of a principle such and so great as this ought the best men in our state, to whom everything is entrusted, to be in the darkness of ignorance?

Certainly not, he said.

I am sure, I said, that he who does not know how the noble and the just are likewise good will be but a sorry guardian of them; and I suspect that no one who is ignorant of the good will have a true knowledge of them.

That, he said, is a shrewd suspicion of yours.

And if only we have a guardian who has this knowledge our state will be perfectly ordered?

Of course, he replied; but I wish that you would tell me whether you conceive this supreme principle of the good to be knowledge or pleasure, or different from either?

Sir, I said, I could see quite well all along that you would not be contented with the thoughts of other people about these matters.

True, Socrates; but I must say that one who like you has passed a lifetime in the study of philosophy should not be always repeating the opinions of others, and never telling his own.

Well, but has anyone a right to say positively what he does not know?

Not, he said, with the assurance of positive certainty; he has no right to do that: but he may say what he thinks, as a matter of opinion.

And have you not observed, I said, that all mere opinions are bad, and the best of them blind? You would not deny that those who have any true notion without intelligence are only like blind men who feel their way along the right road?

Very true.

And do you wish to behold what is blind and crooked and base, when others will tell you of brightness and beauty?

Still, I must implore you, Socrates, said Glaucon, not to turn away just as you are reaching the goal; if you will only give such an explanation of the good as you have already given of justice and temperance and the other virtues, we shall be satisfied.

Yes, my friend, and I shall be at least equally satisfied, but I cannot help fearing that I shall fail, and that my indiscreet zeal will bring ridicule upon me. No, sirs, let us not at present ask what is the actual nature of the good, for to reach what is now in my thoughts would be an effort too great for me. But of the child of the good who is likest him, I am ready to speak, if I could be sure that you wished to hear – otherwise, not.

By all means, he said, tell us about the child, and you shall remain in our debt for the account of the parent.

I do indeed wish, I replied, that I could pay, and you receive, the account of the parent, and not, as now, of the offspring only; take, however, this latter by way of interest, and at the same time have a care that I do not pay you in spurious coin, although I have no intention of deceiving you.

Yes, we will take all the care that we can: proceed.

Yes, I said, but I must first come to an understanding with you, and remind you of what I have mentioned in the course of this discussion, and at many other times.

What?

The old story, that there are many beautiful things and many good. And again there is a true beauty, a true good; and all other things to which the term 'many' has been applied, are now brought under a single idea, and, assuming this unity, we speak of it in every case as 'that which really is'.

Very true.

The many, as we say, are seen but not known, and the ideas are known but not seen.

Exactly.

And what is the organ with which we see the visible things?

The sight, he said.

And with the hearing, I said, we hear, and with the other senses perceive the other objects of sense?

True.

But have you remarked that sight is by far the most costly and complex piece of workmanship which the artificer of the senses ever contrived?

Not exactly, he said.

Then reflect: have the ear and voice need of any third or additional nature in order that the one may be able to hear and the other to be heard?

Nothing of the sort.

No, indeed, I replied; and the same is true of most, if not all, the other senses – you would not say that any of them requires such an addition?

PLATO

Certainly not.

But you see that without the addition of some other nature there is no seeing or being seen?

How do you mean?

Sight being, as I conceive, in the eyes, and he who has eyes wanting to see; colour being also present in the objects, still unless there be a third nature specially adapted to the purpose, sight, as you know, will see nothing and the colours will be invisible.

Of what nature are you speaking?

Of that which you term light, I replied.

True, he said.

Then the bond which links together the sense of sight and the power of being seen, is of an evidently nobler nature than other such bonds – unless sight is an ignoble thing?

Nay, he said, the reverse of ignoble.

And which, I said, of the gods in heaven would you say was the lord of this element? Whose is that light which makes the eye to see perfectly and the visible to appear?

I should answer, as all men would, and as you plainly expect – the sun.

May not the relation of sight to this deity be described as follows?

How?

Neither sight nor the organ in which it resides, which we call the eye, is the sun?

No.

Yet of all the organs of sense the eye is the most like the sun?

By far the most like.

And the power which the eye possesses is a sort of effluence which is dispensed from the sun?

Exactly.

Then the sun is not sight, but the author of sight who is recognised by sight?

True, he said.

And this, you must understand, is he whom I call the child of the good, whom the good begat in his own likeness, to be in the visible world, in relation to sight and the things of sight, what the good is in the intellectual world in relation to mind and the things of mind:

Will you be a little more explicit? he said.

Why, you know, I said, that the eyes, when a person directs them towards objects on which the light of day is no longer shining, but the moon and stars only, see dimly, and are nearly blind; they seem to have no clearness of vision in them?

Very true.

But when they are directed towards objects on which the sun shines, they see clearly and there is sight in them?

Certainly.

And the soul is like the eye: when resting upon that on which truth and being shine, the soul perceives and understands, and is radiant with intelligence; but when turned towards the twilight and to those things which come into being and perish, then she has opinion only, and goes blinking about, and is first of one opinion and then of another, and seems to have no intelligence?

Just so.

Now, that which imparts truth to the known and the power of knowing to the knower is, as I would have you say, the idea of good, and this idea, which is the cause of science and of truth, you are to conceive as being apprehended by knowledge, and yet, fair as both truth and knowledge are, you will be right to esteem it as different from these and even fairer; and as in the previous instance light and sight may be truly said to be like the sun and yet not to be the sun, so in this other sphere science and truth may be deemed to be like the good, but it is wrong to think that they are the good; the good has a place of honour yet higher.

What a wonder of beauty that must be, he said, which is the author of science and truth, and yet surpasses them in beauty; for you surely cannot mean to say that pleasure is the good?

God forbid, I replied; but may I ask you to consider the image in another point of view?

In what point of view?

You would say, would you not, that the sun is not only the author of visibility in all visible things, but of generation and nourishment and growth, though he himself is not generation?

Certainly.

In like manner you must say that the good not only infuses the power of being known into all things known, but also bestows upon them their being and existence, and yet the good is not existence, but lies far beyond it in dignity and power.

Glaucon said, with a ludicrous earnestness: By the light of heaven, that is far beyond indeed!

Yes, I said, and the exaggeration may be set down to you; for you made me utter my fancies.

And pray continue to utter them; at any rate let us hear if there is anything more to be said about the similitude of the sun.

Yes, I said, there is a great deal more.

Then omit nothing, however slight.

I expect that I shall omit a great deal, I said, but shall not do so deliberately, as far as present circumstances permit.

I hope not, he said.

You have to imagine, then, that there are two ruling powers, and that one of them is set over the intellectual world, the other over the visible. I do not say heaven, lest you should fancy that I am playing upon the name.[1] May I suppose that you have this distinction of the visible and intelligible fixed in your mind?

I have.

Now take a line which has been cut into two unequal parts, and divide each of them again in the same proportion, and suppose the two main divisions to answer, one to the visible and the other to the intelligible, and then compare the subdivisions in respect of their clearness and want of clearness, and you will find that the first section in the sphere of the visible consists of images. And by images I mean, in the first place, shadows, and in the second place, reflections in water and in solid, smooth and polished bodies and the like: do you understand?

Yes, I understand.

Imagine, now, the other section, of which this is only the resemblance, to include the animals which we see, and every thing that grows or is made.

Very good.

Would you not admit that both the sections of this division have different degrees of truth, and that the copy is to the original as the sphere of opinion is to the sphere of knowledge?

Most undoubtedly.

1 οὐρανός, ὁρατός

277

Next proceed to consider the manner in which the sphere of the intellectual is to be divided.

In what manner?

Thus: there are two subdivisions, in the lower of which the soul, using as images those things which themselves were reflected in the former division, is forced to base its enquiry upon hypotheses, proceeding not towards a principle but towards a conclusion; in the higher of the two, the soul proceeds *from* hypotheses, and goes up to a principle which is above hypotheses, making no use of images as in the former case, but proceeding only in and through the ideas themselves.

I do not quite understand your meaning, he said.

Then I will try again; you will understand me better when I have made some preliminary remarks. You are aware that students of geometry, arithmetic, and the kindred sciences assume the odd and the even and the figures and three kinds of angles and the like in their several branches of science; these are their hypotheses, which they and everybody are supposed to know, and therefore they do not deign to give any account of them either to themselves or others; but they begin with them, and go on until they arrive at last, and in a consistent manner, at the solution which they set out to find?

Yes, he said, I know.

And do you not know also that although they make use of the visible forms and reason about them, they are thinking not of these, but of the ideals which they resemble; not of the figures which they draw, but of the absolute square and the absolute diameter, and so on – the forms which they draw or make, and which themselves have shadows and reflections in water, are in turn converted by them into images; for they are really seeking to behold the things themselves, which can only be seen with the eye of the mind?

That is true.

And this was what I meant by a subdivision of the intelligible, in the search after which the soul is compelled to use hypotheses; not ascending to a first principle, because she is unable to rise above the region of hypothesis, but employing now as images those objects from which the shadows below were derived, even these being deemed clear and distinct by comparison with the shadows.

I understand, he said, that you are speaking of the province of geometry and the sister arts.

And when I speak of the other division of the intelligible, you will understand me to speak of that other sort of knowledge which reason herself attains by the power of dialectic, using the hypotheses not as first principles, but literally as hypotheses – that is to say, as steps and points of departure into a world which is above hypotheses, in order that she may soar beyond them to the first principle of the whole; and clinging to this and then to that which depends on this, by successive steps she descends again without the aid of any sensible object, from ideas, through ideas, and in ideas she ends.

I understand you, he replied; not perfectly, for you seem to me to be describing a task which is really tremendous; but, at any rate, I understand you to say that that part of intelligible being, which the science of dialectic contemplates, is clearer than that which falls under the arts, as they are termed, which take hypotheses as their principles; and though the objects are of such a kind that they must be viewed by the understanding, and not by the senses, yet, because they start from hypotheses and do not ascend to a principle, those who contemplate them appear to you not to exercise the higher reason upon them, although when a first principle is added to them they are cognisable by the higher reason. And the habit which is concerned with geometry and the cognate sciences I suppose that you would term understanding and not reason, as being intermediate between opinion and reason.

You have quite conceived my meaning, I said; and now, corresponding to these four divisions, let there be four faculties in the soul – reason answering to the highest, understanding to the second, faith (or conviction) to the third, and perception of shadows to the last – and let there be a scale of them, and let us suppose that the several faculties have clearness in the same degree that their objects have truth.

I understand, he replied, and give my assent, and accept your arrangement.

BOOK SEVEN

And now, I said, let me show in a figure how far our nature is enlightened or unenlightened: Behold! human beings housed in an underground cave, which has a long entrance open towards the light and as wide as the interior of the cave; here they have been from their childhood, and have their legs and necks chained, so that they cannot move and can only see before them, being prevented by the chains from turning round their heads. Above and behind them a fire is blazing at a distance, and between the fire and the prisoners there is a raised way; and you will see, if you look, a low wall built along the way, like the screen which marionette players have in front of them, over which they show the puppets.

I see.

And do you see, I said, men passing along the wall carrying all sorts of vessels, and statues and figures of animals made of wood and stone and various materials, which appear over the wall? While carrying their burdens, some of them, as you would expect, are talking, others silent.

You have shown me a strange image, and they are strange prisoners.

Like ourselves, I replied; for in the first place do you think they have seen anything of themselves, and of one another, except the shadows which the fire throws on the opposite wall of the cave?

How could they do so, he asked, if throughout their lives they were never allowed to move their heads?

And of the objects which are being carried in like

manner they would only see the shadows?

Yes, he said.

And if they were able to converse with one another, would they not suppose that the things they saw were the real things?

Very true.

And suppose further that the prison had an echo which came from the other side, would they not be sure to fancy when one of the passers-by spoke that the voice which they heard came from the passing shadow?

No question, he replied.

To them, I said, the truth would be literally nothing but the shadows of the images.

That is certain.

And now look again, and see in what manner they would be released from their bonds, and cured of their error, whether the process would naturally be as follows. At first, when any of them is liberated and compelled suddenly to stand up and turn his neck round and walk and look towards the light, he will suffer sharp pains; the glare will distress him, and he will be unable to see the realities of which in his former state he had seen the shadows; and then conceive someone saying to him that what he saw before was an illusion, but that now, when he is approaching nearer to being and his eye is turned towards more real existence, he has a clearer vision – what will be his reply? And you may further imagine that his instructor is pointing to the objects as they pass and requiring him to name them – will he not be perplexed? Will he not fancy that the shadows which he formerly saw are truer than the objects which are now shown to him?

Far truer.

And if he is compelled to look straight at the light, will he not have a pain in his eyes which will make him turn away to take refuge in the objects of vision which he can see, and which he will conceive to be in reality clearer than the things which are now being shown to him?

True, he said.

And suppose once more, that he is reluctantly dragged up that steep and rugged ascent, and held fast until he is forced into the presence of the sun himself, is he not likely to be pained and irritated? When he approaches the light his eyes will be dazzled, and he will not be able to see anything at all of what are now called realities.

Not all in a moment, he said.

He will require to grow accustomed to the sight of the upper world. And first he will see the shadows best, next the reflections of men and other objects in the water, and then the objects themselves; and, when he turned to the heavenly bodies and the heaven itself, he would find it easier to gaze upon the light of the moon and the stars at night than to see the sun or the light of the sun by day?

Certainly.

Last of all he will be able to see the sun, not turning aside to the illusory reflections of him in the water, but gazing directly at him in his own proper place, and contemplating him as he is.

Certainly.

He will then proceed to argue that this is he who gives the seasons and the years, and is the guardian of all that is in the visible world, and in a certain way the cause of all things which he and his fellows have been accustomed to behold?

Clearly, he said, he would arrive at this conclusion after what he had seen.

And when he remembered his old habitation, and the wisdom of the cave and his fellow-prisoners, do you not suppose that he would felicitate himself on the change, and pity them?

Certainly, he would.

And if they were in the habit of conferring honours among themselves on those who were quickest to observe the passing shadows and to remark which of them went before and which followed after and which were together, and who were best able from these observations to divine the future, do you think that he would be eager for such honours and glories, or envy those who attained honour and sovereignty among those men? Would he not say with Homer,

'Better to be a serf, labouring for a landless master', and to endure anything, rather than think as they do and live after their manner?

Yes, he said, I think that he would consent to suffer anything rather than live in this miserable manner.

Imagine once more, I said, such a one coming down suddenly out of the sunlight, and being replaced in his old seat; would he not be certain to have his eyes full of darkness?

To be sure, he said.

And if there were a contest, and he had to compete in measuring the shadows with the prisoners who had never moved out of the cave, while his sight was still weak, and before his eyes had become steady (and the time which would be needed to acquire this new habit of sight might be very considerable), would he not make himself ridiculous? Men would say of him that he had returned from the place above with his eyes ruined; and that it was better not even to think of ascending; and if anyone tried to loose another and lead him up to the light, let them only catch the offender, and they would put him to death.

No question, he said.

This entire allegory, I said, you may now append, dear Glaucon, to the previous argument; the prison-house is the world of sight, the light of the fire is the power of the sun, and you will not misapprehend me if you interpret the journey upwards to be the ascent of the soul into the intellectual world according to my surmise, which, at your desire, I have expressed – whether rightly or wrongly god knows. But, whether true or false, my opinion is that in the world of knowledge the idea of good appears last of all, and is seen only with an effort; although, when seen, it is inferred to be the universal author of all things beautiful and right, parent of light and of the lord of light in the visible world, and the immediate and supreme source of reason and truth in the intellectual; and that this is the power upon which he who would act rationally either in public or private life must have his eye fixed.

I agree, he said, as far as I am able to understand you.

Moreover, I said, you must agree once more, and not wonder that those who attain to this vision are unwilling to take any part in human affairs; for their souls are ever hastening into the upper world where they desire to dwell; which desire of theirs is very natural, if our allegory may be trusted.

Yes, very natural.

And is there anything surprising in one who passes from divine contemplations to the evil state of man, appearing grotesque and ridiculous; if, while his eyes are blinking and before he has become accustomed to the surrounding darkness, he is compelled to fight in courts of law, or in other places, about the images or the shadows of images of justice, and must strive against some rival about opinions of these things which are entertained by men who have never yet seen the true justice?

Anything but surprising, he replied.

Anyone who has common sense will remember that the bewilderments of the eyes are of two kinds and arise from two causes, either from coming out of the light or from going into the light, and, judging that the soul may be affected in the same way, will not give way to foolish laughter when he sees anyone whose vision is perplexed and weak; he will first ask whether that soul of man has come out of the brighter life and is unable to see because unaccustomed to the dark, or having turned from darkness to the day is dazzled by excess of light. And he will count the one happy in his condition and state of being, and he will pity the other; or, if he have a mind to laugh at the soul which comes from below into the light, this laughter will not be quite so laughable as that which greets the soul which returns from above out of the light into the cave.

That, he said, is a very just distinction.

But then, if I am right, certain professors of education must be wrong when they say that they can put a knowledge into the soul which was not there before, like sight into blind eyes.

They undoubtedly say this, he replied.

Whereas our argument shows that the power and capacity of learning exists in the soul already; and that just as if it were not possible to turn the eye from darkness to light without the whole body, so too the instrument of knowledge can only by the movement of the whole soul be turned from the world of becoming to that of being, and learn by degrees to endure the sight of being, and of the brightest and best of being, or in other words, of the good.

Very true.

And must there not be some art which will show how the conversion can be effected in the easiest and quickest manner; an art which will not implant the faculty of sight, for that exists already, but will set it straight when it has been turned in the wrong direction, and is looking away from the truth?

Yes, he said, such an art may be presumed.

And whereas the other so-called virtues of the soul seem to be akin to bodily qualities, for even when they are not originally innate they can be implanted later by habit and exercise, the virtue of wisdom more than anything else contains a divine element which never loses its power, and by this conversion is rendered useful and profitable; or, by conversion of another sort, hurtful and useless. Did you never observe the narrow intelligence flashing from the keen eye of a clever rogue – how eager he is, how clearly his paltry soul sees the way to his end; he is the reverse of blind, but his keen eyesight is forced into the service of evil, and he is mischievous in proportion to his cleverness?

Very true, he said.

But what if such natures had been gradually stripped, beginning in childhood, of the leaden weights which sink them in the sea of becoming, and which, fastened upon the soul through gluttonous indulgence in eating and other such pleasures, forcibly turn its vision downwards – if, I say, they had been released from these impediments and turned in the opposite direction, the very same faculty in them would have seen the truth as keenly as they see what their eyes are turned to now.

Very likely.

Yes, I said; and there is another thing which is likely, or rather a necessary inference from what has preceded, that neither the uneducated and uninformed of the truth, nor yet those who are suffered to prolong their education without end, will be able ministers of state; not the former, because they have no single aim of duty which is the rule of all their actions, private as well as public; nor the latter, because they will not act at all except upon compulsion, fancying that they are already dwelling apart in the islands of the blest.

Very true, he replied.

Then, I said, the business of us who are the founders of the state will be to compel the best minds to attain that knowledge which we have already shown to be the greatest of all, namely, the vision of the good; they must make the ascent which we have described; but when they have ascended and seen enough we must not allow them to do as they do now.

What do you mean?

They are permitted to remain in the upper world, refusing to descend again among the prisoners in the cave, and partake of their labours and honours, whether they are worth having or not.

But is not this unjust? he said; ought we to give them a worse life, when they might have a better?

You have again forgotten, my friend, I said, the intention of our law, which does not aim at making any one class in the state happy above the rest; it seeks rather to spread happiness over the whole state, and to hold the citizens together by persuasion and necessity, making each share with others any benefit which he can confer upon the state; and the law aims at producing such citizens, not that they may be left to please themselves, but that they may serve in binding the state together.

True, he said, I had forgotten.

Observe, Glaucon, that we shall do no wrong to our philosophers but rather make a just demand, when we oblige them to have a care and providence of others; we shall explain to them that in other states, men of their class are not obliged to share in the toils of politics: and this is reasonable, for they grow up spontaneously, against the will of the governments in their several states; and things which grow up of themselves, and are indebted to no one for their nurture, cannot fairly be expected to pay dues for a culture which they have never received. But we have brought you into the world to be rulers of the hive, kings of yourselves and of the other citizens, and have educated you far better and more perfectly than they have been educated, and you are better able to share in the double duty. Wherefore each of you, when his turn comes, must go down to rejoin his companions, and acquire with them the habit of seeing things in the dark. As you acquire that habit, you will see ten thousand times better than the inhabitants of the cave, and you will know what the several images are and what they represent, because you have seen the beautiful and just and good in their truth. And thus our state, which is also yours, will be a reality and not a dream only, and will be administered in a spirit unlike that of other states, in which men fight with one another about shadows only and are distracted in the struggle for power, which in their eyes is a great good. Whereas the truth is that the state in which those who are to govern have least ambition to do so is always the best and most quietly governed, and the state in which they are most eager, the worst.

Quite true, he replied.

And will our pupils, when they hear this, refuse to take their turn at the toils of state, when they are allowed to spend the greater part of their time with one another in the heavenly light?

Impossible, he answered; for they are just men, and the commands which we impose upon them are just. But there can be no doubt that every one of them will take office as a stern necessity, contrary to the spirit of our present rulers of state.

Yes, my friend, I said; and there lies the point. You must contrive for your future rulers another and a better life than that of a ruler, and then you may have a well-ordered state; for only in the state which offers this, will they rule who are truly rich, not in gold, but in virtue and wisdom, which are the true blessings of life. Whereas if men who are destitute and starved of such personal goods go to the administration of public affairs, thinking to enrich themselves at the public expense, order there can never be; for they will be fighting about office, and the civil and domestic broils which thus arise will be the ruin of the rulers themselves and of the whole state.

Most true, he replied.

And the only life which looks down upon the life of political ambition is that of true philosophy. Do you know of any other?

Indeed, I do not, he said.

And those who govern should not 'make love to

their employment'? For, if they do there will be rival lovers, and they will fight.

No question.

Whom, then, will you compel to become guardians of the state? Surely those who excel in judgment of the means by which a state is administered, and who at the same time have other honours and another and a better life than that of politics?

None but these, he replied.

[*there follows a description of the rulers' higher education, and the subjects they will study*]

BOOK EIGHT

And so, Glaucon, we have arrived at the conclusion that in the perfect state wives and children are to be in common; and that all education and the pursuits of war and peace are also to be common, and that those who have proved to be both the best philosophers and the bravest warriors are to be their kings?

That, replied Glaucon, has been acknowledged.

Yes, I said; and we have further acknowledged that the governors, when appointed themselves, will take their soldiers and place them in houses such as we were describing, which are common to all, and contain nothing private or individual; and, apart from houses, you remember what sort of possessions we agreed to allow them?

Yes, I remember that no one was to have any of the ordinary possessions of mankind; they were to be warrior athletes and guardians, receiving from the other citizens, as their annual stipend, only the maintenance necessary for their duties, and they were to be responsible for themselves and for the whole state.

True, I said; and now that this division of our task is concluded, let us recall the point at which we digressed, that we may return into the old path.

There is no difficulty in returning; you implied, then as now, that you had finished the description of the state: you said that such a state as you had described was good, and the man was good who answered to it, although, as now appears, you had more excellent things to relate both of state and man. However that may be, you said that if this was the right form, then the others were wrong; and of the false forms, you said, as I remember, that four were worthy of notice, and that their defects, and the defects of the individuals corresponding to them, were worth examining. When we had seen all the individuals, and finally agreed as to who was the best and who was the worst of them, we were to consider whether the best was, or was not, also the happiest, and the worst the most miserable. I asked you what were the four forms of government of which you spoke, and then Polemarchus and Adeimantus put in their word; and you began again, and have found your way to the point at which we have now arrived.

Your recollection, I said, is most exact.

Then, like a wrestler, he replied, you must let me take my former hold; and let me ask the same questions, and do you give me the same answer which you were about to give me then.

Yes, if I can, I will, I said.

I shall particularly wish to hear what were the four constitutions of which you were speaking.

That question, I said, is easily answered: the four governments of which I spoke, so far as they have distinct names, are, first, this Cretan and Spartan kind, which is generally applauded; next, and second in order of approbation, comes what is termed oligarchy – a form of government which teems with evils: thirdly, the form which is antagonistic to this and succeeds it, democracy: and lastly comes tyranny, great and famous, which differs from them all, and is the fourth and worst disorder of a state. I do not know, do you, of any other constitution which can be said to have a distinct character. There are hereditary monarchies which are bought and sold, and principalities and some other intermediate forms of government. But these are nondescripts and may be found equally among Hellenes and among barbarians.

Yes, he replied, we certainly hear of many curious forms of government.

Do you know, I said, that governments vary as the dispositions of men vary, and that there must be as many of the one as there are of the other? Or do you suppose that states spring from 'oak and rock', and not from the human natures which are in them, and as it were, turn the scale and draw other things after them?

By no means, he said, they can spring from no other source.

Then if the constitutions of states are five, the dispositions of individual minds will also be five?

Certainly.

Him who answers to aristocracy, and whom we rightly call just and good, we have already described.

We have.

Then let us now proceed to describe the inferior sort of natures, being the contentious and ambitious, who answer to the Spartan polity; also the oligarchical, democratical, and tyrannical, so that we may place the most just by the side of the most unjust, and so complete our comparison between pure justice and pure injustice, in respect of the happiness or misery which they bring to their possessor. And we shall know whether we ought to pursue injustice, as Thrasymachus advises, or in accordance with the argument which is now coming to light, to prefer justice.

Certainly, he replied, we must do as you say.

Shall we follow our old plan, which we adopted with a view to clearness, of taking the state first and then proceeding to the individual, and begin with the government based upon the love of honour? I know of no name for such a government other than timocracy, or perhaps timarchy. We will compare with this the like character in the individual; and, after that, consider oligarchy and the oligarchical man; and then again we will turn our attention to democracy and the democratical man; and lastly, we will go and view the city of tyranny, and once more take a look into the tyrant's soul, and try to arrive at a satisfactory decision.

That way of viewing and judging of the matter will be very suitable.

First, then, I said, let us inquire how timocracy (the government of honour) would arise out of aristocracy (the government of the best). Clearly, all political changes originate in divisions of the actual governing power; a government which is united, however small, cannot be moved.

Very true, he said.

In what way, then, will our city be disturbed, and in what manner will the two classes of auxiliaries and rulers disagree among themselves or with one another? Shall we, after the manner of Homer, pray the Muses to tell us 'how discord first arose'? Shall we imagine them in solemn mockery to play and jest with us as if we were children, and to address us in a lofty tragic vein, making believe to be in earnest?

How would they address us?

After this manner: 'A city which is thus constituted can hardly be shaken; but, seeing that everything which has a beginning has also an end, even a constitution such as yours will not last for ever, but will in time be dissolved. And this is the dissolution: as in plants that grow in the earth, so in animals that move on the earth's surface, fertility and sterility of soul and body occur when the circumferences of the circles of each are completed, which in short-lived existences pass over a short space, and in long-lived ones over a long space. But to the knowledge of human fecundity and sterility all the wisdom and education of your rulers will not attain; the laws which regulate them will not be discovered by any blend of reasoning and sensation, but will escape them, and they will bring children into the world when they ought not. Now that which is of divine birth has a period which is contained in a perfect number, but the period of human birth is comprehended in a number in which first increments by involution and evolution [*or* squared and cubed] obtaining three intervals and four terms of like and unlike, waxing and waning numbers, make all the terms commensurable and agreeable to one another. The base of these (3) with a third added (4) when combined with five (20) and raised to the third power furnishes two harmonies; the first a square which is a hundred times as great (400 = 4 x 100), and the other a figure having one side equal to the former, but oblong, consisting of a hundred numbers squared upon rational diameters of a square (i.e. omitting fractions), the side of which is five (7 x 7 = 49 x 100 = 4900), each of them being less by one (than the perfect square which includes the fractions, sc. 50) or less by two perfect squares of irrational diameters (of a square the side of which is five = 50 + 50 = 100); and a hundred cubes of three (27 x 100 = 2700 + 4900 + 400 = 8000). Now this number represents a geometrical figure which has control over the good and evil of births. For when your guardians are ignorant of the law of births and unite bride and bridegroom out of season, the children will not be goodly or fortunate. And though only the best of them will be appointed by their predecessors, still they will be unworthy to hold their fathers' places, and when they come into power as guardians, they will soon be found to fail in taking care of us, the Muses; first by undervaluing music, which neglect will soon extend to gymnastic, and hence the young men of your state will be less cultivated. In the succeeding generation rulers will be appointed who have lost the guardian power of testing the metal of your different races, which, like Hesiod's, are of gold and silver and brass and iron. And so iron will be mingled with silver, and brass with gold, and hence there will arise dissimilarity and inequality and irregularity, which always and in all places are causes of hatred and war.' This the Muses affirm to be the stock from which discord has sprung, wherever arising; and this is their answer to us.

Yes, and we may assume that they answer truly.

Why, yes, I said, of course they answer truly; how can the Muses speak falsely?

And what do the Muses say next?

When discord arose, then the two races began to pull in opposite directions – the iron and brass towards the acquisition of money and land and houses and gold and silver; but the gold and silver races, not wanting money but having the true riches in their own natures, inclined towards virtue and the ancient order of things. There was tension and opposition between them, and at last they came to a compromise, agreeing to distribute their land and houses among individual owners; and their friends and maintainers, whom they had formerly protected in the condition of freemen, were to be enslaved and held as subjects and servants; and they themselves were to keep watch against them, besides attending to warfare.

I believe that you have rightly conceived the origin of the change.

And the new government which thus arises will be of a form intermediate between oligarchy and aristocracy?

Very true.

Such will be the change, and after the change has been made, what kind of life will they live? Clearly, the new state, being in a mean between oligarchy and the perfect state, will partly follow one and partly the other, and will also have some peculiarities.

True, he said.

In the honour given to rulers, in the abstinence of the warrior class from agriculture, handicrafts, and trade in general, in the institution of common meals, and in the attention paid to gymnastics and military training – in all these respects this state will resemble the former.

True.

But in the fear of admitting philosophers to power, because such men are no longer to be had simple and earnest, but are made up of mixed elements; and in turning from them to passionate and less complex characters, who are by nature fitted for war rather than peace; and in the value set by them upon military stratagems and contrivances, and in the waging of everlasting wars – this state will be for the most part peculiar.

Yes.

Yes, I said; and men of this stamp will be covetous of money, like those who live in oligarchies; they will have a fierce secret longing after gold and silver, which they will hoard in dark places, having magazines and treasuries of their own for the deposit and concealment of them; also castles which are just nests for their eggs, and in which they will spend large sums upon women, or on any others whom they please.

That is most true, he said.

And they are miserly because they have no means of openly acquiring the money which they prize; they will spend that which is another man's on the gratification of their desires, stealing their pleasures and running away like children from the law, their father: they have been schooled not by persuasion but by force, for they have neglected her who is the true Muse, the companion of reason and philosophy, and have honoured gymnastic more than music.

The form of government which you describe, he said, is a complete mixture of good and evil.

Why, there is a mixture, I said; but one thing, and one thing only, is predominantly seen – the spirit of contention and ambition; and these are due to the prevalence of the passionate or spirited element.

Assuredly, he said.

Such is the origin and such the character of this state, which has been described in outline only; the more perfect execution was not required, for a sketch is enough to show the type of the most perfectly just and most perfectly unjust; and to go through all the states and all the characters of men, omitting no detail, would be an interminable labour.

Very true, he replied.

Now what man answers to this form of government – how did he come into being, and what is he like?

I think, said Adeimantus, that in the spirit of

contention which characterises him, he is not unlike our friend Glaucon.

Perhaps, I said, he may be like him in that one point; but there are other respects in which he is very different.

In what respects?

He should have more of self-assertion and be less cultivated, though still a friend of culture; and a good listener, but no speaker. Such a person is apt to be rough with slaves, unlike the educated man, who esteems them beneath his notice; and he will also be courteous to freemen, and remarkably obedient to authority; he is a lover of power and a lover of honour; claiming to be a ruler, not because he is eloquent or on any ground of that sort, but because he is a soldier and has performed feats of arms; he is also a lover of gymnastic exercises and of the chase.

Yes, that is the type of character which answers to timocracy.

Such a one will despise riches so long as he is young; but as he gets older he will be more and more attracted to them, because he has a piece of the avaricious nature in him and is not single-minded towards virtue, having lost his best guardian.

Who was that? said Adeimantus.

Reason, I said, tempered with music, which alone, when established within a man, can maintain his excellence throughout life.

Good, he said.

Such, I said, is the timocratical youth, and he is like the timocratical state.

Exactly.

His origin is as follows: he is often the young son of a brave father, who dwells in an ill-governed city, declining its honours and offices, and avoiding its lawsuits and other such business; and quite ready to waive his rights in order that he may escape trouble.

And how does the son come into being?

The character of the son begins to develop when he hears his mother complaining that her husband has no place in the government, of which the consequence is that she has no precedence among other women. Further, when she sees her husband not very eager about money, and instead of battling and railing in the law courts or assembly, taking whatever happens to him quietly; and when she observes that his thoughts always centre in himself, while he treats her with no special honour and no great disrespect, she is annoyed, and says to her son that his father is only half a man and far too easygoing, adding all the other complaints about her own ill-treatment which women are so fond of rehearsing.

Yes, said Adeimantus, they give us plenty of them, and their complaints are so like themselves.

And you know, I said, that the old servants also, who are supposed to be attached to the family, from time to time talk privately in the same strain to the son; and if they see anyone who owes money to his father or is wronging him in any way, and he fails to prosecute them, they tell the youth that when he grows up he must retaliate upon all people of this sort, and be more of a man than his father. He has only to walk abroad and he hears and sees the same sort of thing: those who mind their own business in the city are called simpletons and held in no esteem, while the busybodies are honoured and applauded. The result is that the young man, hearing and seeing all these things – hearing, too, the words of his father, and having a nearer view of his way of life, and making comparisons of him and others – is drawn opposite ways: while his father is watering and nourishing the rational principle in his soul, the others are encouraging the passionate and appetitive; and he being not originally of a bad nature, but having kept bad company, is at last brought by their joint influence to a middle point, and gives up the kingdom which is within him to the middle principle of contentiousness and passion, and, in his maturity, becomes arrogant and ambitious.

You seem to me to have described his origin perfectly.

Then we have now, I said, the second form of government and the second type of character?

We have.

Shall we, then, next look at another man who, as Aeschylus says, 'is set over against another city'; or rather, as our plan requires, begin with the state?

By all means.

I believe that oligarchy follows next in order.

And what manner of government do you term oligarchy?

A government resting on a valuation of property, in which the rich have power and the poor man is deprived of it.

I understand, he replied.

Ought I not to begin by describing how the change from timocracy to oligarchy arises?

Yes.

Well, I said, no eyes are required in order to see how the one passes into the other.

How?

The accumulation of gold in the treasury of private

individuals is the ruin of timocracy; for first, they invent for themselves new modes of expenditure and wrest the laws to allow of these; for what do they or their wives care about the law?

Yes, that is probable.

And then one, seeing another grow rich, seeks to rival him, and thus the great mass of the citizens become lovers of money.

Likely enough.

And so they grow richer and richer, and the more they think of making a fortune the less they honour virtue; for when riches and virtue are placed together in the scales of the balance, the one always rises as the other falls.

True.

Therefore, in proportion as riches and rich men are honoured in the state, virtue and the virtuous are dishonoured.

Clearly.

And what is honoured is practised, and that which has no honour is neglected.

That is obvious.

And so at last, instead of loving contention and glory, men become lovers of money and money-making; they honour and look up to the rich man, and promote him to high office, and dishonour the poor man.

They do so.

They next proceed to make a law which fixes a sum of money as the qualification of citizenship; the sum is higher in one place and lower in another, as the oligarchy is more or less exclusive; and they allow no one whose property falls below the amount fixed to have any share in the government. These changes in the constitution they effect by force of arms, if intimidation has not already done their work.

Very true.

And this, speaking generally, is the way in which oligarchy is established.

Yes, he said; but what are the characteristics of this form of government, and what are the defects in it of which we were speaking?

First of all, I said, consider the nature of the qualification. Just think what would happen if pilots were to be chosen according to a census of their property, and a poor man were refused permission to steer, even though he were a better pilot?

You mean that the voyage would be very unpleasant?

Yes; and is not this true of the government of anything?

I should imagine so.

Except a city? Or would you include a city?

Nay, he said, the case of a city is the strongest of all, inasmuch as the rule of a city is the greatest and most difficult of all.

This, then, will be the first great defect of oligarchy?

Clearly.

And here is another defect which is quite as bad.

What defect?

The inevitable division: such a state is not one, but two states, the one of poor, the other of rich men, living on the same spot and always conspiring against one another.

That, surely, is at least as bad.

Another discreditable feature is that, for a like reason, they are incapable of carrying on any war. Either they must arm the multitude, and then they are more afraid of them than of the enemy; or, if they do not call them out in the hour of battle, they are oligarchs indeed, few to fight as they are few to rule. And at the same time their fondness for money makes them unwilling to pay taxes.

Not a good thing.

And, under such a constitution there is the fault which we blamed long ago; the same persons have too many callings – they are husbandmen, tradesmen, warriors, all in one. Does that look well?

Anything but well.

There is another evil which is, perhaps, the greatest of all, and to which this state first begins to be liable.

What evil?

A man may sell all that he has, and another may acquire his property; yet after the sale he may dwell in the city of which he is no longer a part, and being neither trader, nor artisan, nor horseman, nor hoplite, is named a pauper, and destitute.

Yes, that is an evil which begins in this state.

The evil is certainly not prevented there; otherwise oligarchies would not show the extremes of great wealth and utter poverty.

True.

But think again: in his wealthy days, while he was spending his money, was a man of this sort a whit more good to the state for the purposes of which we were now speaking? Or did he only seem to be a member of the ruling body, although in truth he was neither ruler nor subject, but just a spendthrift?

As you say, he seemed to be a ruler, but was only a spendthrift.

May we not say that he is the drone who in his house is like the drone in its cell, and that the one is the plague of the city as the other is of the hive?

Just so, Socrates.

And god has made the flying drones, Adeimantus, all without stings, whereas of the walking drones he has made some, indeed, without stings but others with dreadful stings; of the stingless class are those who in their old age end as paupers; of the stingers come all the criminal class, as they are termed.

Most true, he said.

Clearly then, whenever you see paupers in a state, somewhere in that neighbourhood there are hidden away thieves and cutpurses and robbers of temples, and all sorts of malefactors.

Clearly.

Well, I said, and in oligarchical states do you not find paupers?

Yes, he said; nearly everybody is a pauper who is not a ruler.

And may we be so bold as to affirm that there are also many criminals to be found in them, rogues who have stings, and whom the authorities are careful to restrain by force?

Certainly, we may be so bold.

The existence of such persons is to be attributed to want of education, ill training, and an evil constitution of the state?

True.

Such, then, is the form and such are the evils of an oligarchical city; and there may be many other evils.

Very likely.

Then our picture of this form of government called oligarchy, in which the rulers are elected for their wealth, may be regarded as complete. Let us next proceed to consider the nature and origin of the individual who answers to this state.

By all means.

Does not the timocratical man change into the oligarchical on this wise?

How?

A time arrives when the representative of timocracy has a son: at first he begins by emulating his father and walking in his footsteps, but presently he sees him of a sudden foundering against the state as upon a sunken reef, and he and all that he has is lost; he may have been a general or some other high officer who is brought to trial under a prejudice raised by informers, and either put to death, or exiled, or deprived of the privileges of a citizen, and all his property taken from him.

Nothing more likely.

And the son has seen and known all this – he is a ruined man, and his fear has taught him to knock ambition and passion headforemost from his bosom's throne; humbled by poverty he takes to money-making and by mean and miserly savings and hard work gets a fortune together. Is not such a one likely to seat the concupiscent and covetous element on the vacant throne and to suffer it to play the great king within him, girt with tiara and chain and scimitar?

Most true, he replied.

And when he has made reason and spirit sit down on the ground obediently on either side of their sovereign, and made them his slaves, he compels the one to think only of how lesser sums may be turned into larger ones, and will not allow the other to worship and admire anything but riches and rich men, or to be ambitious of anything so much as the possession of wealth and the means of acquiring it.

In no other way, he said, can the conversion of the ambitious youth into the avaricious one be so speedy and violent.

And the avaricious, I said, is the oligarchical youth?

Yes, he said; at any rate the individual out of whom he came is like the state out of which oligarchy came.

Let us then consider whether there is any likeness between them.

Very good.

First, then, they resemble one another in the supreme value which they set upon wealth?

Certainly.

Also in their penurious, laborious character; the individual only satisfies his necessary appetites, and confines his expenditure to them; his other desires he subdues, under the idea that they are unprofitable.

True.

He is a shabby fellow, who saves something out of everything and makes a purse for himself; and this is the sort of man whom the vulgar applaud. Is he not a true image of the state which he represents?

He appears to me to be so; at any rate money is highly valued by this type of man as well as by the state.

You see that he is not a man of cultivation, I said.

I imagine not, he said; had he been educated he would never have made a blind god director of his chorus, or given him chief honour.

Excellent! I said. Yet consider: must we not further admit that owing to this want of cultivation there will be found in him dronelike desires as of pauper and rogue, which are forcibly kept down by his prudent habit of life?

True.

Do you know where you will have to look if you want to discover his rogueries?

Where must I look?

You should see him in some position which gives

him complete liberty to act dishonestly, as in the guardianship of an orphan.

Aye.

Now does not this make it clear that in his ordinary dealings which give him a reputation for honesty he coerces his bad passions by an enforced virtue; not making them see that they are wrong, or taming them by reason, but by necessity and fear constraining them, because he trembles for his possessions?

To be sure.

Yes, indeed, my dear friend, but you will find that the natural desires of the drone commonly exist in him all the same whenever he has to spend what is not his own.

Yes, and they will be strong in him too.

Such a man, then, will not be at peace with himself; he will be two men, and not one; but, in general, his better desires will be found to prevail over his inferior ones.

True.

For these reasons such a one will be more respectable than many people; yet the true virtue of a unanimous and harmonious soul will flee far away and never come near him.

I should expect so.

And surely, the miser individually will be an ignoble competitor in a state for any prize of victory, or other object of honourable ambition; he will not spend his money in the contest for glory, so afraid is he of awakening his expensive appetites and inviting them to help and join in the struggle; in true oligarchical fashion he fights with a small part only of his resources, and the result commonly is that he loses the prize and saves his money.

Very true.

Can we any longer doubt, then, that the miser and money-maker answers to the oligarchical state?

There can be no doubt.

Next comes democracy; of this the origin and nature have still to be considered by us; and then we will inquire into the ways of the democratic man, and bring him up for judgment.

At any rate, he said, we shall then proceed consistently.

Well, I said, and how does the change from oligarchy into democracy arise? Is it not on this wise? The good at which such a state aims is to become as rich as possible, a desire which is insatiable?

What then?

The rulers, being aware that their power rests upon their wealth, refuse to curtail by law the liberty of undisciplined young men to spend and waste their money, wishing to buy up their estates or lend money on them, and thus increase their own wealth and importance?

To be sure.

There can be no doubt that the love of wealth and the spirit of moderation cannot exist together in citizens of the same state to any considerable extent; one or the other will be disregarded.

That is tolerably clear.

And so in oligarchical states, where no one has troubled to check self-indulgence, men of good family have often been reduced to beggary?

Yes, often.

And still they remain in the city; there they are, ready to sting and fully armed, either owing money, or having forfeited their citizenship, or both; and they hate and conspire against those who have got their property, and against everybody else, and are eager for revolution.

That is true.

On the other hand, the men of business, stooping as they walk, and pretending not even to see those whom they have already ruined, insert their sting – that is, their money – into someone else who is not on his guard against them, and recover the parent sum many times over multiplied into a family of children: and so they make drone and pauper to abound in the state.

Yes, he said, there are plenty of them – that is certain.

The evil blazes up like a fire; and they will not extinguish it, either by restricting a man's use of his own property, or by another legal remedy for evils of this kind.

What other?

One which is the next best, and has the advantage of compelling the citizens to look to their characters: let there be a general rule that every one shall enter into voluntary contracts at his own risk, and there will be less of this scandalous money-making, and the evils of which we were speaking will be greatly lessened in the state.

Yes, they will be greatly lessened.

At present the governors, induced by the various motives which I have named, reduce their subjects to this condition; while as for themselves and their adherents, all the young men of the governing class are habituated to lead a life of luxury and idleness both of body and mind; they will not work, and have not the hardihood to resist either pleasure or pain.

Very true.

And they themselves care only for making money, and are as indifferent as the pauper to the cultivation of virtue.

Yes, quite as indifferent.

Such is the state of affairs which prevails among them. And often rulers and their subjects may come in one another's way, whether on a journey or on some other occasion of meeting, on a pilgrimage or a march, as fellow soldiers or fellow sailors; aye, and they may observe the behaviour of each other in the very moment of danger – for where danger is, there is no fear that the poor will be despised by the rich – and very likely the wiry sunburnt poor man may be placed in battle at the side of a wealthy one who has never spoilt his complexion and has plenty of superfluous flesh – when he sees such a one puffing and at his wit's end, how can he avoid drawing the conclusion that men like him are only rich because no one has the courage to despoil them? And when they meet in private will they not pass the word round, 'We have them in our power; they are good for nothing'?

Yes, he said, I am quite aware that this is their way of talking.

And, as in a body which is diseased the addition of a touch from without may bring on illness, and sometimes even when there is no external provocation a commotion may arise within – in the same way an enfeebled state may, upon some slight occasion (for instance if the one party introduce from without their oligarchical, or the other their democratical allies), fall sick, and be at war with herself; and may be at times distracted, even when there is no external cause.

Yes, surely.

And then democracy comes into being after the poor have conquered their opponents, slaughtering some and banishing some, while to the remainder they give an equal share of freedom and power; and in this form of government the magistrates are commonly elected by lot.

Yes, he said, that is the genesis of democracy, whether the revolution has been effected by arms, or whether fear has caused the opposite party to withdraw.

And now what is their manner of life, and what sort of a government have they? For as the government is, such will be the man.

Clearly, he said.

In the first place, are they not free; and is not the city full of freedom and frankness – a man may say and do what he likes?

'Tis said so, he replied.

And where freedom is, the individual is clearly able to order for himself his own life as he pleases?

Clearly.

Then in this kind of state there will be the greatest variety of human natures?

There will.

This, then, seems likely to be the fairest of states, being like an embroidered robe which is spangled with every sort of flower. And just as women and children think a variety of colours to be of all things most charming, so there are many men to whom this state, which is spangled with the manners and characters of mankind, will appear to be the fairest of states.

Yes.

Yes, my good sir, and there will be no better in which to look for a government.

Why?

Because, owing to the liberty which reigns there, it offers a complete assortment of constitutions; and he who has a mind to establish a state, as we have been doing, must go to a democratic city as he would to a bazaar at which they sell constitutions, and pick out the one that suits him; then, when he has made his choice, he may found his state.

He will be sure to find patterns enough.

And there being no necessity, I said, for you to govern in this state even if you have the capacity, or to be governed unless you like, or to go to war when the rest go to war, or to be at peace when others are at peace, unless you are so disposed – there being no necessity also, because some law forbids you to hold office or be a dicast, that you should not hold office or be a dicast, if you have a fancy – is not this a way of life which for the moment is supremely delightful?

For the moment, yes.

And is not their humanity to the condemned in some cases quite charming? Have you not observed how, in a democracy, many persons, although they have been sentenced to death or exile, just stay where they are and walk about the world – the gentleman parades like a hero, and nobody sees or cares?

Yes, he replied, many and many a one.

See too, I said, the forgiving spirit of democracy, and the 'don't care' about trifles, and the disregard which she shows of all the fine principles which we solemnly laid down at the foundation of the city – as when we said that, except in the case of some rarely gifted nature, there never will be a good man who has not from his childhood been used to play amid things of beauty and pursue only what is honourable – how grandly does she trample all these fine notions of ours under her feet, never giving a thought to the pursuits from which a man has come into political life, and promoting to honour anyone who professes to be the people's friend.

Yes, she is of a noble spirit.

These and other kindred characteristics are proper to democracy, which will be, so it seems, a charming form of government, full of variety and disorder, and dispensing a sort of equality to equals and unequals alike.

We know her well.

Consider now, I said, what manner of man the individual is; or should we first consider, as in the case of the state, how he comes into being?

Yes, he said.

Is not this the way – he is the son of the miserly and oligarchical father who has trained him in his own habits?

Exactly.

And, like his father, he keeps under by force the pleasures which are of the spending and not of the getting sort, being those which are called unnecessary?

Obviously.

Would you like, for the sake of clearness, to distinguish which are the necessary and which are the unnecessary pleasures?

I should.

May not those desires be rightly termed necessary, of which we cannot get rid, and of which the satisfaction is a benefit to us? For it is a necessity of our nature to desire both what is beneficial and what cannot be suppressed – is it not so?

True.

We shall not be wrong therefore in calling them necessary?

No.

And the desires of which a man may get rid, if he takes pains from his youth upwards – of which the presence, moreover, does no good, and in some cases the reverse of good – shall we not be right in saying that all these are unnecessary?

Yes, certainly.

Suppose we select an example of either kind, in order that we may have a general notion of them?

Very good.

Will not the desire of eating, that is, of simple food and condiments, in so far as they are required for health and strength, be of the necessary class?

That is what I should suppose.

The desire for simple food is necessary, both as beneficial, and because it is one which a man cannot check as long as he lives.

Yes.

But the condiments are only necessary in so far as they are good for health?

Certainly.

But what of the desire which goes beyond this, or extends to other kinds of food, which might generally be got rid of if beaten down and trained in youth, and is hurtful to the body, and hurtful to the soul in the pursuit of wisdom and virtue? May this be rightly called unnecessary?

Very true.

May we not say that these desires spend, and that the others make money because they conduce to production?

Certainly.

And of the pleasures of love, and all other pleasures, the same holds good?

True.

And the drone of whom we spoke just now was, I suppose, meant to be one who was surfeited in pleasures and desires of this sort, and was the slave of the unnecessary desires, whereas he who was subject to the necessary only was miserly and oligarchical?

Very true.

Again, let us see how the democratical man grows out of the oligarchical: the following, as I suspect, is commonly the process.

What is the process?

When a young man who has been brought up as we were just now describing, in a vulgar and miserly way, has tasted drones' honey and has come to associate with fierce and crafty natures who are able to provide for him all sorts of refinements and varieties of pleasure – then, as you may imagine, the change will begin of the oligarchical principle within him into the democratical?

Inevitably.

And as in the city the change was effected by an alliance from without assisting one division of the citizens, like giving help to like, so too the young man is changed by a class of desires coming from without to assist the desires within him, to which they are akin and alike?

Certainly.

And if there be any ally which aids the oligarchical principle within him, whether the influence of a father or of kindred advising or rebuking him, then there arises in his soul a faction and an opposite faction, and so he comes to be at war with himself.

It must be so.

And there are times when the democratical principle

gives way to the oligarchical, and some of his desires die, and others are banished; a spirit of reverence enters into the young man's soul and order is restored.

Yes, he said, that sometimes happens.

And then, again, after the old desires have been driven out, fresh ones spring up which are akin to them, and because he their father does not know how to educate them, wax fierce and numerous.

Yes, he said, that is apt to be the way.

They draw him to his old associates, and holding secret intercourse with them, breed and multiply in him.

Very true.

At length they seize upon the citadel of the young man's soul, which they perceive to be void of all noble studies and pursuits and principles, such as make their abode in the minds of men who are dear to the gods, and are their best guardians and sentinels.

None better.

But now false and boastful conceits and phrases mount upwards and take possession of the stronghold.

They are certain to do so.

And so the young man returns into the country of the lotus-eaters, and takes up his dwelling there in the face of all men; and if any help be sent by his friends to the economical part of him, the aforesaid vain conceits shut the gate of the king's fastness; and they will neither allow his allies themselves to enter, nor if private advisers offer the fatherly counsel of the aged will they listen to them or receive them. There is a battle and they gain the day; the sense of honour, which they call silliness, is ignominiously thrust into exile by them, and temperance, which they nickname unmanliness, is trampled in the mire and cast forth;

they persuade men that moderation and orderly expenditure are vulgarity and meanness, and so, by the
help of a rabble of unprofitable appetites, they drive
them beyond the border.

Yes, with a will.

And when they have emptied and swept clean the
soul of him who is now in their power and who is being
initiated by them in great mysteries, the next thing is to
bring back to their house insolence and anarchy and
waste and impudence in bright array having garlands
on their heads, and a great company with them;
hymning their praises and calling them by sweet names,
they term insolence breeding, and anarchy liberty, and
waste magnificence, and impudence courage. Is it not
thus that a man, while still young, passes out of his
original nature, which was trained in the school of
necessity, into the freedom and libertinism of useless
and unnecessary pleasures?

Yes, he said, the change in him is visible enough.

After this he lives on, spending his money and labour
and time on unnecessary pleasures quite as much as on
necessary ones; but if he be fortunate and is not too
much disordered in his wits, when years have elapsed
and the heyday of passion is over – supposing that he
then re-admits into the city some part of the exiled
virtues, and does not wholly give himself up to their
successors – in that case he balances his pleasures and
lives in a sort of equilibrium, putting the government of
himself into the hands of the one which comes first and
wins the turn; and when he has had enough of that,
then into the hands of another; he despises none of
them but encourages them all equally.

Very true, he said.

Neither does he receive or let pass into the fortress

any true word of advice; if any one says to him that some pleasures are the satisfactions of good and noble desires, and others of evil desires, and that he ought to use and honour some and chastise and master the others – whenever this is repeated to him he shakes his head and says that they are all alike, and that one is as good as another.

Yes, he said; that is the way with a man in this condition.

Yes, I said, he lives from day to day indulging the appetite of the hour; and sometimes he is lapped in drink and strains of the flute; then he becomes a water-drinker, and tries to get thin; then he takes a turn at gymnastics; sometimes idling and neglecting every-thing, then once more living the life of a philosopher; often he is busy with politics, and starts to his feet and says and does whatever comes into his head; and if he is emulous of anyone who is a warrior, off he goes in that direction, or if of men of business, once more in that. His life has neither law nor order; and this distracted existence, which he terms joy and bliss and freedom, continues throughout his life.

You describe exactly, he replied, the life of one whose law is liberty and equality.

Yes, I said; his life is motley and manifold and an epitome of the lives of many; he answers to the state which we described as fair and spangled. And many a man and many a woman will take him for their pattern, and many a constitution and many an example of manners is contained in him.

Just so.

Shall he then be set over against democracy, as one who may truly be called the democratic man?

Let that be his place, he said.

Last of all comes the most beautiful of all, man and state alike, tyranny and the tyrant; these we have now to consider.

Quite true, he said.

Say then, my friend, what do we find the character of tyranny to be? That it has a democratic origin is evident.

Clearly.

And does not tyranny spring from democracy in the same manner, so to speak, as democracy from oligarchy?

How?

The good which oligarchy proposed to itself and the object for which it was established was wealth – am I not right?

Yes.

Thus, the insatiable desire of wealth and the neglect of all other things for the sake of money-getting was also the ruin of oligarchy?

True.

And democracy also is brought to dissolution by an insatiable desire for that which she designates as good?

What do you suppose that to be?

Freedom, I replied; which, as they tell you in a democracy, is the glory of the state – and that therefore in a democracy alone will the freeman of nature deign to dwell.

Yes; the saying is in everybody's mouth.

To return, then, to the question I was going to ask: is it true that the insatiable desire of this good, and the neglect of other things, introduces change in this constitution also, and occasions a demand for tyranny?

How so?

When a democracy which has begun to thirst for

freedom has evil cup-bearers presiding over the feast, and has drunk too deeply of the strong wine of freedom, then, unless her rulers are very amenable and give a plentiful draught, she calls them to account and punishes them, and says that they are cursed oligarchs.

Yes, he replied, a very common occurrence.

Yes, I said; and men who obey their rulers are insultingly termed by her 'slaves who hug their chains' and 'men of naught'; she would have subjects who are like rulers, and rulers who are like subjects: these are men after her own heart, whom she praises and honours both in private and public. Now, in such a state, can there be anything to stop the progress of liberty?

Certainly not.

By degrees the anarchy must find a way into private houses, and end by getting among the animals and infecting them?

How do you mean?

I mean that the father grows accustomed to descend to the level of his sons and to fear them, and the son is on a level with his father; he shows no respect or reverence for either of his parents, such being his notion of freedom. And the metic is equal with the citizen and the citizen with the metic, and the stranger is quite as good as either.

Yes, he said, that is the way.

And these are not the only evils, I said – there are several lesser ones: In such a state of society the master fears and flatters his scholars, and the scholars despise their masters and their tutors also; young and old are all alike; and the young man is on a level with the old, and is ready to compete with him in word or deed; and old men condescend to the young and are full of pleasantry and gaiety; they are loth to be thought morose and authoritative, and therefore they adopt the manners of the young.

Quite true, he said.

But the last extreme of popular liberty is when the slave bought with money, whether male or female, is just as free as his or her purchaser; nor must I forget to tell of the liberty and equality of the two sexes in relation to each other.

Why not, as Aeschylus says, utter the word which rises to our lips?

That is what I am doing, I replied; and I must add that no one who does not know would believe how much greater is the liberty which the animals who are under the dominion of man have in a democracy than in any other state: for truly, the she-dogs, as the proverb says, are as good as their she-mistresses, and the horses and asses have a way of marching along with all the rights and dignities of freemen; and they will run at any body who comes in their way if he does not leave the road clear for them: and all things are just ready to burst with liberty.

When I am on my way to the country, he said, I often experience what you describe. You and I have dreamed the same thing.

And above all, I said, and as the result of all, see how sensitive the citizens become; they chafe impatiently at the least touch of authority, and at length, as you know, they cease to care even for the laws, written or unwritten; they will have no master over them at all.

Yes, he said, I know it too well.

Such, my friend, I said, is the fair and glorious beginning out of which springs tyranny.

Glorious indeed, he said. But what is the next step?

The ruin of oligarchy is the ruin of democracy; the same disease magnified and intensified by liberty overmasters democracy – the truth being that the excessive increase of anything often causes a reaction in the opposite direction; and this is the case not only in the seasons and in vegetable and animal life, but above all in forms of government.

True.

The excess of liberty, whether in states or individuals, seems only to pass into excess of slavery.

Yes, the natural order.

And so it is from democracy, and from no other source, that tyranny naturally arises, and the harshest and most complete form of tyranny and slavery out of the most extreme form of liberty?

As we might expect, he said.

That, however, was not, as I believe, your question – you rather desired to know what is that disorder which is generated alike in oligarchy and democracy, and is the ruin of both?

Just so, he said.

Well, I said, I meant to refer to the class of idle spendthrifts, of whom the more courageous are the leaders and the more timid the followers, the same whom we compare to drones, some stingless, and others having stings.

A very just comparison.

These two classes create disturbance in every city in which they are generated, being what phlegm and bile are to the body. And the good physician and lawgiver of the state ought, like the wise bee-master, to keep them at a distance and prevent, if possible, their ever coming in; and if they have anyhow found a way in, then he should have them and their cells cut out as speedily as possible.

Yes, by all means, he said.

Then, in order that we may obtain a more distinct view of our subject, let us imagine democracy to be divided, as indeed it is, into three classes; for in the first place freedom creates rather more drones in the democratic than there were in the oligarchical state.

That is true.

And in the democracy they are certainly more aggressive.

How so?

Because in the oligarchical state they are disqualified and driven from office, and therefore they cannot train or gather strength; whereas in a democracy they are almost the entire ruling power, and while the keener sort speak and act, the rest keep buzzing about the bema and do not suffer a word to be said on the other side; hence in democracies almost everything is managed by the drones.

Very true, he said.

Then there is another class which is always being severed from the mass.

What is that?

Those who are most orderly by nature – a class, which in a nation of traders is sure to be the richest.

Naturally so.

They are the most squeezable persons and yield the largest amount of honey to the drones.

Why, yes, he said, there is little to be squeezed out of people who have little.

And this is called the wealthy class, and is the food of the drones.

That is pretty much the case, he said.

The people are a third class, consisting of those who work with their own hands; they are not politicians, and have not much to live upon. This, when assembled, is the largest and most powerful class in a democracy.

True, he said; but then the multitude is seldom willing to congregate unless they get a little honey.

But then they do share, I said, in so far as their leaders can deprive the rich of their estates and distribute them among the people, at the same time taking care to reserve the larger part for themselves.

Why, yes, he said, to that extent the people do share.

And the persons whose property is taken from them are compelled to defend themselves by speech before the people and by action as they best can?

What else can they do?

And then, although they may have no desire of change, the others charge them with plotting against the people and being friends of oligarchy?

True.

And the end is that when they see the people, not of their own accord, but through ignorance and because they are deceived by informers, seeking to do them wrong, then at last they are forced to become oligarchs in reality; they do not wish to be, but the sting of the drones torments them and breeds revolution in them.

That is exactly the truth.

Then come impeachments and judgments and trials of one another.

True.

The people have always some champion whom they are wont to set over them and nurse into greatness.

Yes, that is their way.

So much then is clear, that whenever tyranny appears, the protectorship of the people is the root from which it springs.

Yes, that is quite clear.

How then does a protector begin to change into a tyrant? Clearly when he begins to do what the man is said to do in the tale of the Arcadian temple of Lycaean Zeus.

What tale?

The tale is that he who has tasted the entrails of a single human victim minced up with the entrails of other victims is destined to become a wolf. Did you never hear it?

O yes.

And the protector of the people is like him; having a mob entirely at his disposal, he is not restrained from shedding the blood of kinsmen; by the favourite method of false accusation he brings them into court and murders them, making the life of man to disappear, and with unholy tongue and lips tasting the blood of his fellow citizens; some he kills and others he banishes, at the same time hinting at the abolition of debts and partition of lands: and after this, what will be his destiny? Must he not either perish at the hands of his enemies, or from being a man become a wolf – that is, a tyrant?

Inevitably.

This, I said, is he who forms a party against the owners of property.

The same.

After a while he is driven out, but comes back, in spite of his enemies, a tyrant full grown.

That is clear.

And if they are unable to expel him, or to get him

condemned to death by a public accusation, they conspire to assassinate him secretly.

Yes, he said, that is their usual way.

Then comes the famous request for a bodyguard, which is the device of all those who have got thus far in their tyrannical career – 'Let not the people's friend,' as they say, 'be lost to them.'

Exactly.

The people readily assent; probably because all their fears are for him – they have none for themselves.

Very true.

And when a man who is wealthy and is also accused of being an enemy of the people sees this, then, my friend, as the oracle said to Croesus,

'By pebbly Hermus' shore he flees and rests not, and is not ashamed to be a coward.'

And quite right too, said he, for if he were, he would never be ashamed again.

But if he is caught he dies.

Of course.

And he, the protector of whom we spoke, is to be seen, not 'larding the plain' with his bulk, but himself the overthrower of many, standing up in the chariot of state with the reins in his hand, no longer protector, but tyrant absolute.

No doubt, he said.

And now let us consider the happiness of the man, and also of the state in which a creature like him is generated.

Yes, he said, let us consider that.

At first, in the early days of his power, he is full of smiles, and he salutes every one whom he meets – he to be called a tyrant, who is making promises in public and also in private, releasing men from their debts, and distributing land to the people and his followers, and professing to be so gracious and kind to every one!

Of course, he said.

But when he has disposed of foreign enemies by conquest or treaty, and there is nothing to fear from them, then he is always stirring up some war or other, in order that the people may require a leader.

To be sure.

Has he not also another object, which is that they may be impoverished by payment of taxes, and thus compelled to devote themselves to their daily wants and therefore less likely to conspire against him?

Clearly.

And if any of them are suspected by him of having such notions of freedom as may make them rebellious to his authority, he will have a good pretext for destroying them by placing them at the mercy of the enemy; and for all these reasons the tyrant must be always getting up a war.

He must.

Now he begins to grow unpopular.

A necessary result.

Then some of those who joined in setting him up, and who are in power, speak their minds to him and to one another, and the more courageous of them cast in his teeth what is being done.

Yes, that may be expected.

And the tyrant, if he means to rule, must get rid of them all; he cannot stop while he has a friend or an enemy who is good for anything.

He cannot.

And therefore he must look about him and see who is valiant, who is high-minded, who is wise, who is wealthy; happy man, he must be the enemy of them all, and must plot their destruction whether he will or no, until he has made a purgation of the state.

Yes, he said, and a rare purgation.s

Yes, I said, not the sort of purgation which the physicians make of the body; for they take away the worse and leave the better part, but he does the reverse.

If he is to rule, I suppose that he cannot help himself.

What a blessed alternative, I said: to be compelled to dwell only with the many bad and to be by them hated, or not to live at all!

Yes, that is the alternative.

And the more detestable such actions make him to the citizens the more satellites and the greater devotion in them will he require?

Certainly.

And who are the devoted band, and where will he procure them?

They will flock to him, he said, of their own accord, if he pays them.

By the dog! I said, you seem to foresee a new invasion of drones, of every sort and from every land.

Yes, he said, and I am right.

But whom will he enlist on the spot? Will he not be ready –

To do what?

To rob the citizens of their slaves, and set them free and enrol them in his bodyguard?

To be sure, he said; and he will be able to trust them best of all.

What a blessed creature, I said, must this tyrant be, if he has put to death the others and has these for his trusted friends.

Why, yes, he said; these are really the kind of men he employs.

Yes, I said, and these new citizens whom he has called into existence admire him and are his companions, while the good hate and avoid him.

Of course.

So it is not without reason that tragedy is reputed a wise thing and Euripides a great tragedian.

Why so?

Why, because he is the author of the pregnant saying,

'Tyrants are wise by living with the wise'; and he clearly meant to say that they are the wise whom the tyrant makes his companions.

Yes, he said, and he also praises tyranny as godlike; and many other things of the same kind are said by him and by the other poets.

And therefore, I said, the tragic poets being wise men will forgive us and any others who live after our manner if we do not receive them into our state, because they are the eulogists of tyranny.

Yes, he said, those who have the wit will doubtless forgive us.

But they will continue to go to other cities and attract mobs, and hire voices fair and loud and persuasive, and draw the cities over to tyrannies and democracies.

Very true.

Moreover, they are paid for this and receive honour – the greatest honour, as might be expected, from tyrants, and the next greatest from democracies; but the higher they ascend our constitution hill, the more their reputation fails, and seems unable from shortness of breath to proceed further.

True.

But we are wandering from the subject: let us

therefore return and inquire how the tyrant will maintain that fair and numerous and various and ever-changing army of his.

Evidently, he said, if there are sacred treasures in the city, he will confiscate and spend them; and in so far as the fortunes of his victims may suffice, he will be able to diminish the taxes which he would otherwise have to impose upon the people.

And when these fail?

Why, clearly, he said, then he and his boon companions, whether male or female, will be maintained out of his father's estate.

You mean to say that the people, from whom he has derived his being, will maintain him and his companions?

Yes, he said; they will be obliged to do so.

But what if the people fly into a passion, and aver that a grown-up son ought not to be supported by his father, but that the father should be supported by the son? The father did not bring him into being, or settle him in life, in order that when his son became a man he should himself be the servant of his own servants and should support him and his rabble of slaves and companions; but that his son should protect him, and that by his help he might be emancipated from the government of the rich and aristocratic, as they are termed. And so he bids him and his companions depart, just as any other father might drive out of the house a riotous son and his undesirable associates.

By heaven, he said, then the parent will discover what a monster he has been fostering in his bosom; and, when he wants to drive him out, he will find that he is weak and his son strong.

Why, you do not mean to say that the tyrant will

use violence? What! beat his father if he opposes him?

Yes, he will, having first disarmed him.

Then he is a parricide, and a cruel guardian of an aged parent; and this is real tyranny, about which there can be no longer a mistake: as the saying is, the people who would escape the smoke which is the slavery of freemen, has fallen into the fire which is the tyranny of slaves. And instead of that abundant and ill-timed liberty, it puts on the harshest and bitterest form of slavery, that is, slavery to slaves.

That, he said, is indeed what happens.

Very well; and may we not rightly say that we have sufficiently discussed the manner of the transition from democracy to tyranny, and the nature of tyranny when it has come into being?

Yes, quite enough, he said.

BOOK NINE

Last of all comes the tyrannical man; about whom we have once more to ask, how is he formed out of the democratical? What is his character? And how does he live, in happiness or in misery?

Yes, he said, he is the only one remaining.

There is, however, I said, one thing which I still miss.

What is it?

I do not think that we have adequately determined the nature and number of the appetites, and until this is accomplished our inquiry will always be confused.

Well, he said, it is not too late to supply the omission.

Very true, I said; and observe the point which I want to understand: certain of the unnecessary pleasures and appetites I conceive to be unlawful; everyone appears to have them, but in some persons they are controlled by the laws and by the better desires with the help of reason, and either they are wholly banished or they become few and weak; while in others they are stronger, and there are more of them.

Which appetites do you mean?

I mean those which wake when the rest of the soul – the reasoning and human and ruling power – is asleep; then the wild beast within us, gorged with meat or drink, starts up and having shaken off sleep goes forth to satisfy his desires; and you know that there is no action which at such a time, when he has parted company with all shame and sense, a man may not be ready to commit; for he does not, in his imagination, shrink from incest with his mother, or from any unnatural union with man, or god, or beast, or from parricide, or the eating of forbidden food. And in a word, no action is too irrational or indecent for him.

Most true, he said.

But when a man's pulse is healthy and temperate, and when before going to sleep he has awakened his rational powers, and fed them on noble thoughts and inquiries, collecting himself in meditation, after having first indulged his appetites neither too much nor too little, but just enough to lay them to sleep, and prevent them and their enjoyments and pains from interfering with the higher principle – which he leaves in the solitude of pure abstraction, free to contemplate and aspire to the knowledge of the unknown, whether in past, present, or future: when again he has allayed the passionate element, so that he does not go to sleep with his spirit still excited by anger against anyone – I say, when, after pacifying the two irrational principles, he rouses up the third, in which resides reason, before he takes his rest, then, as you know, he attains truth most nearly, and is least likely to be the sport of fantastic and lawless visions.

I quite agree.

In saying this I have been running into a digression; but the point which I desire to note is that in all of us, even the most highly respectable, there is a lawless wild-beast nature, which peers out in sleep. Pray, consider whether I am right, and you agree with me.

Yes, I agree.

And now remember the character which we attributed to the democratic man. He was supposed from his youth upwards to have been trained under a miserly parent, who encouraged only the saving appetites in him, but discountenanced the unnecessary, which aim only at amusement and ornament?

True.

And then he got into the company of a more refined sort of people who are full of the appetites we have just described, and taking to all their wanton ways rushed into the opposite extreme from an abhorrence of his father's meanness. At last, being a better man than his corruptors, he was drawn in both directions until he halted midway and led a life neither of the frugal nor of the anarchical kind, but of what he deemed moderate indulgence in various pleasures. After this manner the democrat was generated out of the oligarch.

Yes, he said; that was our view of him, and is so still.

And now, I said, years will have passed away, and you must conceive this man, in turn, to have a son, who is brought up in his father's way of life.

I can imagine him.

Then you must further imagine the same thing to happen to the son which has already happened to the father: he is drawn into a perfectly lawless life, which by his seducers is termed perfect liberty; and his father and friends take part with his moderate desires, and the opposite party assist the opposite ones. As soon as these dire magicians and tyrant-makers find that they cannot keep their hold on him otherwise, they contrive to implant in him a master passion, to be the champion of his idle and spendthrift lusts – a sort of monstrous winged drone – that is the only image which will adequately describe him.

Yes, he said, that is the only adequate image of him.

And when other lusts, amid clouds of incense and perfumes and garlands and wines, and all the dissolute pleasures of such company, come buzzing around him, and when they implant in his dronelike nature the sting of desire, while they fatten and nourish him, then at last this lord of the soul, having Madness for the captain of his guard, breaks out into a frenzy; and if he finds in the man such opinions or appetites as are deemed to be good, or still have the sense of shame about them, he kills them and casts them forth until he has purged away all temperance and brought in madness to the full.

Yes, he said, that is the way in which the tyrannical man is generated.

And is not this the reason why of old love has been called a tyrant?

I should not wonder.

Further, I said, has not a drunken man also the spirit of a tyrant?

He has.

And you know that a man who is deranged and not right in his mind, will fancy that he is able to rule, not only over men, but also over the gods?

That he will.

And the tyrannical man in the true sense of the word comes into being when, either under the influence of nature, or habit, or both, he becomes drunken, lustful, passionate? O my friend, is not that so?

Assuredly.

Such is the man and such is his origin. And next, how does he live?

Suppose, as people facetiously say, you were to tell me.

I imagine, I said, that at the next step in his progress there will be feasts and carousals and revellings and courtesans, and all that sort of thing; Love is the lord of the house within him, and orders all the concerns of his soul.

That is certain.

Yes; and every day and every night new offshoots of desire grow up many and formidable, and their demands are many.

They are indeed, he said.

His revenues, if he has any, are soon spent.

True.

Then comes borrowing and the cutting down of his capital.

Of course.

When he has nothing left, must not his desires, crowding in the nest like young ravens, be crying aloud for food; and he, goaded on by them, and especially by Lust himself, who has all the other passions for his bodyguard, is in a frenzy, and would fain discover whom he can defraud or despoil of his property, in order that he may gratify them?

Yes, that is sure to be the case.

He must plunder, no matter how, if he is to escape horrid pains and pangs.

He must.

And as in himself there was a succession of pleasures, and the new got the better of the old and took away their rights, so he being younger will claim to have more than his father and his mother, and if he has spent his own share of the property, he will take a slice of theirs.

No doubt he will.

And if his parents will not give way, then he will try first of all to cheat and deceive them.

Very true.

And if he fails, then he will use force and plunder them.

Yes, probably.

And if the old man and woman fight for their own, what then, my friend? Will he feel any compunction or shrink from any act of a tyrant?

Nay, he said, I should not feel at all comfortable about his parents.

But, O heavens! Adeimantus, on account of some sudden fancy for a harlot, who is anything but a necessary connection, can you believe that he would strike the mother who is his ancient friend and necessary to his very existence, and would place her under the authority of the other, when she is brought under the same roof with her; or that, under like circumstances, he would do the same to his withered old father, first and most indispensable of friends, for the sake of some newly found blooming youth who is the reverse of indispensable?

Yes, indeed, he said; I believe that he would.

Truly, then, I said, a tyrannical son is a blessing to his father and mother.

He is indeed, he replied.

But when the property of his father and mother has been spent, and pleasures are beginning to swarm in the hive of his soul, then he breaks into a house, or steals the garments of some nightly wayfarer; next he proceeds to clear a temple. Meanwhile the old opinions about good and evil, which he has had from childhood, and which have been accounted just, are overthrown by those others which were lately emancipated, and are now the bodyguard of Lust and share his empire. These in his democratic days, when he was still subject to the laws and to his father, were only let loose in the dreams of sleep. But now that he is under the dominion of Lust, he becomes always and in waking reality what he was then very rarely and in a dream only; he will not abstain from the foulest murder, or from forbidden food, or from any other horrid act. Lust is his tyrant, and lives in him in complete anarchy and lawlessness, and being himself sole king leads him on, as a tyrant leads a state, to the performance of any reckless deed by which he can maintain himself and the rabble of his associates, whether those whom evil communications have brought in from without, or those whom he himself has allowed to break loose within him by reason of a similar evil nature in himself. Have we not here a picture of his way of life?

Yes, indeed, he said.

And if there are only a few of them in the state and the rest of the people are well disposed, they go away and become the bodyguard of some other tyrant, or mercenary soldiers if there is war anywhere; and if they arise in time of peace and quiet, they stay at home and do many little pieces of mischief in the city.

What sort of mischief?

For example, they are the thieves, burglars, cut-purses, footpads, robbers of temples, man-stealers of the community; or if they are able to speak they turn informers, and bear false witness, and take bribes.

Such mischief is slight, perhaps, if the perpetrators are few in number.

Yes, I said; but small and great are comparative terms, and all these things, in the misery and evil which they inflict upon a state, do not come within a thousand miles of the tyrant; when this noxious class and their followers grow numerous and become conscious of their strength, it is they who, assisted by the infatuation of the people, create the tyrant, choosing from among themselves the one who has most of the tyrant in his own soul.

Naturally, he said, since he will be the most fit to be a tyrant.

If the people yield, well and good; but if they resist him, as he began by beating his own father and mother, so now, if he has the power, he beats them, and will keep his dear old fatherland, or motherland as the Cretans say, in subjection to his young retainers whom he has introduced to be their rulers and masters. And so such a man attains the end of his passions and desires.

Exactly in this way.

When such men are only private individuals and before they get power, this is their character; they associate entirely with their own flatterers or ready tools; or if they want anything from anybody, they in their turn are equally ready to bow down before them and perform every gesture of friendship for them; but when they have gained their point they know them no more.

Yes, truly.

They are always either the masters or servants and never the friends of anybody; the tyrannical nature never tastes of true freedom or friendship.

Certainly not.

And may we not rightly call such men faithless?

No question.

Also they are utterly unjust, if we were right in our agreement as to the nature of justice?

Indeed, he said, we were perfectly right.

Let us then sum up in a word, I said, the character of the worst man: he is the waking reality of what we dreamed.

Most true.

And this is he who being by nature most of a tyrant bears rule, and the longer he lives the more of a tyrant he becomes.

That is certain, said Glaucon, taking his turn to answer.

And will not he who has been shown to be the wickedest, also be proved the most miserable? And he who has tyrannised longest and most, most continually and deeply miserable, although this may not be the opinion of men in general?

Yes, he said, inevitably.

And must not the tyrannical man be like the tyrannical state, and the democratical man like the democratical state; and the same of the others?

Certainly.

And as state is to state in virtue and happiness, so is man in relation to man?

To be sure.

Then comparing our original city, which was under a king, and the city which is under a tyrant, how do they stand as to virtue?

They are the opposite extremes, he said, for one is the very best and the other is the very worst.

I will not ask you, I said, which is which, for it is evident; but would you arrive at a similar decision about their relative happiness and misery? And here we must not allow ourselves to be panic-stricken at the apparition of the tyrant, who is only a unit and may perhaps have a few retainers about him; but let us go as we ought into every corner of the city and look all about, and then we will give our opinion.

A fair challenge, he replied; and everyone must see that no city is more miserable than that which is governed by a tyrant, and none happier than that ruled by a king.

And in estimating the men too, may I not fairly offer a like challenge, that I should have a judge whose mind can enter into and see through human nature? He must not be like a child who looks at the outside and is dazzled at the pompous aspect which the tyrannical nature assumes to the beholder, but let him be one who has a clear insight. May I suppose that the judgment is given in the hearing of us all by one who is able to judge, and has dwelt in the same place with him, and been present at his domestic life and known him in his family relations, where he may best be seen stripped of his tragedy attire, and again in the hour of public danger – he shall tell us about the happiness and misery of the tyrant when compared with other men?

That again, he said, is a very fair proposal.

Do you permit me, then, to assume that we ourselves are able and experienced judges who have before now met with such persons? We shall then have someone who will answer our inquiries.

By all means.

Let me ask you not to forget the parallel of the individual and the state; bearing this in mind, and glancing in turn from one to the other of them, will you tell me their respective conditions?

To what do you refer? he asked.

Beginning with the state, I replied, would you say that a city which is governed by a tyrant is free or enslaved?

No city, he said, can be more completely enslaved.

And yet, as you see, there are freemen as well as masters in such a state?

Yes, he said, I see that there are – a few; but the people, speaking generally, and the best of them, are miserably degraded and enslaved.

Then if the man is like the state, I said, must not the same rule prevail? His soul is full of meanness and vulgarity – the best elements in him are enslaved; and he is despotically governed by that small part, which is also the worst and maddest.

Inevitably.

And would you say that the soul of such a one is the soul of a freeman, or of a slave?

He has the soul of a slave, in my opinion.

And the state which is enslaved under a tyrant is utterly incapable of acting as it desires?

Utterly incapable.

And also the soul which is under a tyrant (I am speaking of the soul taken as a whole) will be least capable of doing what she desires; there is a gadfly which goads her, and she will be full of confusion and remorse?

Certainly.

And is the city which is under a tyrant of necessity rich or poor?

Poor.

Therefore, the tyrannical soul also must be always poor and insatiable?

True.

Again, must not such a state, and likewise such a man, be always full of fear?

Yes, indeed.

Is there any state in which you will find more of lamentation and mourning and groaning and pain?

Certainly not.

And is there any man in whom you will find more of

this sort of misery than in this tyrannical man, who is maddened by his desires and passions?

Impossible.

Reflecting upon these and similar evils, you held the tyrannical state to be the most miserable of states?

Was I not right? he said.

Certainly, I said. And when you see the same evils in the tyrannical man, what do you say of him?

I say that he is by far the most miserable of all men.

There, I said, I think that you are beginning to go wrong.

What do you mean?

I do not think that he has as yet reached the utmost extreme of misery.

Then who is more miserable?

One of whom I am about to speak.

Who is that?

He who is of a tyrannical nature, and instead of leading a private life has been cursed with the further misfortune of becoming a public tyrant.

From what has been said, I gather that you are right.

Yes, I replied, but this high argument requires not mere belief, but earnest logical inquiry; for of all questions, this respecting a good or an evil life is the greatest.

Very true, he said.

Let me then offer you an illustration, which may, I think, throw a light upon this subject.

What is your illustration?

The case of rich individuals in cities who possess many slaves: for they have this in common with the tyrant, that they are masters of many; the only difference is that he is master of more.

Yes, that is the difference.

You know that they live securely and have nothing to apprehend from their servants?

What should they fear?

Nothing. But do you observe the reason of this?

Yes; the reason is, that the whole city is leagued together for the protection of each individual.

Very true, I said. But imagine one of these owners, the master say of some fifty slaves, or even more, together with his family and property and slaves, carried off by a god into the wilderness, where there are no freemen to help him – will he not be in an agony of fear lest he and his wife and children should be put to death by his slaves?

Yes, he said, he will be in the utmost fear.

The time has arrived when he will be compelled to fawn upon some of his slaves, and make large promises to them, and set them free, though he is under no obligation to do so – he will find himself the flatterer of his own servants.

Yes, he said, that will be the only way of saving himself.

And suppose the same god, who carried him away, to surround him with neighbours who will not suffer one man to be the master of another, and who, if they could catch any offender, would inflict extreme punishment upon him?

His case will be still worse, if you suppose him to be everywhere surrounded and watched by enemies.

And is not this the sort of prison in which the tyrant will be bound – he who being by nature such as we have described, is full of all sorts of fears and lusts? His soul craves for pleasure and yet, alone of all men in the city, he is never allowed to go on a journey, or to see the things which other freemen desire to see, but he lives hidden in his house like a woman, and is jealous of any other citizen who goes into foreign parts and sees anything of interest.

Very true, he said.

So that these ills must be added to the account of the man who is ill-governed in his own person – the tyrannical man, I mean, whom you just now decided to be the most miserable of all – when, instead of leading a private life, he is constrained by fortune to be a public tyrant? He has to be master of others when he is not master of himself: he is like a diseased or paralytic man who is compelled to pass his life, not in retirement, but fighting and combating with other men.

Yes, Socrates, he said, the similitude is most exact and true.

Is not his case utterly miserable, my dear Glaucon? and does not the actual tyrant lead a more grievous life than he whose life you determined to be the most grievous?

Certainly.

He who is the real tyrant, whatever men may think, is the real slave, and is obliged to practise the greatest adulation and servility, and to be the flatterer of the vilest of mankind. He has desires which he is utterly unable to satisfy, and has more wants than anyone, and is truly poor, if you know how to inspect the whole soul of him: all his life long he is beset with fear and is full of convulsions and distractions, if his condition is like that of the state which he governs: and surely the resemblance holds?

Indeed it does, he said.

Moreover, we have still to add to his score something which we have already mentioned – that he is, and owing to his power steadily becomes, more jealous, more faithless, more unjust, more friendless, more impious, than he was at first; he is the purveyor and cherisher of every sort of vice, and the consequence is that he is supremely miserable, and that he makes his neighbours as miserable as himself.

No man of any sense will dispute your words.

Come then, I said, and as the final judge in a competition proclaims the result, do you also decide who in your opinion is first in the scale of happiness, and who second, and in what order the others follow: there are five of them in all – they are the royal, timocratical, oligarchical, democratical, tyrannical.

The decision will be easily given, he replied; the order of the entrance of these choruses upon the stage is also their order of merit in respect of virtue and vice, happiness and misery.

Need we hire a herald, or shall I announce, that the son of Ariston [the best] has decided that the best and justest is also the happiest, and that this is he who is the most royal man and king over himself; and that the worst and most unjust man is also the most miserable, and that this is he who being the greatest tyrant of himself is also the greatest tyrant of his state?

You may make that proclamation, he said.

And shall I add, 'whether the character of each is seen or unseen by gods and men'?

Let the words be added.

Then this, I said, will be our first proof; now consider another, which may also have some weight.

What is that?

Seeing that the individual soul, like the state, has been divided by us into three principles, the division may, I think, furnish a new demonstration.

Of what nature?

It is this. It seems to me that to these three principles three pleasures correspond; also three desires and governing powers.

How do you mean? he said.

There is one principle with which, according to our view, a man learns, another with which he is angry; the third has so many forms that we have not been able to give it a special name, but have denoted it by the general term appetitive, from the extraordinary strength and vehemence of the desires of eating and drinking and the other sensual appetites which are the main elements of it; also money-loving, because such desires are generally satisfied by the help of money.

We were right, he said.

If we were to say that the loves and pleasures of this third part were concerned with gain, we should then be back on a single general term, which would remind us of our meaning when we referred to this part of the soul; and we might truly describe it as loving gain or money.

I agree with you.

Again, is not the passionate principle always wholly set on ruling and conquering and getting fame?

True.

Suppose we call it the contentious or ambitious – would the term be suitable?

Extremely suitable.

On the other hand, everyone sees that the principle by which we learn is always wholly directed to the truth, and cares less than either of the others for gain or fame.

Far less.

'Lover of learning', 'lover of wisdom', are titles which we may fitly apply to that part of the soul?

Certainly.

Now does not this principle prevail in the souls of one class of men, and one of the others, as may happen, in those of other men?

Yes.

And this is the reason for our saying that there are three primary classes of men – lovers of wisdom, lovers of honour, lovers of gain?

Exactly.

And there are three kinds of pleasure, which are their several objects?

Very true.

Do you know that, if you examine the three classes of men, and ask of them in turn which of their lives is pleasantest, each will give the highest praise to his own life: the money-maker will contrast the vanity of honour or of learning if they bring no money with the advantages of gain?

True, he said.

And the lover of honour – what will be his opinion? Will he not think that the pleasure of riches is vulgar, while the pleasure of learning, if it brings no distinction, is all smoke and nonsense to him?

Very true.

And, lastly, the philosopher, I said, what worth are we to suppose that he ascribes to other pleasures in comparison with the pleasure of knowing the truth or of continual learning, which is a pleasure of the same order? Would he not think them far indeed from true pleasure? Does he not call the other pleasures necessary, under the idea that if there were no necessity for them, he would rather not have them?

There can be no doubt of that, he replied.

Since, then, the pleasures of each class are in

dispute, and concerning the lives also the question is asked, not which is more or less honourable, or better or worse, but which is the more pleasant or painless – how shall we know who speaks most truly?

I cannot myself tell, he said.

Well, ask yourself what critical powers are needed for any sound judgment. Could a man have better ones than experience and wisdom and reason?

Surely not, he said.

Then, I said, reflect. Of the three individuals, which has the greatest experience of all the pleasures which we enumerated? Would the lover of gain, learning the nature of essential truth, have greater experience of the pleasure of knowledge than the philosopher has of the pleasure of gain?

The philosopher, he replied, has greatly the advantage; for he has of necessity always known the taste of the other pleasures from his childhood upwards: but the lover of gain in all his experience has not of necessity tasted – or, I should rather say, even had he urgently desired, could hardly have tasted – the sweetness of learning and knowing truth.

Then the lover of wisdom has a great advantage over the lover of gain, for he has a double experience?

Yes, very great.

Compare him now with the lover of honour. Is he more inexperienced in the pleasures of honour, than the lover of honour in the pleasures of wisdom?

Nay, he said, all three are honoured in proportion as they attain the object which they set out to gain; for the rich man and the brave man and the wise man alike have their crowd of admirers, and as they all receive honour they all have experience of the pleasures of honour; but the delight which is to be found in the contemplation of true being is known to the philosopher only.

His experience, then, will enable him to judge better than any one?

Far better.

And then he is the only one who has wisdom as well as experience?

Certainly.

Further, the very instrument of judgment is not possessed by the covetous or ambitious man, but only by the philosopher?

What instrument?

We have said, I think, that the decision ought to be secured by reasoning?

Yes.

And reasoning is peculiarly his instrument?

Certainly.

If wealth and gain were the criterion, then the praise or blame of the lover of gain would surely be the most trustworthy?

Assuredly.

Or if honour or victory or courage, in that case the judgment of the ambitious or pugnacious would be the truest?

Clearly.

But since experience and wisdom and reason are the judges –

The only inference possible, he replied, is that pleasures which are approved by the lover of wisdom and reason are the truest.

And so we arrive at the result that the pleasure of the intelligent part of the soul is the pleasantest of the three, and that he of us in whom this is the ruling principle has the pleasantest life.

Unquestionably, he said, the wise man speaks with authority when he approves of his own life.

And what does the judge affirm to be the life which is next, and the pleasure which is next?

Clearly that of the soldier and lover of honour; who is nearer to himself than the money-maker.

Last comes the lover of gain?

Very true, he said.

Twice in succession, then, has the just man overthrown the unjust in this conflict; and now comes the third trial, which is dedicated to Olympian Zeus the saviour: a sage whispers in my ear that no pleasure except that of the wise is quite true and pure – all others are a shadow only; and surely this will prove the greatest and most decisive of falls?

Yes, the greatest; but what is your meaning?

I hope to find out the truth by searching while you answer my questions.

Proceed.

Say, then, do we not think that pleasure is opposed to pain?

True.

And that there is a neutral state which is neither pleasure nor pain?

There is.

A state which, being intermediate, is a sort of repose of the soul in respect of either – that is what you mean?

Yes.

You remember what people say when they are sick?

What do they say?

That after all nothing is pleasanter than health; but that they never knew this to be the greatest of pleasures until they were ill.

I remember, he said.

And when persons are suffering from acute pain, you must have heard them say that there is nothing pleasanter than to get rid of one's pain?

I have.

And you are aware of many other cases of suffering in which the mere relief from and cessation of pain, and not any positive enjoyment, is extolled by the sufferers as the greatest pleasure?

Perhaps, he said, their notion of pleasure at such a time is rest, and this contents them.

It should follow that, when pleasure ceases, that sort of rest or cessation will be painful?

Perhaps, he said.

Then the intermediate state of rest will be pleasure and will also, at another time, be pain?

So it would seem.

But can that which is neither become both?

I should say not.

Then again, both pleasure and pain are motions occurring in the soul, are they not?

Yes.

But that which is neither was just now shown to be a state of rest, intermediate between these?

It was.

How, then, can it be right to suppose that the absence of pain is pleasure, or that the absence of pleasure is pain?

Impossible.

This then is an appearance only and not a reality; that is to say, the tranquil state appears to be pleasure at the moment and in comparison with what is painful, and painful in comparison with what is pleasant; but all these representations, when tried by the test of true pleasure, are not real but a sort of imposition?

That is the inference.

Look at a new class of pleasures, which have no antecedent pains, and you will no longer suppose, as you perhaps may at present, that pleasure is only the cessation of pain, or pain of pleasure.

What are they, he said, and where shall I find them?

There are many of them: but as an example I would have you notice the pleasures of smell, which occur suddenly, without previous pain, and in great intensity, and when they depart leave no pain behind them.

Most true, he said.

Let us not, then, be induced to believe that pure pleasure is the cessation of pain, or pain of pleasure.

No.

Still, the more numerous and violent of the pleasures so called which reach the soul through the body are generally of this sort – they are reliefs of pain.

They are.

And the anticipatory pleasures and pains which arise from the expectation of these are of a like nature?

Yes.

Shall I give you an illustration of them?

Let me hear.

You would allow, I said, that there is in nature an upper and lower and middle region?

I should.

And if a person were to go from the lower to the middle region, would he not imagine that he is going up; and he who is standing in the middle and sees whence he has come, would imagine that he is already in the upper region, if he has never seen the true upper world?

To be sure, he said; how, in his position, can he think otherwise?

But if he were taken back again he would imagine, and truly imagine, that he was descending?

No doubt.

All that would arise out of his ignorance of the true upper and middle and lower regions?

Yes.

Then can you wonder that persons who are inexperienced in the truth, as they have wrong ideas about many other things, should also have wrong ideas about pleasure and pain and the intermediate state; so that when they are only being drawn towards the painful they feel pain and think the pain which they experience to be real, and in like manner, when drawn away from pain to the neutral or intermediate state, they firmly believe that they have reached the goal of satiety and pleasure; having no experience of pleasure, they can only compare pain with the absence of pain, and are subject to the same sort of illusion as those who contrast black with grey from inexperience of white – can you wonder, I say, at this?

No, indeed; I should be much more disposed to wonder at the opposite.

Look at the matter thus: hunger, thirst, and the like, are inanitions of the bodily state?

Yes.

And ignorance and folly are states of emptiness in the soul?

True.

And taking food and the acquisition of wisdom are the corresponding processes of replenishment?

Certainly.

And is the satisfaction derived from that which has less or from that which has more existence the truer?

Clearly, from that which has more.

What classes of things have a greater share of pure existence in your judgment – those of which food and drink and condiments and all kinds of sustenance are examples, or the class which contains true opinion and knowledge and mind and all the different kinds of virtue? Put the question in this way: which has a more pure being – that which is concerned with the invariable, the immortal, and the true, and is itself of such a nature, and is found in such natures, or that which is concerned with and found in the ever variable and mortal, and is itself variable and mortal?

Far purer, he replied, is the being of that which is concerned with the invariable.

And does the real being of the invariable partake of knowledge in any less degree than of reality?

By no means.

And of truth in the same degree?

Yes.

And, conversely, that which has less of truth will also have less of reality?

Necessarily.

Then, in general, those kinds of things which are in the service of the body have less of both truth and reality than those which are in the service of the soul?

Far less.

And do you not agree that the body itself has less of these than the soul?

Yes.

That which is being filled with things more real, and itself has a more real existence, is more really filled than that which is being filled with less real existence and is less real?

Of course.

And if pleasure consists in being filled with that which

is naturally suitable, that which is more really filled with more real being will more really and truly enjoy true pleasure; whereas that which participates in less real being will be less truly and surely satisfied, and will participate in a less trustworthy and less real pleasure?

Unquestionably.

Those then who know not wisdom and virtue, and are always busy with gluttony and sensuality, are carried down and up again as far as the mean; and in this region they move at random throughout life, but they never pass beyond into the true upper world; thither they neither look, nor do they ever find their way, neither are they truly filled with true being, nor do they taste of pure and abiding pleasure. Like cattle, with their eyes always looking down and their heads stooping to the earth, that is, to the dining-table, they fatten and feed and breed, and, in order to obtain the chief share of these delights, they kick and butt at one another with horns and hoofs which are made of iron; and they kill one another by reason of their insatiable lust. For they fill themselves with that which is not real, and the part of themselves which they fill is also neither real nor retentive.

Verily, Socrates, said Glaucon, you describe the life of the many like an oracle.

Must they not, then, embrace pleasures which are mixed with pains and which are mere shadows and sketches of the true, and are so coloured by the contrast, which exaggerates both light and shade, that they implant in the minds of fools insane desires of themselves; and they are fought about as Stesichorus says that the Greeks fought about the shadow of Helen at Troy in ignorance of the truth?

Something of that sort must inevitably happen.

And must not the like happen with the spirited or

passionate element of the soul? Will not the passionate man who carries his passion into action be in the like case, whether he is envious and ambitious, or violent and contentious, or angry and discontented, if he be seeking to satisfy his anger or his passion for honour and victory without reason or sense?

Yes, he said, the same will happen with the spirited element also.

Then may we not confidently assert that whatever desires are associated with the love of money and honour, when they seek their pleasures under the guidance and in the company of reason and knowledge, and pursue after and win the pleasures which wisdom shows them, will also secure the truest pleasures in the highest degree which is attainable to them, inasmuch as they follow truth; and they will have the pleasures which are natural to them, if that which is best for each one is also most natural to him?

Yes, certainly; the best is the most natural.

And so, when the whole soul follows the philosophical principle and there is no division, the several parts are just and do each of them their own business; but besides this they enjoy severally the best and truest pleasures of which they are capable?

Exactly.

But when either of the two other principles prevails, it fails in attaining its own pleasure, and compels the rest to pursue after a pleasure which is a shadow only and which is not their own?

True.

And the greater the interval which separates them from philosophy and reason, the more strange and illusive will be the pleasure?

Yes, much more.

And is not that farthest from reason which is at the greatest distance from law and order?

Clearly.

And the lustful and tyrannical desires are, as we saw, at the greatest distance?

Yes, by far.

And the royal and orderly desires are nearest?

Yes.

Then the tyrant will live at the greatest distance from true or natural pleasure, and the king at the least?

Certainly.

But if so, the tyrant will live most unpleasantly, and the king most pleasantly?

Inevitably.

Would you know the measure of the interval which separates them?

Will you tell me?

There appear to be three pleasures, one genuine and two spurious: now the transgression of the tyrant reaches a point beyond the spurious; he has run away from the region of law and reason, and taken up his abode with certain slave pleasures which are his satellites, and the measure of his inferiority cannot easily be expressed, except in this way.

How? he asked.

I assume, I said, that the tyrant is in the third place from the oligarch; the democrat was in the middle?

Yes.

And if there is truth in what has preceded, he will be wedded to an image of pleasure which is thrice removed as to truth from the pleasure of the oligarch?

He will.

And the oligarch is third from the royal; since we count as one royal and aristocratical?

Yes, he is third.

Then the tyrant is removed from true pleasure by the space of a number which is three times three?

Apparently.

The shadow then of tyrannical pleasure determined by the number of length will be a plane figure.

Certainly.

And if you raise the power and make the plane a solid, it is clear how vast is the interval by which the tyrant is parted from the king.

Clear, he said, to the arithmetician.

Or if some person begins at the other end and measures the interval by which the king is parted from the tyrant in truth of pleasure, he will find him, when the multiplication is completed, living 729 times more pleasantly, and the tyrant more painfully by this same interval.

What a wonderful calculation! And what an over-whelming expression of the distance which separates the just from the unjust in regard to pleasure and pain!

Yet a true calculation, I said, and a number which nearly concerns human life, if human beings are concerned with days and nights and months and years.

Yes, he said, human life is certainly concerned with them.

Then if the good and just man be thus superior in pleasure to the evil and unjust, his superiority will be infinitely greater in propriety of life and in beauty and virtue?

Immeasurably greater.

[*the final conclusion is drawn that injustice is never beneficial – not even to someone who acts unjustly and gets away with it*]

361

*[after a short digression on poets, and imitation in art,
the benefits of justice are reviewed]*

And yet we have not described the greatest prizes and
rewards which await virtue.

What, are there any greater still? If there are, they
must be of an inconceivable greatness.

Why, I said, what was ever great in a short time? The
whole period from childhood to age is surely but a little
thing in comparison with eternity?

Say rather 'nothing', he replied.

And should an immortal being be anxious for this
little time rather than for the whole?

For the whole, certainly. But why do you ask?

Are you not aware, I said, that the soul of man is
immortal and imperishable?

He looked at me in astonishment, and said: No, by
heaven: and are you really prepared to maintain this?

Yes, I said, I ought to be, and you too – there is no
difficulty in proving it.

I see a great difficulty; but I should like to hear you
state this argument of which you make so light.

Listen then.

I am attending.

There is a thing which you call good and another
which you call evil?

Yes, he replied.

Would you agree with me in thinking that the
corrupting and destroying element is the evil, and the
saving and improving element the good?

True.

And you admit that everything has a good and also an evil; as ophthalmia is the evil of the eyes and disease of the whole body; as blight is of corn, and rot of timber, or rust of copper and iron: in everything, or in almost everything, there is an inherent evil and disease?

Yes, he said.

And any of these evils, when it attacks a thing, first makes it rotten and at last wholly dissolves and destroys it?

True.

The vice and evil which is inherent in each is the destruction of each; or if this does not destroy them there is nothing else that will; for good certainly will never destroy anything, nor, again, will that which is neither good nor evil.

Certainly not.

If, then, we find any nature which has indeed some inherent corruption, but of a kind whereby it cannot be dissolved or destroyed, we may be certain that of such a nature there is no destruction?

That may be assumed.

Well, I said, and is there no evil which corrupts the soul?

Yes, he said, there are all the evils which we were just now passing in review: unrighteousness, intemperance, cowardice, ignorance.

But does any of these dissolve and destroy her? And here do not let us fall into the error of supposing that the unjust and foolish man, when he is detected, perishes through his own injustice, which is an evil of the soul. You should represent it rather in this way: The evil of the body is a disease which dissolves and wastes it, till it is no longer a body at all; and all the things of which we were just now speaking come to annihilation through their own corruption attaching to them and inhering in them and so destroying them. Is not this true?

Yes.

Consider the soul in like manner. Does injustice, or vice in some other form, waste and consume her? Do they by attaching to the soul and inhering in her at last bring her to death, and so separate her from the body?

Certainly not.

And yet, I said, it is unreasonable to suppose that anything can perish under a disease proper to another thing, which could not be destroyed by a corruption of its own?

It is, he replied.

Consider, I said, Glaucon, that even the badness of food, whether staleness, decomposition, or any other bad quality, when confined to the actual food, is not supposed to destroy the body; although, if the badness of food causes the body to become corrupt in its own fashion, then we should say that the body has been destroyed by a corruption of itself, which is disease, brought on by this; but that the body, being one thing, can be destroyed by the badness of food, which is another, unless it has implanted the corruption peculiar to the body – this we shall absolutely deny?

Very true.

On the same principle, then, unless some bodily evil can produce in the soul an evil of the soul, we must not suppose that the soul, which is one thing, can be dissolved, in the absence of its own disease, by any evil which belongs to another?

Yes, he said, there is reason in that.

Either, then, let us refute this conclusion, or, while it remains unrefuted, let us never say that fever, or any other disease, or the knife put to the throat, or even the cutting up of the whole body into the minutest pieces, can destroy the soul, until she herself is proved to become more unholy or unrighteous in consequence of these things being done to the body; but that the soul or anything else can be free from its special evil and yet be destroyed because a foreign evil is found in something else, is not to be affirmed by any man.

And surely, he replied, no one will ever prove that the souls of dying men become more unjust in consequence of death.

But if someone, lest he be obliged to admit the immortality of the soul, boldly goes out to meet our argument, and says that the dying do really become more evil and unrighteous, then, if the speaker is right, I suppose that injustice, like disease, must be assumed to be fatal to the unjust, and that those who take this disorder die by the natural inherent power of destruction which evil has, and which kills them sooner or later, but in quite another way from that in which, at present, the wicked receive death at the hands of others as the penalty of their deeds?

Nay, he said, in that case injustice, if fatal to the unjust, will not be so very terrible to him, for he will thus be delivered from evil. But I rather suspect the opposite will prove to be the truth, and that injustice which, if it have the power, will murder others, gives the murderer greater vitality – aye, and keeps him well awake too; so far removed is her dwelling-place from being a house of death.

True, I said; if the inherent natural vice or evil of the soul has not the force to kill or destroy her, hardly will that which is appointed to be the destruction of some other body destroy a soul, or anything else except that of which it was appointed to be the destruction.

Yes, that can hardly be.

But the soul which cannot be destroyed by any evil, whether its own or that of something else, must exist for ever, and if existing for ever, must be immortal?

Certainly.

Let that be our conclusion, I said; and, if it is a true conclusion, you will observe that the souls must always be the same, for if none be destroyed they will not diminish in number. Neither will they increase, for the increase of the immortal natures must, as you know, come from something mortal, and all things would thus end in immortality.

Very true.

But this we cannot believe – reason will not allow us – any more than we can believe the soul, in her truest nature, to be a thing full of variety and internal difference and dissimilarity.

What do you mean? he said.

It is not easy, I said, for that thing to be immortal which is a compound of many elements not perfectly adapted to each other, as the soul has appeared to us to be.

Certainly not.

Her immortality is demonstrated by the previous argument, and there are many other proofs; but to see her as she really is, not, as we now behold her, marred by association with the body and other miseries, you must contemplate her with the eye of reason, in her original purity; and then her greater beauty will be revealed, and the forms of justice and injustice and all the things which we have described will be more vividly discerned. Thus far, we have spoken the truth concerning her as she appears at present, but we have seen her only in a condition which may be compared to that of the sea-god Glaucus, whose original nature could hardly be discerned by those who saw him because his natural members were either broken off or crushed and damaged by the waves in all sorts of ways, and encrustations had grown over them of seaweed and shells and stones, so that he was more like some monster than to his own natural form. And the soul which we behold is in a similar condition, disfigured by ten thousand ills. But not there, Glaucon, not there must we look.

Where then?

At her love of wisdom. Let us see whom she affects, and what society and converse she seeks in virtue of her near kindred with the immortal and eternal and divine; also how different she would become if wholly following this superior principle, and borne by a divine impulse out of the ocean in which she now is, and disengaged from the stones and shells and things of earth and rock which in wild variety spring up around her because she feeds upon earth, and is overgrown by the good things of this life as they are termed: then you would see her as she is, and know whether she have one shape only or many, or what her nature and state may be. Of her affections and of the forms which she takes in this present life I think that we have now given a very fair description.

True, he replied.

And thus, I said, we have disproved the charges brought against justice without introducing the rewards and glories, which, as you were saying, are to be found ascribed to her in Homer and Hesiod;

but justice in her own nature has been shown to be best for the soul in her own nature. Let a man do what is just, whether he have the ring of Gyges or not, and even if in addition to the ring of Gyges he put on the helmet of Hades.

Very true.

And now, Glaucon, there will be no harm in further enumerating how many and how great are the rewards which justice and the other virtues procure to the soul from gods and men, both in life and after death.

Certainly not, he said.

Will you repay me, then, what you borrowed in the argument?

What did I borrow?

The assumption that the just man should appear unjust and the unjust just: for you were of opinion that even if the true state of the case could not possibly escape the eyes of gods and men, still this admission ought to be made for the sake of the argument, in order that pure justice might be weighed against pure injustice. Do you remember?

The injustice would be mine if I had forgotten.

Then, as the cause is decided, I demand on behalf of justice that we should admit the estimation in which she is held by gods and men to be what it really is; since she has been shown to confer the blessings which come from reality, and not to deceive those who truly possess her, let what has been taken from her be given back, that so she may win that palm of appearance which is hers also, and which she gives to her own.

The demand, he said, is just.

In the first place, I said – and this is the first thing which you will have to give back – the nature both of the just and unjust is truly known to the gods.

Granted.

And if they are both known to them, one must be the friend and the other the enemy of the gods, as we admitted from the beginning?

True.

And the friend of the gods may be supposed to receive in its best form whatever the gods bestow, excepting only such evil as may have been the necessary consequence of former sins?

Certainly.

Then this must be our notion of the just man, that even when he is in poverty or sickness, or any other seeming misfortune, these things will bring him finally to some good end, either in life, or perhaps in death; for the gods surely will not neglect anyone whose earnest desire is to become just and by the pursuit of virtue to be like god, as far as man can attain the divine likeness?

Yes, he said; if he is like god he will surely not be neglected by him.

And of the unjust must not the opposite be supposed?

Certainly.

Such, then, are the palms of victory which the gods give the just?

That, at least, is my conviction.

And what do they receive of men? Look at things as they really are, and you will see that the clever unjust are in the case of runners, who run well from the starting-place to the goal but not back again from the goal: they go off at a great pace, but in the end only look foolish, slinking away with their ears draggling on their shoulders, and without a crown; but the true runner comes to the finish and receives the prize and is crowned. And this is the way with the just; they endure to the end of every action and association, and of life itself, and so win a good report and carry off the prizes which men have to bestow.

True.

Will you then allow me to repeat of the just the blessings which you were attributing to the fortunate unjust? I shall say of them that as they grow older they become rulers in their own city if they care to be; they marry whom they like and give in marriage to whom they will; all that you said of the others I now say of these. And, on the other hand, of the unjust I say that the greater number, even though they escape in their youth, are found out at last and look foolish at the end of their course, and when they come to be old and miserable are flouted alike by stranger and citizen; they are beaten, and then come those things unfit for ears polite, as you truly term them; they will be racked and have their eyes burned out, as you were saying. And you may suppose that I have repeated the remainder of your tale of horrors. I ask once more, will you allow all this?

Certainly, he said, for what you say is true.

These, then, are the prizes and rewards and gifts which are bestowed upon the just by gods and men in this present life, in addition to the other good things which justice of herself provides.

Yes, he said; and they are fair and lasting.

And yet, I said, all these are as nothing either in number or greatness in comparison with those other recompenses which await both just and unjust after death. And you ought to hear them, and then both just and unjust will have received from us a full payment of the debt which the argument owes to them.

Speak, he said; there are few things which I would more gladly hear.

Well, I said, I will tell you a tale; not one of the tales which Odysseus tells to the hero Alcinous, yet this too is a tale of a hero, Er the son of Armenius, a Pamphylian by birth. He was slain in battle, and ten days afterwards, when the bodies of the dead were taken up already in a state of corruption, his body was found unaffected by decay, and carried away home to be buried. And on the twelfth day, as he was lying on the funeral pile, he returned to life and told them what he had seen in the other world. He said that when his soul left the body it went on a journey with a great company, and that they came to a mysterious place at which there were two openings in the earth; they were near together, and over against them were two other openings in the heaven above. In the intermediate space there were judges seated, who commanded the just, after they had given judgment on them and had bound their sentences in front of them, to ascend by the way up through the heaven on the right hand; and in like manner the unjust were bidden by them to descend by the lower way on the left hand; these also bore tokens of all their deeds, but fastened on their backs. He drew near, and they told him that he was to be the messenger who would carry the report of the other world to men, and they bade him hear and see all that was to be heard and seen in that place. Then he beheld and saw on one side the souls departing at either opening of heaven and earth when sentence had been given on them; and at the two other openings other souls, some ascending out of the earth dusty and worn with travel, some descending out of heaven clean and bright. And arriving ever and anon they seemed to have come from a long journey, and they went forth with gladness into the meadow, where they encamped as at a festival; and those who knew one another embraced and conversed, the souls which came from earth curiously inquiring about the things above, and the souls which came from heaven about the things beneath. And they told one another of what had happened by the way, those from below weeping and sorrowing at the remembrance of the things which they had endured and seen in their journey beneath the earth (now the journey lasted a thousand years), while those from above were describing heavenly delights and visions of inconceivable beauty. The full story, Glaucon, would take too long to tell; but the sum was this: he said that for every wrong which they had done and every person whom they had injured they had suffered tenfold; or once in a hundred years – such being reckoned to be the length of man's life, and the penalty being thus paid ten times in a thousand years. If, for example, there were any who had been the cause of many deaths by the betrayal of cities or armies, or had cast many into slavery, or been accessory to any other ill treatment, for all their offences, and on behalf of each man wronged, they were afflicted with tenfold pain, and the rewards of beneficence and justice and holiness were in the same proportion. I need hardly repeat what he said concerning young children dying almost as soon as they were born. Of piety and impiety to gods and parents, and of murder, there were retributions other and greater far which he described. He mentioned that he was present when one of the spirits asked another, 'Where is Ardiaeus the Great?' (Now this Ardiaeus lived a thousand years before the time of Er: he had been the tyrant of some

city of Pamphylia and had murdered his aged father
and his elder brother, and was said to have committed
many other abominable crimes.) The answer of the
other spirit was: 'He comes not hither and will never
come. And this', said he, 'was one of the dreadful
sights which we ourselves witnessed. We were at the
mouth of the cavern, and, having completed all our
experiences, were about to re-ascend, when of a
sudden, we saw Ardiaeus and several others, most of
whom were tyrants; but there were also some private
individuals who had been great criminals: they were
just, as they fancied, about to return into the upper
world, but the mouth, instead of admitting them, gave
a roar, whenever any of these whose wickedness was
incurable or who had not been sufficiently punished
tried to ascend; and then wild men of fiery aspect, who
were standing by and heard the sound, seized and
carried them off; but Ardiaeus and others they bound
head and foot and hand, and threw them down, and
flayed them with scourges, and dragged them along
the road outside the entrance, carding them on thorns
like wool, and declaring to the passers-by what were
their crimes, and that they were being taken away to be
cast into Tartarus.' And of all the many terrors of every
kind which they had endured, he said that there was
none like the terror which each of them felt at that
moment, lest they should hear the voice; and when
there was silence, one by one they ascended with
exceeding joy. These, said Er, were the penalties and
retributions, and there were blessings as great.

Now when each band which was in the meadow had
tarried seven days, on the eighth they were obliged to
proceed on their journey, and, on the fourth day after,
he said that they came to a place where they could

see from above a line of light, straight as a column, extending right through the whole heaven and through the earth, in colour resembling the rainbow, only brighter and purer; another day's journey brought them to the place, and there, in the midst of the light, they saw the ends of the chains of heaven let down from above: for this light is the belt of heaven, and holds together the circumference of the universe, like the under-girders of a trireme. From these ends is extended the spindle of Necessity, on which all the revolutions turn. The shaft and hook of this spindle are made of adamant, and the whorl is made partly of steel and also partly of other materials. The nature of the whorl is as follows; it is, in outward shape, like the whorl used on earth; and his description of it implied that there is one large hollow whorl which is quite scooped out, and into this is fitted another lesser one, and another, and another, and four others, making eight in all, like vessels which fit into one another; the whorls show their circular edges on the upper side, and on their lower side all together form one continuous whorl. This is pierced by the shaft which is driven home through the centre of the eighth. The first and outermost whorl has the rim broadest, and the seven inner whorls are narrower, in the following proportions – the sixth is next to the first in size, the fourth next to the sixth; then comes the eighth; the seventh is fifth, the fifth is sixth, the third is seventh, last and eighth comes the second. The largest [or fixed stars] is spangled, and the seventh [or sun] is brightest; the eighth [or moon] coloured by the reflected light of the seventh; the second and fifth [Saturn and Mercury] are in colour like one another, and yellower than the preceding; the third [Venus] has the whitest light;

374

the fourth [Mars] is reddish; the sixth [Jupiter] is in whiteness second. Now the whole spindle has the same motion; but, as the whole revolves in one direction, the seven inner circles move slowly in the other, and of these the swiftest is the eighth; next in swiftness are the seventh, sixth, and fifth, which move together; third in swiftness appeared to move, because of this contrary motion, the fourth; the third appeared fourth and the second fifth. The spindle turns on the knees of Necessity; and on the upper surface of each circle stands a siren, who goes round with them, chanting a single tone or note. The eight together form one harmony; and round about, at equal intervals, there is another band, three in number, each sitting upon her throne: these are the Fates, daughters of Necessity, who are clothed in white robes and have chaplets upon their heads, Lachesis and Clotho and Atropos, who accompany with their voices the harmony of the sirens – Lachesis singing of the past, Clotho of the present, Atropos of the future; Clotho from time to time assisting with a touch of her right hand the revolution of the outer circle of the whorl or spindle, and Atropos with her left hand touching and guiding the inner ones, and Lachesis laying hold of either in turn, first with one hand and then with the other.

When Er and the spirits arrived, their duty was to go at once to Lachesis; but first of all there came a prophet who arranged them in order; then he took from the knees of Lachesis lots and samples of lives, and having mounted a high pulpit, spoke as follows: 'Hear the word of Lachesis, the daughter of Necessity. Mortal souls, behold a new cycle of life and mortality. Your genius will not be allotted to you, but you will choose your genius; and let him who draws the first lot have the first choice, and the life which he chooses shall be his destiny. Virtue is free, and as a man honours or dishonours her he will have more or less of her; the responsibility is with the chooser – God is not responsible.' When the Interpreter had thus spoken he scattered lots indifferently among them all, and each of them took up the lot which fell near him, all but Er himself (he was not allowed), and each as he took his lot perceived the number which he had obtained. Then the Interpreter placed on the ground before them the patterns of lives; and there were many more lives than the souls present, and they were of all sorts. There were lives of every animal and of man in every condition. And there were tyrannies among them, some lasting out the tyrant's life, others which broke off in the middle and came to an end in poverty and exile and beggary; and there were lives of famous men, some who were famous for their form and beauty as well as for their strength and success in games, or, again, for their birth and the qualities of their ancestors; and some who were the reverse of famous for the opposite qualities. And of women likewise. The disposition of the soul was not, however, included in them, because the soul, when choosing a new life, must of necessity become different. But there was every other quality, and they all mingled with one another, and also with elements of wealth and poverty, and disease and health; and there were also states intermediate in these respects.

And here, my dear Glaucon, is the supreme peril of our human state; and therefore each one of us must take the utmost care to forsake every other kind of knowledge and seek and study one thing only, if peradventure he may be able to discover someone who will make him able to discern between a good and an evil life, and so to choose always and everywhere the better life as he has opportunity. He should consider the bearing of all these things which have been mentioned severally and collectively upon the excellence of a life; he should know what the effect of beauty is, for good or evil, when combined with poverty or wealth in this or that kind of soul, and what are the good and evil consequences of noble and humble birth, of private and public station, of strength and weakness, of cleverness and dullness, and of all the natural and acquired gifts of the soul, and the operation of them when blended with one another; he will then look at the nature of the soul, and from the consideration of all these qualities he will be able to determine which is the better and which is the worse; and so he will choose, giving the name of evil to the life which will tend to make his soul more unjust, and good to the life which will make his soul more just; all else he will disregard. For we have seen and know that this is the best choice both in life and after death. A man must take with him into the world below an adamantine faith in truth and right, that there too he may be undazzled by the desire of wealth or the other allurements of evil, lest he be drawn into tyrannies and similar activities, and do irremediable wrongs to others and suffer yet worse himself; but may know how to choose a life moderate in these respects and avoid the extremes on either side, as far as possible, not only in this life but in all that which is to come. For this way brings men to their greatest happiness.

And according to the report of the messenger from

the other world this was what the prophet said at the time: 'Even for the last comer, if he chooses wisely and will live diligently, there is appointed a happy and not undesirable existence. Let not him who chooses first be careless, and let not the last despair.' And when he had spoken, he who had the first choice came forward and in a moment chose the greatest tyranny; his mind having been darkened by folly and sensuality, he had not made any thorough inspection before he chose, and did not perceive that he was fated, among other evils, to devour his own children. But when he had time to examine the lot and saw what was in it, he began to beat his breast and lament over his choice, forgetting the proclamation of the prophet; for, instead of throwing the blame of his misfortune on himself, he accused chance and the gods, and everything rather than himself. Now he was one of those who came from heaven, and in a former life had dwelt in a well-ordered state, virtuous from habit only, and without philosophy. And for the most part it was true of others who were caught in this way, that the greater number of them came from heaven and therefore they had never been schooled by trial, whereas the pilgrims who came from earth having themselves suffered and seen others suffer were not in a hurry to choose. And owing to this inexperience of theirs, and also to the accident of the lot, the majority of the souls exchanged a good destiny for an evil or an evil for a good. For if a man had always on his arrival in this world dedicated himself from the first to sound philosophy, and had been moderately fortunate in the number of the lot, he might, as the messenger reported, be happy here, and also his journey to another life and return to this, instead of being rough and underground, would be smooth and heavenly. Most curious, he said, was the spectacle – sad and laughable and strange; for the choice of the souls was in most cases based on their experience of a previous life. There he saw the soul which had once been Orpheus choosing the life of a swan out of enmity to the race of women, hating to be born of a woman because they had been his murderers; he beheld also the soul of Thamyras choosing the life of a nightingale; birds, on the other hand, like the swan and other musicians, wanting to be men. The soul which obtained the twentieth lot chose the life of a lion, and this was the soul of Ajax the son of Telamon, who would not be a man, remembering the injustice which was done him in the judgment about the arms. The next was Agamemnon, who took the life of an eagle, because, like Ajax, he hated human nature by reason of his sufferings. About the middle came the lot of Atalanta; she, seeing the great fame of an athlete, was unable to resist the temptation: and after her there followed the soul of Epeus the son of Panopeus passing into the nature of a woman skilled in some craft; and far away among the last who chose, the soul of the jester Thersites was putting on the form of a monkey. There came also the soul of Odysseus having yet to make a choice, and his lot happened to be the last of them all. Now the recollection of former toils had disenchanted him of ambition, and he went about for a considerable time in search of the life of a private man who had no cares; he had some difficulty in finding this, which was lying about and had been neglected by everybody else; and when he saw it, he said that he would have done the same had his lot been first instead of last, and gladly chose it. And not only did men pass into animals, but I must also mention that there were animals tame and wild who changed into one another and into corresponding human natures – the righteous into the gentle and the unrighteous into the savage, in all sorts of combinations.

All the souls had now chosen their lives, and they went in the order of their choice to Lachesis, who sent with them the genius whom they had severally chosen, to be the guardian of their lives and the fulfiller of the choice: this genius led the souls first to Clotho, and drew them within the revolution of the spindle impelled by her hand, thus ratifying the destiny of each; and then, when they were fastened to this, carried them to Atropos, who spun the threads and made them irreversible, whence without turning round they passed beneath the throne of Necessity; and when they had all passed, they marched on to the plain of Forgetfulness, in intolerable scorching heat, for the plain was a barren waste destitute of trees and verdure; and then towards evening they encamped by the river of Unmindfulness, whose water no vessel can hold; of this they were all obliged to drink a certain quantity, and those who were not saved by wisdom drank more than was necessary; and each one as he drank forgot all things. Now after they had gone to rest, about the middle of the night there was a thunderstorm and earthquake, and then in an instant they were driven upwards in all manner of ways to their birth, like stars shooting. He himself was hindered from drinking the water. But in what manner or by what means he returned to the body he could not say; only in the morning, awaking suddenly, he found himself lying on the pyre.

And thus, Glaucon, the tale has been saved and has not perished, and will save us if we are obedient to the word spoken; and we shall pass safely over the river of Forgetfulness and our soul will not be defiled. Wherefore my counsel is that we hold fast ever to the heavenly way and follow after justice and virtue always, considering that the soul is immortal and able to endure every sort of good and every sort of evil. Thus shall we live dear to one another and to the gods, both while remaining here and when, like conquerors in the games who go round to gather gifts, we receive our reward. And it shall be well with us both in this life and in the pilgrimage of a thousand years which we have been describing.

PHAEDRUS

PHAEDRUS

[*this short extract presents a slightly different picture of the tripartite soul from that given in the Republic*]

The soul through all her being is immortal, for that which is ever in motion is immortal; but that which moves another and is moved by another, in ceasing to move ceases also to live. Only the self-moving, since it cannot depart from itself, never ceases to move, and is the fountain and beginning of motion to all that moves besides. Now, the beginning is unbegotten, for that which is begotten must have a beginning; but this itself cannot be begotten of anything, for if it were dependent upon something, then the begotten would not come from a beginning. But since it is unbegotten, it must also be indestructible. For surely if a beginning were destroyed, then it could neither come into being itself from any source, nor serve as the beginning of other things, if it be true that all things must have a beginning.

Thus it is proved that the self-moving is the beginning of motion; and this can neither be destroyed nor begotten, else the whole heavens and all creation would collapse and stand still, and, lacking all power of motion, never again have birth. But whereas the self-moving is proved to be immortal, he who affirms that this is the very meaning and essence of the soul will not be put to confusion. For every body which is moved from without is soulless, but that which is self-moved from within is animate, and our usage makes it plain what is the nature of the soul. But if this be true, that the soul is identical with the self-moving, it must follow of necessity that the soul is unbegotten and immortal. Enough of her immortality: let us pass to the description of her form.

To show her true nature would be a theme of large and more than mortal discourse, but an image of it may be given in a briefer discourse within the scope of man; in this way, then, let us speak. Let the soul be compared to a pair of winged horses and charioteer joined in natural union. Now the horses and the charioteers of the gods are all of them noble and of noble descent, but those of other races are mixed. First, you must know that the human charioteer drives a pair; and next, that one of his horses is noble and of noble breed, and the other is ignoble and of ignoble breed; so that the management of the human chariot cannot but be a difficult and anxious task. I will endeavour to explain to you in what way the mortal differs from the immortal creature.

The soul in her totality has the care of inanimate being everywhere, and traverses the whole heaven in divers forms appearing; when perfect and fully winged she soars upward, and orders the whole world; whereas the imperfect soul, losing her wings and drooping in her flight at last settles on the solid ground – there, finding a home, she receives an earthly frame which appears to be self-moved, but is really moved by her power; and this composition of soul and body is called a living and mortal creature. For immortal no such union can be reasonably believed to be; although fancy, not having seen nor surely known the nature of god, may imagine an immortal creature having both a body and also a soul which are united throughout all time. Let that, however, be as god wills, and be spoken of acceptably to him. And now let us ask the reason why the soul loses her wings.

The wing is the corporeal element which is most akin to the divine, and which by nature tends to soar aloft and carry that which gravitates downwards into the upper region, which is the habitation of the gods. The divine is beauty, wisdom, goodness, and the like; and by these the wing of the soul is nourished, and grows apace; but when fed upon evil and foulness and the opposite of good, wastes and falls away. Zeus, the mighty lord, holding the reins of a winged chariot, leads the way in heaven, ordering all and taking care of all; and there follows him the array of gods and demi-gods, marshalled in eleven bands; Hestia alone abides at home in the house of heaven; of the rest they who are reckoned among the princely twelve march in their appointed order.

They see many blessed sights in the inner heaven, and there are many ways to and fro, along which the blessed gods are passing, every one doing his own work; he may follow who will and can, for jealousy has no place in the celestial choir. But when they go to banquet and festival, then they move up the steep to the top of the vault of heaven. The chariots of the gods in even poise, obeying the rein, glide rapidly; but the others labour, for the vicious steed goes heavily, weighing down the charioteer to the earth when his steed has not been thoroughly trained: and this is the hour of agony and extremest conflict for the soul. For the immortals, when they are at the end of their course, go forth and stand upon the outside of heaven; its revolution carries them round, and they behold the things beyond.

But of the heaven which is above the heavens, what earthly poet ever did or ever will sing worthily? It is such as I will describe; for I must dare to speak the truth, when truth is my theme. There abides the very being with which true knowledge is concerned; the colourless, formless, intangible essence, visible only to mind, the pilot of the soul. The divine intelligence, being nurtured upon mind and pure knowledge, and the intelligence of every soul which is capable of receiving the food proper to it, rejoices at beholding reality once more after so long a time, and gazing upon truth, is replenished and made glad, until the revolution of the world brings her round again to the same place. In the revolution she beholds justice, and temperance, and knowledge absolute, not that to which becoming belongs, nor that which is found, in varying forms, in one or other of those regions which we men call real, but real knowledge really present where true being is. And beholding the other true existences in like manner, and feasting upon them, she passes down into the interior of the heavens and returns home; and there the charioteer putting up his horses at the stall, gives them ambrosia to eat and nectar to drink.

Such is the life of the gods; but of other souls, that which follows god best and is likest to him lifts the head of the charioteer into the outer world, and is carried round in the revolution, troubled indeed by the steeds, and with difficulty beholding true being; while another only rises and falls, and sees, and again fails to see by reason of the unruliness of the steeds. The rest of the souls are also longing after the upper world and they all follow, but not being strong enough they are carried round below the surface, plunging, treading on one another, each striving to be first; and there is confusion and perspiration and the extremity of effort; and many of them are lamed or have their wings broken through the ill driving of the charioteers; and all of them after a fruitless toil, not having attained to the mysteries of true being, go away, and feed upon opinion [or appearance].

The reason why the souls exhibit this exceeding eagerness to behold the Plain of Truth is that pasturage is found there which is suited to the highest part of the soul; and the wing on which the soul soars is nourished with this. And there is a law of Destiny, that the soul which attains any vision of truth in company with a god is preserved from harm until the next period, and if attaining always is always unharmed. But when she is unable to follow, and fails to behold the truth, and through some ill-hap sinks beneath the double load of forgetfulness and vice, and her wings fall from her and she drops to the ground, then the law ordains that this soul shall at her first birth pass, not into any other animal, but only into man; and the soul which has seen most of truth shall be placed in the seed from which a philosopher, or artist, or some musical and loving nature will spring; that which has seen truth in the second degree shall be some righteous king or warrior chief; the soul which is of the third class shall be a politician, or economist, or trader; the fourth shall be a lover of gymnastic toils, or a physician; the fifth shall lead the life of a prophet or hierophant; to the sixth the character of a poet or some other imitative artist will be assigned; to the seventh the life of an artisan or husbandman; to the eighth that of a sophist or demagogue; to the ninth that of a tyrant; all these are states of probation, in which he who does righteously improves, and he who does unrighteously deteriorates, his lot.

Ten thousand years must elapse before the soul of each one can return to the place from whence she came, for she cannot grow her wings in less, save only the soul of a philosopher, guileless and true, or of a lover who has been guided by philosophy. And these when the third period comes round, if they have chosen this life three times in succession, have wings given them, and go away at the end of three thousand years. But the others receive judgment when they have completed their first life, and after the judgment they go, some of them to the houses of correction which are under the earth, and are punished; others to some place in heaven whither they are lightly borne by justice, and there they live in a manner worthy of the life which they led here when in the form of men.

And in the thousandth year, both arrive at a place where they must draw lots and choose their second life, and they may take any which they please. And now the soul of a man may pass into the life of a beast, or that which has once been a man return again from the beast into human form. But the soul which has never seen the truth will not pass into the human form. For a man must have intelligence by what is called the idea, a unity gathered together by reason from the many particulars of sense. This is the recollection of those things which our soul once saw while following god – when regardless of that which we now call being she raised her head up towards the true being.

And therefore the mind of the philosopher alone has wings; and this is just, for he is always, according to the measure of his abilities, clinging in recollection to those things in which god abides, and in beholding which he is what he is. And he who employs aright these memories is ever being initiated into perfect mysteries and alone becomes truly perfect. But, as he forgets earthly interests and is rapt in the divine, the vulgar deem him mad, and rebuke him; they do not see that he is inspired.

Thus far I have been speaking of the fourth and last kind of madness, which is imputed to him who, when he sees the beauty of earth, is transported with the recollection of the true beauty; he would like to fly away, but he cannot; he is like a bird fluttering and looking upward and careless of the world below; and he is therefore thought to be mad. And I have shown this of all inspirations to be the noblest and highest and the offspring of the highest to him who has or shares in it, and that he who loves the beautiful is called a lover because he partakes of it. For, as has been already said, every soul of man has in the way of nature beheld true being; this was the condition of her passing into the form of man. But all souls do not easily recall the things of the other world; they may have seen them for a short time only, or they may have been unfortunate in their earthly lot, and, having had their hearts turned to unrighteousness through some corrupting influence, they may have lost the memory of the holy things which once they saw. Few only retain an adequate remembrance of them; and they, when they behold here any image of that other world, are rapt in amazement; but they are ignorant of what this rapture means, because they do not clearly perceive. For there is no radiance in our earthly copies of justice or temperance or those other things which are precious to souls: they are seen through a glass dimly; and there are few who, going to the images, behold in them the realities, and these only with difficulty. But beauty could be seen, brightly shining, by all who were with that happy band – we philosophers following in the train of Zeus, others in company with other gods; at which time we beheld the beatific vision and were initiated into a mystery which may be truly called most blessed, celebrated by us in our state of innocence, before we had any experience of evils to come, when we were admitted to the sight of apparitions innocent and simple and calm and happy, which we beheld shining in pure light, pure ourselves and not yet enshrined in that living tomb which we carry about, now that we are imprisoned in the body, like an oyster in his shell. Let me linger over the memory of scenes which have passed away.

But of beauty, I repeat that we saw her there shining in company with the celestial forms; and coming to earth we find her here too, shining in clearness through the clearest aperture of sense. For sight is the most piercing of our bodily senses, though not by that is wisdom seen; her loveliness would have been transporting if there had been a visible image of her, and the other ideas, if they had visible counterparts, would be equally lovely. But this is the privilege of beauty, that being the loveliest she is also the most palpable to sight.

Now he who is not newly initiated or who has become corrupted, does not easily rise out of this world to the sight of true beauty in the other, when he contemplates her earthly namesake, and instead of being awed at the sight of her, he is given over to pleasure, and like a brutish beast he rushes on to enjoy and beget; he consorts with wantonness, and is not afraid or ashamed of pursuing pleasure in violation of nature.

But he whose initiation is recent, and who has been

the spectator of many glories in the other world, is amazed when he sees anyone having a godlike face or form, which is the expression of divine beauty; and at first a shudder runs through him, and again the old awe steals over him; then looking upon the face of his beloved as of a god he reverences him, and if he were not afraid of being thought a downright madman, he would sacrifice to his beloved as to the image of a god; then while he gazes on him there is a sort of reaction, and the shudder passes into an unusual heat and perspiration; for, as he receives the effluence of beauty through the eyes, the wing moistens and he warms. And as he warms, the parts out of which the wing grew, and which had been hitherto closed and rigid, and had prevented the wing from shooting forth, are melted, and as nourishment streams upon him, the lower end of the wing begins to swell and grow from the root upwards; and the growth extends under the whole soul – for once the whole was winged.

During this process the whole soul is all in a state of ebullition and effervescence – which may be compared to the irritation and uneasiness in the gums at the time of cutting teeth – bubbles up, and has a feeling of uneasiness and tickling; but when in like manner the soul is beginning to grow wings, the beauty of the beloved meets her eye and she receives the sensible warm motion of particles which flow towards her, therefore called emotion, and is refreshed and warmed by them, and then she ceases from her pain with joy. But when she is parted from her beloved and her moisture fails, then the orifices of the passage out of which the wing shoots dry up and close, and intercept the germ of the wing; which, being shut up with the emotion, throbbing as with the pulsations of an artery,

pricks the aperture which is nearest, until at length the
entire soul is pierced and maddened and pained, and
at the recollection of beauty is again delighted. And
from both of them together the soul is oppressed at the
strangeness of her condition, and is in a great strait and
excitement, and in her madness can neither sleep by
night nor abide in her place by day. And wherever she
thinks that she will behold the beautiful one, thither in
her desire she runs.

And when she has seen him, and bathed herself in
the waters of beauty, her constraint is loosened, and
she is refreshed, and has no more pangs and pains; and
this is the sweetest of all pleasures at the time, and is the
reason why the soul of the lover will never forsake his
beautiful one, whom he esteems above all; he has
forgotten mother and brethren and companions, and
he thinks nothing of the neglect and loss of his
property; the rules and proprieties of life, on which he
formerly prided himself, he now despises, and is ready
to sleep like a servant, wherever he is allowed, as near
as he can to his desired one, who is the object of his
worship, and the physician who can alone assuage the
greatness of his pain. And this state, my dear imaginary
youth to whom I am talking, is by men called love, and
among the gods has a name at which you, in your
simplicity, may be inclined to mock; there are lines in
the apocryphal writings of Homer in which the name
occurs. One of them is rather outrageous, and not
altogether metrical. They are as follows:

Mortals call him fluttering love,
But the immortals call him winged one,
Because the growing of wings is a necessity to him.

You may believe this, but not unless you like. At any

rate the plight of lovers and its cause are such as I have described.

Now the lover who is taken to be the attendant of Zeus is better able to bear the winged god, and can endure a heavier burden; but the attendants and companions of Ares, who made the circuit in his company, when under the influence of love they fancy that they have been at all wronged, are ready to kill and put an end to themselves and their beloved. And he who followed in the train of any other god, while he is unspoiled and the impression lasts, honours and imitates him, as far as he is able; and after the manner of his god he behaves in his intercourse with his beloved and with the rest of the world during the first period of his earthly existence. Every one chooses his love from the ranks of beauty according to his character, and this he makes his god, and fashions and adorns as a sort of image which he is to fall down and worship.

The followers of Zeus desire that their beloved should have a soul like him; and therefore they seek out someone of a philosophical and imperial nature, and when they have found him and loved him, they do all they can to confirm such a nature in him, and if they have no experience of such a disposition hitherto, they learn of anyone who can teach them, and themselves follow in the same way. And they have the less difficulty in finding the nature of their own god in themselves, because they have been compelled to gaze intensely on him; their recollection clings to him, and they become possessed of him, and receive from him their character and disposition, so far as man can participate in god. The qualities of their god they attribute to the beloved, wherefore they love him all the more, and if, like the Bacchic nymphs, they draw inspiration from Zeus, they pour out their own fountain upon him, wanting to make him as like as possible to their own god.

But those who were the followers of Hera seek a royal love, and when they have found him they do just the same with him; and in like manner the followers of Apollo and of every other god, walking in the ways of their god, seek a love who is to be made like him whom they serve; and when they have found him, they themselves imitate their god, and persuade their love to do the same, and educate him into the manner and nature of the god as far as they each can; for no feelings of envy or jealousy are entertained by them towards their beloved, but they do their utmost to create in him the greatest likeness of themselves and of the god whom they honour. Thus fair and blissful to the beloved is the desire of the inspired lover, and the initiation of which I speak into the mysteries of true love, if he be captured by the lover and their purpose is effected. Now the beloved is taken captive in the following manner.

At the beginning of this tale, I divided each soul into three parts – two having the form of horses and the third being like a charioteer; the division may remain. I have said that one horse was good, the other bad, but I have not yet explained in what the goodness or badness of either consists, and to that I will now proceed. The right-hand horse is upright and cleanly made; he has a lofty neck and an aquiline nose; his colour is white, and his eyes dark; he is one who loves honour with modesty and temperance, and the follower of true opinion; he needs no touch of the whip, but is guided by word and admonition only. The other is a crooked, lumbering animal, put together anyhow; he has a short, thick neck; he is flat-faced and of a dark colour, with grey eyes and blood-red complexion; the mate of insolence and pride, shag-eared and deaf, hardly yielding to whip and spur.

Now when the charioteer beholds the vision of love, and has his whole soul warmed through sense, and is full of the prickings and ticklings of desire, the obedient steed, then as always under the government of shame, refrains from leaping on the beloved; but the other, heedless of the pricks and of the blows of the whip, plunges and runs away, giving all manner of trouble to his companion and the charioteer, whom he forces to approach the beloved and to remember the joys of love. They at first indignantly oppose him and will not be urged on to do terrible and unlawful deeds; but at last, when he persists in plaguing them, they yield and agree to do as he bids them.

And now they are at the spot and behold the flashing beauty of the beloved; which when the charioteer sees, his memory is carried to the true beauty, whom he beholds in company with Modesty like an image placed upon a holy pedestal. He sees her, but he is afraid and falls backwards in adoration, and by his fall is compelled to pull back the reins with such violence as to bring both the steeds on their haunches, the one willing and unresisting, the unruly one very unwilling; and when they have gone back a little, the one is overcome with shame and wonder, and his whole soul is bathed in perspiration; the other, when the pain is over which the bridle and the fall had given him, having with difficulty taken breath, is full of wrath and reproaches, which he heaps upon the charioteer and his fellow steed, for want of courage and manhood, declaring that they have been false to their agreement and guilty of desertion. Again they refuse, and again he urges them on, and will scarce yield to their prayer that he would wait until another time.

When the appointed hour comes, they make as if they had forgotten, and he reminds them, fighting and neighing and dragging them on, until at length he, on the same thoughts intent, forces them to draw near again. And when they are near he stoops his head and puts up his tail, and takes the bit in his teeth and pulls shamelessly. Then the charioteer is worse off than ever; he falls back like a racer at the barrier, and with a still more violent wrench drags the bit out of the teeth of the wild steed and covers his abusive tongue and jaws with blood, and forces his legs and haunches to the ground and punishes him sorely. And when this has happened several times and the villain has ceased from his wanton way, he is tamed and humbled, and follows the will of the charioteer, and when he sees the beautiful one he is ready to die of fear. And from that time forward the soul of the lover follows the beloved in modesty and holy fear.

And so the beloved who, like a god, has received every true and loyal service from his lover, not in pretence but in reality, being also himself of a nature friendly to his admirer, if in former days he has blushed to own his passion and turned away his lover, because his youthful companions or others slanderously told him that he would be disgraced, now as years advance, at the appointed age and time, is led to receive him into communion. For fate which has ordained that there shall be no friendship among the evil has also ordained that there shall ever be friendship among the good. And the beloved when he has received him into communion and intimacy, is quite amazed at the good will of the lover; he recognises that the inspired friend is worth all other friends or kinsmen; they have nothing of friendship in them worthy to be compared with his.

And when this feeling continues and he is nearer to him and embraces him, in gymnastic exercises and at other times of meeting, then the fountain of that stream, which Zeus when he was in love with Ganymede named Desire, overflows upon the lover, and some enters into his soul, and some when he is filled flows out again; and as a breeze or an echo rebounds from the smooth rocks and returns whence it came, so does the stream of beauty, passing through the eyes which are the windows of the soul, come back to the beautiful one, there arriving and quickening the passages of the wings, watering them and inclining them to grow, and filling the soul of the beloved also with love. And thus he loves, but he knows not what; he does not understand and cannot explain his own state; he appears to have caught the infection of blindness from another; the lover is his mirror in whom he is beholding himself, but he is not aware of this.

When he is with the lover, both cease from their pain, but when he is away then he longs as he is longed for, and has love's image, love for love [Anteros] lodging in his breast, which he calls and believes to be not love but friendship only, and his desire is as the desire of the other, but weaker; he wants to see him, touch him, kiss, embrace him, and probably not long afterwards his desire is accomplished. When they meet, the wanton steed of the lover has a word to say to the charioteer; he would like to have a little pleasure in return for many pains, but the wanton steed of the beloved says not a word, for he is bursting with passion which he understands not; he throws his arms round the lover and embraces him as his dearest friend; and, when they are side by side, he is not in a state in which he can refuse the lover anything, if he ask him, although his fellow steed and the charioteer oppose him with the arguments of shame and reason.

After this their happiness depends upon their self-control; if the better elements of the mind which lead to order and philosophy prevail, then they pass their life here in happiness and harmony – masters of themselves and orderly – enslaving the vicious and emancipating the virtuous elements of the soul; and when the end comes, they are light and winged for flight, having conquered in one of the three heavenly or truly Olympian victories; nor can human discipline or divine inspiration confer any greater blessing on man than this. If, on the other hand, they leave philosophy and lead the lower life of ambition, then probably, after wine or in some other careless hour, the two wanton animals take the two souls when off their guard and bring them together, and they accomplish that desire of their hearts which to the many is bliss; and this having once enjoyed they continue to enjoy, yet rarely, because they have not the approval of the whole soul.

They too are dear, but not so dear as the others; and it is for each other that they live, throughout the time of their love and afterwards. They consider that they have given and taken from each other the most sacred pledges, and they may not break them and fall into enmity. At last they pass out of the body, unwinged, but eager to soar, and thus obtain no mean reward of love and madness. For those who have once begun the heavenward pilgrimage may not go down again to darkness and the journey beneath the earth, but they live in light always; happy companions in their pilgrimage, and when the time comes at which they receive their wings they have the same plumage because of their love.

Thus great are the heavenly blessings which the friendship of a lover will confer upon you, my youth. Whereas the attachment of the non-lover, which is alloyed with a worldly prudence and has worldly and niggardly ways of doling out benefits, will breed in your soul those vulgar qualities which the populace applaud, will send you bowling round the earth during a period of nine thousand years, and leave you a fool in the world below.

And thus, dear Eros, I have made and paid my recantation, as well and as fairly as I could; more especially in the matter of the poetical figures which I was compelled to use, because Phaedrus would have them. And now forgive the past and accept the present, and be gracious and merciful to me, and do not in thine anger deprive me of sight, or take from me the art of love which thou hast given me, but grant that I may be yet more esteemed in the eyes of the fair. And if Phaedrus or I myself said anything rude in our first speeches, blame Lysias, who is the father of the brat, and let us have no more of his progeny; bid him study philosophy, like his brother Polemarchus; and then his lover Phaedrus will no longer halt between two opinions, but will dedicate himself wholly to love and to philosophical discourses.

GORGIAS

GORGIAS

Persons of the dialogue
CALLICLES
SOCRATES
CHAEREPHON
GORGIAS
POLUS

SCENE: *The house of Callicles*

[*The dialogue begins by discussing rhetoric, and goes on to discuss what is just; the selection given here omits the discussion of rhetoric – first between Socrates and Gorgias, and then between Socrates and Polus – and begins with Socrates' paradoxical conclusions and the indignant intervention of Callicles*]

SOCRATES: Then rhetoric is of no use to us, Polus, in helping a man to excuse his own injustice, that of his parents or friends, or children or country; but may be of use to anyone who holds that instead of excusing he ought to accuse – himself above all, and in the next degree his family or any of his friends who may be doing wrong; he should bring to light the iniquity and not conceal it, that so the wrongdoer may suffer and be made whole; and he should even force himself and others not to shrink, but with closed eyes like brave men to let the physician operate with knife or searing iron, not regarding the pain, in the hope of attaining the good and the honourable; let him who has done things worthy of stripes, allow himself to be scourged, if of bonds, to be bound, if of a fine, to be fined, if of exile, to be exiled, if of death, to die, himself being the first to accuse himself and his own relations, and using rhetoric to this end, that his and their unjust actions may be made manifest, and that they themselves may be delivered from injustice, which is the greatest evil. Then, Polus, rhetoric would indeed be useful. Do you say 'Yes' or 'No' to that?

POLUS: To me, Socrates, what you are saying appears very strange, though probably in agreement with your premises.

SOCRATES: Is not this the conclusion, if the premises are not disproven?

POLUS: Yes; it certainly is.

SOCRATES: And from the opposite point of view, if indeed it be our duty to harm another, whether an enemy or not – I except the case of self-defence – then I have to be upon my guard – but if my enemy injures a third person, then in every sort of way, by word as well as deed, I should try to prevent his being punished, or appearing before the judge; and if he appears, I should contrive that he should escape, and not suffer punishment: if he has stolen a sum of money, let him keep what he has stolen and spend it on him and his, regardless of religion and justice; and if he have done things worthy of death, let him not die, but rather be immortal in his wickedness; or, if this is not possible, let him at any rate be allowed to live as long as he can. For such purposes, Polus, rhetoric may be useful, but is of small if of any use to him who is not intending to commit injustice; at least, there was no such use discovered by us in the previous discussion.

CALLICLES: Tell me, Chaerephon, is Socrates in earnest, or is he joking?

CHAEREPHON: I should say, Callicles, that he is in most profound earnest; but you may well ask him.

CALLICLES: By the gods, and I will. Tell me, Socrates, are you in earnest, or only in jest? For if you are in earnest, and what you say is true, is not the whole of human life turned upside down; and are we not doing, as would appear, in everything the opposite of what we ought to be doing?

SOCRATES: O Callicles, if there were not some community of feelings among mankind, however varying in different persons – I mean to say, if every man's feelings were peculiar to himself and were not shared by the rest of his species – I do not see how we could ever communicate our impressions to one another. I make this remark because I perceive that you and I have a common feeling. For we are lovers both, and both of us have two loves apiece: I am the lover of Alcibiades, the son of Cleinias, and of philosophy; and you of the Athenian demos, and of Demos the son of Pyrilampes. Now, I observe that you, with all your cleverness, do not venture to contradict your favourite in any word or opinion of his; but as he changes you change, backwards and forwards. When the Athenian demos denies anything that you are saying in the assembly, you go over to his opinion; and you do the same with Demos, the fair young son of Pyrilampes. For you have not the power to resist the words and ideas of your loves; and if a person were to express surprise at the strangeness of what you say from time to time when under their influence, you would probably reply to him, if you were honest, that you cannot help saying what your loves say unless they are prevented; and that you can only be silent when they are. Now you must understand that my words are an echo too, and therefore you need not wonder at me; but if you want to silence me, silence philosophy, who is my love, for she is always telling me what I am now telling you, my friend; neither is she capricious like my other love, for the son of Cleinias says one thing today and another thing tomorrow, but philosophy is always true. She is the teacher at whose words you are now wondering, and you have heard her yourself. Her you must refute, and either show, as I was saying, that to do injustice and to escape punishment is not the worst of all evils; or, if you leave her word unrefuted, by the dog the god of Egypt, I declare, O Callicles, that Callicles will never be at one with himself, but that his whole life will be a discord. And yet, my friend, I would rather that my lyre should be inharmonious, and that there should be no music in the chorus which I provided; aye, or that the whole world should be at odds with me, and oppose me, rather than that I myself should be at odds with myself, and contradict myself.

CALLICLES: O Socrates, you are a regular declaimer, and seem to be running riot in the argument. And now you are declaiming in this way because Polus has fallen into the same error himself of which he accused Gorgias: for he said that when Gorgias was asked by you whether, if someone came to him who wanted to learn rhetoric and did not know justice, he would teach him justice, Gorgias in his modesty replied that he would, because he thought that mankind in general would be displeased if he answered 'No'; and then in consequence of this admission, Gorgias was compelled to contradict himself, that being just the sort of thing in which you delight. Whereupon Polus laughed at you deservedly, as I think; but now he has himself fallen into the same trap. I cannot say very much for his wit when he conceded to you that to do is more dishonourable than to suffer injustice, for this was the admission which led to his being entangled by you; and because he was too modest to say what he thought, he had his mouth stopped. For the truth is, Socrates, that you, who pretend to be engaged in the pursuit of truth, are appealing now to the popular and vulgar notions of right, which are not natural, but only conventional. Convention and nature are generally at variance with one another: and hence, if a person is too modest to say what he thinks, he is compelled to contradict himself; and you, in your ingenuity perceiving the advantage to be thereby gained, slyly ask of him who is arguing conventionally a question which is to be determined by the rule of nature; and if he is talking of the rule of nature, you slip away to custom: as, for instance, you did in this very discussion about doing and suffering injustice. When Polus was speaking of the conventionally dishonourable, you assailed him from the point of view of nature; for by the rule of nature, to suffer injustice is the greater disgrace because the greater evil; but conventionally, to do evil is the more disgraceful. For the suffering of injustice is not the part of a man, but of a slave, who indeed had better die than live, since when he is wronged and trampled upon, he is unable to help himself, or any other about whom he cares. The reason, as I conceive, is that the makers of laws are the majority who are weak; and they make laws and distribute praises and censures with a view to themselves and to their own interests; and they terrify the stronger sort of men, and those who are able to get the better of them, in order that they may not get the better of them; and they say, that dishonesty is shameful and unjust; meaning, by the word injustice, the desire of a man to have more than his neighbours; for knowing their own inferiority, I suspect that they are too glad of equality. And therefore the endeavour to have more than the many, is conventionally said to be shameful and unjust, and is called injustice, whereas nature herself intimates that it is just for the better to have more than the worse, the more powerful than the weaker; and in many ways she shows, among men as well as among animals, and indeed among whole cities and races, that justice consists in the superior ruling over and having more than the inferior. For on what principle of justice did Xerxes invade Hellas, or his father the Scythians (not to speak of numberless other examples)? Nay, but these are the men who act according to nature; yes, by heaven, and according to the law of nature: not, perhaps, according to that artificial law, which we invent and impose upon our fellows, of whom we take the best and strongest from their youth upwards, and tame them like young lions, charming them with the sound of the voice, and saying to them, that with equality they must be content, and that the equal is the honourable and the just. But if there were a man who had sufficient force, he would shake off and break through and escape from all this; he would trample under foot all our formulas and spells and charms, and all our laws which are against nature: the slave would rise in rebellion and be lord over us, and the light of natural justice would shine forth. And this I take to be the sentiment of Pindar, when he says in his poem, that 'Law is the king of all, of mortals as well as of immortals'; this, as he says, 'makes might to be right, doing violence with highest hand; as I infer from the deeds of Heracles, for without buying them ... ' – I do not remember the exact words, but the meaning is, that without buying them, and without their being given to him, he carried off the oxen of Geryon, according to the law of natural right, and that the oxen and other possessions of the weaker and inferior properly belong to the stronger and superior. And this is true, as you may ascertain, if you will leave philosophy and go on to higher things: for philosophy, Socrates, if pursued in moderation and at the proper age, is an elegant accomplishment, but too much philosophy is the ruin of human life. Even if a man has good parts, still, if he carries philosophy into later life, he is necessarily ignorant of all those things which a gentleman and a person of honour ought to know; he is inexperienced in the laws of the state, and in the language which ought to be used in the dealings of man with man, whether private or public, and utterly ignorant of the pleasures and desires of mankind and of human character in general. And people of this sort, when they betake themselves to politics or business, are as ridiculous as I imagine the politicians to be, when they make their appearance in the arena of philosophy. For, as Euripides says, 'Every man shines in that and pursues that, and devotes the greatest portion of the day to that in which he most excels,' but anything in which he is inferior, he avoids and depreciates, and praises the opposite from partiality to himself, and because he thinks that he will thus praise himself. The true principle is to unite them. Philosophy, as a part of education, is an excellent thing, and there is no disgrace to a man while he is young in pursuing such a study; but when he is more advanced in years, the thing becomes ridiculous, and I feel towards philosophers as I do towards those who lisp and imitate children. For I love to see a little child, who is not of an age to speak plainly, lisping at his play; there is an appearance of grace and freedom in his utterance, which is natural to his childish years. But when I hear some small creature carefully articulating its words, I am offended; the sound is disagreeable, and has to my ears the twang of slavery. So when I hear a man lisping, or see him playing like a child, his behaviour appears to me ridiculous and unmanly and worthy of stripes. And I have the same feeling about students of philosophy; when I see a youth thus engaged – the study appears to me to be in character, and becoming a man of liberal education, and him who neglects philosophy I regard as an inferior man, who will never aspire to anything great or noble. But if I see him continuing the study in later life, and not leaving off, I should like to beat him, Socrates; for, as I was saying, such a one, even though he have good natural parts, becomes effeminate. He flies from the busy centre and the marketplace, in which, as the poet says, men become distinguished; he creeps into a corner for the rest of his life, and talks in a whisper with three or four admiring youths, but never speaks out like a free man in a satisfactory manner. Now I, Socrates, am very well inclined towards you, and my feeling may be compared with that of Zethus towards Amphion, in the play of Euripides, whom I was mentioning just now: for I am disposed to say to you much what Zethus said to his brother, that you, Socrates, are careless about the things of which you ought to be careful; and that you 'who have a soul so noble, are remarkable for a puerile exterior; neither in a court of justice could you state a case, or give any reason or proof, or offer valiant counsel on another's

behalf.' And you must not be offended, my dear
Socrates, for I am speaking out of goodwill towards
you, if I ask whether you are not ashamed of being thus
defenceless; which I affirm to be the condition not of
you only but of all those who will carry the study of
philosophy too far. For suppose that someone were
to take you, or any one of your sort, off to prison,
declaring that you had done wrong when you had
done no wrong, you must allow that you would not
know what to do: there you would stand giddy and
gaping, and not having a word to say; and when you
went up before the court, even if the accuser were a
poor creature and not good for much, you would die
if he were disposed to claim the penalty of death.
And yet, Socrates, what is the value of 'an art which
converts a man of sense into a fool', who is helpless,
and has no power to save either himself or others,
when he is in the greatest danger and is going to be
despoiled by his enemies of all his goods, and has to
live, simply deprived of his rights of citizenship – he
being a man who, if I may use the expression, may be
boxed on the ears with impunity? Then, my good
friend, take my advice, and refute no more: 'Learn the
philosophy of business, and acquire the reputation of
wisdom. But leave to others these niceties,' whether
they are to be described as follies or absurdities: 'For
they will only give you poverty for the inmate of your
dwelling.' Cease, then, emulating these paltry splitters
of words, and emulate only the man of substance and
honour, who is well to do.

SOCRATES: If my soul, Callicles, were made of gold,
should I not rejoice to discover one of those stones
with which they test gold, and the very best possible
one to which I might bring my soul; and if the stone

and I agreed in approving of her training, then I should know that I was in a satisfactory state, and that no other test was needed by me.

CALLICLES: What is your meaning, Socrates?

SOCRATES: I will tell you; I think that I have found in you the desired touchstone.

CALLICLES: Why?

SOCRATES: Because I am sure that if you agree with me in any of the opinions which my soul forms, I have at last found the truth indeed. For I consider that if a man is to make a complete trial of the good or evil of the soul, he ought to have three qualities – knowledge, goodwill, outspokenness, which are all possessed by you. Many whom I meet are unable to make trial of me, because they are not wise as you are; others are wise, but they will not tell me the truth, because they have not the same interest in me which you have; and these two strangers, Gorgias and Polus, are undoubtedly wise men and my very good friends, but they are not outspoken enough, and they are too modest. Why, their modesty is so great that they are driven to contradict themselves, first one and then the other of them, in the face of a large company, on matters of the highest moment. But you have all the qualities in which these others are deficient, having received an excellent education; to this many Athenians can testify. And you are my friend. Shall I tell you why I think so? I know that you, Callicles, and Tisander of Aphidnae, and Andron the son of Androtion, and Nausicydes of the deme of Cholarges, studied together: there were four of you, and I once heard you advising with one another as to the extent to which the pursuit of philosophy should be carried, and, as I know, you came to the conclusion that the study should not be pushed too much into detail. You were cautioning one another not to be overwise; you were afraid that too much wisdom might unconsciously to yourselves be the ruin of you. And now when I hear you giving the same advice to me which you then gave to your most intimate friends, I have a sufficient evidence of your real goodwill to me. And of the frankness of your nature and freedom from modesty I am assured by yourself, and the assurance is confirmed by your last speech. Well then, the inference in the present case clearly is, that if you agree with me in an argument about any point, that point will have been sufficiently tested by us, and will not require to be submitted to any further test. For you could not have agreed with me either from lack of knowledge or from superfluity of modesty, nor yet from a desire to deceive me, for you are my friend, as you tell me yourself. And therefore when you and I are agreed, the result will be the attainment of perfect truth. Now there is no nobler enquiry, Callicles, than that which you censure me for making – what ought the character of a man to be, and what his pursuits, and how far is he to go, both in maturer years and in youth? For be assured that if I err in my own conduct I do not err intentionally, but from ignorance. Do not then desist from advising me, now that you have begun, until I have learned clearly what this is which I am to practise, and how I may acquire it. And if you find me assenting to your words, and hereafter not doing that to which I assented, call me 'dolt', and deem me unworthy of receiving further instruction. Once more, then, tell me what you and Pindar mean by natural justice: do you not mean that the superior should take the property of the inferior by force; that the better should rule the worse, the noble have more than the mean? Am I not right in my recollection?

CALLICLES: Yes; that is what I was saying, and so I still aver.

SOCRATES: And do you mean by the better the same as the superior? For I could not make out what you were saying at the time – whether you meant by the superior the stronger, and that the weaker must obey the stronger, as you seemed to imply when you said that great cities attack small ones in accordance with natural right, because they are superior and stronger, as though the superior and stronger and better were the same; or whether the better may be also the inferior and weaker, and the superior the worse, or whether better is to be defined in the same way as superior: this is the point which I want to have cleared up. Are the superior and better and stronger the same or different?

CALLICLES: I say unequivocally that they are the same.

SOCRATES: Then the many are by nature superior to the one, against whom, as you were saying, they make the laws?

CALLICLES: Certainly.

SOCRATES: Then the laws of the many are the laws of the superior?

CALLICLES: Very true.

SOCRATES: Then they are the laws of the better; for the superior class are far better, as you were saying?

CALLICLES: Yes.

SOCRATES: And since they are superior, the laws which are made by them are by nature good?

CALLICLES: Yes.

SOCRATES: And are not the many of opinion, as you were lately saying, that justice is equality, and that to do is more disgraceful than to suffer injustice? Is that so or not? Answer, Callicles, and let no modesty be found to come in the way; do the many think, or do they not think thus? I must beg of you to answer, in order that if you agree with me I may fortify myself by the assent of so competent an authority.

CALLICLES: Yes; the opinion of the many is what you say.

SOCRATES: Then not only custom but nature also affirms that to do is more disgraceful than to suffer injustice, and that justice is equality; so that you seem to have been wrong in your former assertion, when accusing me you said that nature and custom are opposed, and that I, knowing this, was dishonestly playing between them, appealing to custom when the argument is about nature, and to nature when the argument is about custom.

CALLICLES: This man will never cease talking non-sense. At your age, Socrates, are you not ashamed to be catching at words and chuckling over some verbal slip? Do you not see – have I not told you already – that by superior I mean better? Do you imagine me to say, that if a rabble of slaves and nondescripts, who are of no use except perhaps for their physical strength, get together, their ipsissima verba are laws?

SOCRATES: Ho! my philosopher, is that your line?

CALLICLES: Certainly.

SOCRATES: I was thinking, Callicles, that something of the kind must have been in your mind, and that is why I repeated the question – what is the superior? I wanted to know clearly what you meant; for you surely do not think that two men are better than one, or that your slaves are better than you because they are stronger? Then please to begin again, and tell me who the better are, if they are not the stronger; and I will ask you, great sir, to be a little milder in your instructions, or I shall have to run away from you.

CALLICLES: You are ironical.

SOCRATES: No, by the hero Zethus, Callicles, by whose aid you were just now saying many ironical things against me, I am not: tell me, then, whom you mean, by the better?

CALLICLES: I mean the more excellent.

SOCRATES: Do you not see that you are yourself using words which have no meaning and that you are explaining nothing? Will you tell me whether you mean by the better and superior the wiser, or if not, whom?

CALLICLES: Most assuredly, I do mean the wiser.

SOCRATES: Then according to you, one wise man may often be superior to ten thousand fools, and he ought to rule them, and they ought to be his subjects, and he ought to have more than they should. This is what I believe that you mean (and you must not suppose that I am word-catching), if you allow that the one is superior to the ten thousand?

CALLICLES: Yes; that is what I mean, and that is what I conceive to be natural justice – that the better and wiser should rule and have more than the inferior.

SOCRATES: Stop there, and let me ask you what you would say in this case: let us suppose that we are all together as we are now; there are several of us, and we have a large common store of meats and drinks, and there are all sorts of persons in our company having various degrees of strength and weakness, and one of us, being a physician, is wiser in the matter of food than all the rest, and he is probably stronger than some and not so strong as others of us – will he not, being wiser, be also better than we are, and our superior in this matter of food?

CALLICLES: Certainly.

SOCRATES: Either, then, he will have a larger share of the meats and drinks, because he is better, or he will have the distribution of all of them by reason of his authority, but he will not expend or make use of a larger share of them on his own person, or if he does, he will be punished; his share will exceed that of some, and be less than that of others, and if he be the weakest of all, he being the best of all will have the smallest share of all, Callicles: am I not right, my friend?

CALLICLES: You talk about meats and drinks and physicians and other nonsense; I am not speaking of them.

SOCRATES: Well, but do you admit that the wiser is the better? Answer 'Yes' or 'No'.

CALLICLES: Yes.

SOCRATES: And ought not the better to have a larger share?

CALLICLES: Not of meats and drinks.

SOCRATES: I understand: then, perhaps, of coats – the skilfullest weaver ought to have the largest coat, and the greatest number of them, and go about clothed in the best and finest of them?

CALLICLES: Fudge about coats!

SOCRATES: Then the skilfullest and best in making shoes ought to have the advantage in shoes; the shoemaker, clearly, should walk about in the largest shoes, and have the greatest number of them?

CALLICLES: Fudge about shoes! What nonsense are you talking?

SOCRATES: Or, if this is not your meaning, perhaps you would say that the wise and good and true husbandman should actually have a larger share of seeds, and have as much seed as possible for his own land?

CALLICLES: How you go on, always talking in the same way, Socrates!

SOCRATES: Yes, Callicles, and also about the same things.

CALLICLES: Yes, by the gods, you are literally always talking of cobblers and fullers and cooks and doctors, as if this had to do with our argument.

SOCRATES: But why will you not tell me in what a man must be superior and wiser in order to claim a larger share? Will you neither accept a suggestion, nor offer one?

CALLICLES: I have already told you. In the first place, I mean by superiors not cobblers or cooks, but wise politicians who understand the administration of a state, and who are not only wise, but also valiant and able to carry out their designs, and not the men to faint from want of soul.

SOCRATES: See now, most excellent Callicles, how different my charge against you is from that which you bring against me, for you reproach me with always saying the same; but I reproach you with never saying the same about the same things, for at one time you were defining the better and the superior to be the stronger, then again as the wiser, and now you bring forward a new notion; the superior and the better are now declared by you to be the more courageous: I wish, my good friend, that you would tell me, once for all, whom you affirm to be the better and superior, and in what they are better.

CALLICLES: I have already told you that I mean those who are wise and courageous in the administration of a state – they ought to be the rulers of their states, and justice consists in their having more than their subjects.

SOCRATES: But whether rulers or subjects will they or will they not have more than themselves, my friend?

CALLICLES: What do you mean?

SOCRATES: I mean that every man is his own ruler; but perhaps you think that there is no necessity for him to rule himself; he is only required to rule others?

CALLICLES: What do you mean by his 'ruling over himself'?

SOCRATES: A simple thing enough; just what is commonly said, that a man should be temperate and master of himself, and ruler of his own pleasures and passions.

CALLICLES: What innocence! You mean those fools – the temperate?

SOCRATES: Certainly: any one may know that to be my meaning.

CALLICLES: Quite so, Socrates; and they are really fools, for how can a man be happy who is the servant of anything? On the contrary, I plainly assert that he who would truly live ought to allow his desires to wax to the uttermost, and not to chastise them; but when they have grown to their greatest he should have courage and intelligence to minister to them and to satisfy all his longings. And this I affirm to be natural justice and nobility. To this however the many cannot attain; and they blame the strong man because they are ashamed of their own weakness, which they desire to conceal, and hence they say that intemperance is base. As I have remarked already, they enslave the nobler natures, and being unable to satisfy their pleasures, they praise temperance and justice out of their own cowardice. For if a man had been originally the son of a king, or had a nature capable of acquiring an empire or a tyranny or sovereignty, what could be more truly base or evil than temperance – to a man like him, I say, who might freely be enjoying every good, and has no one to stand in his way, and yet has admitted custom and reason and the opinion of other men to be lords over him? Must not he be in a miserable plight whom the reputation of justice and temperance hinders from giving more to his friends than to his enemies, even though he be a ruler in his city? Nay, Socrates, for you profess to be a votary of the truth, and the truth is this: that luxury and intemperance and licence, if they be provided with means, are virtue and happiness – all the rest is a mere bauble, agreements contrary to nature, foolish talk of men, nothing worth.

SOCRATES: There is a noble freedom, Callicles, in your way of approaching the argument; for what you say is what the rest of the world think, but do not like to say. And I must beg of you to persevere, that the true rule of human life may become manifest. Tell me, then: you say, do you not, that in the rightly-developed man the passions ought not to be controlled, but that we should let them grow to the utmost and somehow or other satisfy them, and that this is virtue?

CALLICLES: Yes, I do.

SOCRATES: Then those who want nothing are not truly said to be happy?

CALLICLES: No indeed, for then stones and dead men would be the happiest of all.

SOCRATES: But surely life according to your view is an awful thing; and indeed I think that Euripides may have been right in saying, 'Who knows if life be not death and death life?' and that we are very likely dead; I have heard a philosopher say that at this moment we are actually dead, and that the body[1] is our tomb,[2] and that the part of the soul which is the seat of the desires is liable to be tossed about by words and blown up and down; and some ingenious person, probably a Sicilian or an Italian, playing with the word, invented a tale in which he called the soul – because of its believing and make-believe nature[3] – a vessel, and the ignorant he called the uninitiated or leaky, and the place in the souls of the uninitiated in which the desires are seated, being the intemperate and incontinent part, he compared to a vessel full of holes, because it can never be satisfied. He is not of your way of thinking, Callicles, for he declares that of all the souls in Hades, meaning the invisible world, these uninitiated or leaky persons are the most miserable, and that they pour water into a vessel which is full of holes out of a colander which is similarly perforated. The colander, as my informer assures me, is the soul, and the soul which he compares to a colander is the soul of the ignorant, which is likewise full of holes, and therefore incontinent, owing to a bad memory and want of faith. These notions are strange enough, but they show the principle which, if I can, I would fain prove to you; that you should change your mind and, instead of the intemperate and insatiate life, choose that which is orderly and sufficient and has a due provision for daily needs. Do I make any impression on you, and are you coming over to the opinion that the orderly are happier than the intemperate? Or do I fail to persuade you, and, however many tales I rehearse to you, do you continue of the same opinion still?

CALLICLES: The latter, Socrates, is more like the truth.

---

1 sōma   2 sēma   3 an untranslatable pun

SOCRATES: Well, I will tell you another image, which comes out of the same school: let me request you to consider how far you would accept this as an account of the two lives of the temperate and intemperate in a figure: There are two men, both of whom have a number of casks; the one man has his casks sound and full, one of wine, another of honey, and a third of milk, besides others filled with other liquids, and the streams which fill them are few and scanty, and he can only obtain them with a great deal of toil and difficulty; but when his casks are once filled he has no need to feed them any more, and has no further trouble with them or care about them. The other, in like manner, can procure streams, though not without difficulty; but his vessels are leaky and unsound, and night and day he is compelled to be filling them, and if he pauses for a moment, he is in an agony of pain. Such are their respective lives: And now would you say that the life of the intemperate is happier than that of the temperate? Do I not convince you that the opposite is the truth?

CALLICLES: You do not convince me, Socrates, for the one who has filled himself has no longer any pleasure left; and this, as I was just now saying, is the life of a stone: he has neither joy nor sorrow after he is once filled; but the pleasure depends on the superabundance of the influx.

SOCRATES: But the more you pour in, the greater the waste; and the holes must be large for the liquid to escape.

CALLICLES: Certainly.

SOCRATES: The life which you are now depicting is not that of a dead man, or of a stone, but of a cormorant; you mean that he is to be hungering and eating?

CALLICLES: Yes.

SOCRATES: And he is to be thirsting and drinking?

CALLICLES: Yes, that is what I mean; he is to have all his desires about him, and to be able to live happily in the gratification of them.

SOCRATES: Capital, excellent; go on as you have begun, and have no shame; I, too, must disencumber myself of shame: and first, will you tell me whether you include itching and scratching, provided you have enough of them and pass your life in scratching, in your notion of happiness?

CALLICLES: What a strange being you are, Socrates! A regular mob-orator.

SOCRATES: That was the reason, Callicles, why I scared Polus and Gorgias, until they were too modest to say what they thought; but you will not be too modest and will not be scared, for you are a brave man. And now, answer my question.

CALLICLES: I answer, that even the scratcher would live pleasantly.

SOCRATES: And if pleasantly, then also happily?

CALLICLES: To be sure.

SOCRATES: But what if the itching is not confined to the head? Shall I pursue the question? And here, Callicles, I would have you consider how you would reply if consequences are pressed upon you, especially if in the last resort you are asked, whether the life of a catamite is not terrible, foul, miserable? Or would you venture to say, that they too are happy, if they only get enough of what they want?

CALLICLES: Are you not ashamed, Socrates, of introducing such topics into the argument?

SOCRATES: Well, my fine friend, but am I the introducer of these topics, or he who says without any qualification that all who feel pleasure in whatever

manner are happy, and who admits of no distinction
between good and bad pleasures? And I would still
ask, whether you say that pleasure and good are the
same, or whether there is some pleasure which is not a
good?

CALLICLES: Well, then, for the sake of consistency, I
will say that they are the same.

SOCRATES: You are breaking the original agreement,
Callicles, and will no longer be a satisfactory companion in the search after truth, if you say what
is contrary to your real opinion.

CALLICLES: Why, that is what you are doing too,
Socrates.

SOCRATES: Then we are both doing wrong. Still, my
dear friend, I would ask you to consider whether
pleasure, from whatever source derived, is the good;
for, if this be true, then the disagreeable consequences
which have been darkly intimated must follow, and
many others.

CALLICLES: That, Socrates, is only your opinion.

SOCRATES: And do you, Callicles, seriously maintain
what you are saying?

CALLICLES: Indeed I do.

SOCRATES: Then, as you are in earnest, shall we proceed with the argument?

CALLICLES: By all means.

SOCRATES: Well, if you are willing to proceed,
determine this question for me: there is something,
I presume, which you would call knowledge?

CALLICLES: There is.

SOCRATES: And were you not saying just now, that
some courage implied knowledge?

CALLICLES: I was.

SOCRATES: And you were speaking of courage and

knowledge as two things different from one another?

CALLICLES: Certainly I was.

SOCRATES: And would you say that pleasure and knowledge are the same, or not the same?

CALLICLES: Not the same, O man of wisdom.

SOCRATES: And would you say that courage differed from pleasure?

CALLICLES: Certainly.

SOCRATES: Well, then, let us remember that Callicles the Acharnian says that pleasure and good are the same; but that knowledge and courage are not the same, either with one another, or with the good.

CALLICLES: And what does our friend Socrates of Foxton say – does he assent to this, or not?

SOCRATES: He does not assent; neither will Callicles, when he sees himself truly. You will admit, I suppose, that good and evil fortune are opposed to each other?

CALLICLES: Yes.

SOCRATES: And if they are opposed to each other, then, like health and disease, they exclude one another; a man cannot have them both, or be without them both, at the same time?

CALLICLES: What do you mean?

SOCRATES: Take the case of any bodily affection: a man may have the complaint in his eyes which is called ophthalmia?

CALLICLES: To be sure.

SOCRATES: But he surely cannot have the same eyes well and sound at the same time?

CALLICLES: Certainly not.

SOCRATES: And when he has got rid of his ophthalmia, has he got rid of the health of his eyes too? Is the final result that he gets rid of them both together?

CALLICLES: Certainly not.

427

SOCRATES: That would surely be marvellous and absurd?

CALLICLES: Very.

SOCRATES: I suppose that he is affected by them, and gets rid of them, in turns?

CALLICLES: Yes.

SOCRATES: And he may have strength and weakness in the same way, by fits?

CALLICLES: Yes.

SOCRATES: Or swiftness and slowness?

CALLICLES: Certainly.

SOCRATES: And does he have and not have good and happiness, and their opposites, evil and misery, in a similar alternation?

CALLICLES: Certainly he has.

SOCRATES: If then there be anything which a man has and has not at the same time, clearly that cannot be good and evil – do we agree? Please not to answer without consideration.

CALLICLES: I entirely agree.

SOCRATES: Go back now to our former admissions – did you say that to hunger, I mean the mere state of hunger, was pleasant or painful?

CALLICLES: I said painful, but that to eat when you are hungry is pleasant.

SOCRATES: I know; but still the actual hunger is painful: am I not right?

CALLICLES: Yes.

SOCRATES: And thirst, too, is painful?

CALLICLES: Yes, very.

SOCRATES: Need I adduce any more instances, or would you agree that all wants or desires are painful?

CALLICLES: I agree, and therefore you need not adduce any more instances.

SOCRATES: Very good. And you would admit that to drink, when you are thirsty, is pleasant?

CALLICLES: Yes.

SOCRATES: And in the sentence which you have just uttered, the word 'thirsty' implies pain?

CALLICLES: Yes.

SOCRATES: And the word 'drinking' is expressive of pleasure, and of the satisfaction of the want?

CALLICLES: Yes.

SOCRATES: There is pleasure in drinking?

CALLICLES: Certainly.

SOCRATES: When you are thirsty?

CALLICLES: Yes.

SOCRATES: And in pain?

CALLICLES: Yes.

SOCRATES: Do you see the inference: that pleasure and pain are simultaneous, when you say that being thirsty, you drink? For are they not simultaneous, and do they not affect at the same time the same part, whether of the soul or the body? Which of them is affected cannot be supposed to be of any consequence: is not this true?

CALLICLES: It is.

SOCRATES: You said also, that no man could have good and evil fortune at the same time?

CALLICLES: Yes, I did.

SOCRATES: But you admitted, that when in pain a man might also have pleasure?

CALLICLES: Clearly.

SOCRATES: Then pleasure is not the same as good fortune, or pain the same as evil fortune, and therefore the good is not the same as the pleasant?

CALLICLES: I wish I knew, Socrates, what your quibbling means.

SOCRATES: You know, Callicles, but you affect not to know.

CALLICLES: Well, get on, and don't keep fooling: then you will know what a wiseacre you are in your admonition of me.

SOCRATES: Does not a man cease from his thirst and from his pleasure in drinking at the same time?

CALLICLES: I do not understand what you are saying.

GORGIAS: Nay, Callicles, answer, if only for our sakes; we should like to hear the argument out.

CALLICLES: Yes, Gorgias, but I must complain of the habitual trifling of Socrates; he is always arguing about little and unworthy questions.

GORGIAS: What matter? Your reputation, Callicles, is not at stake. Let Socrates argue in his own fashion.

CALLICLES: Well, then, Socrates, you shall ask these little peddling questions, since Gorgias wishes to have them.

SOCRATES: I envy you, Callicles, for having been initiated into the great mysteries before you were initiated into the lesser. I thought that this was not allowable. But to return to our argument: does not a man cease from thirsting and from the pleasure of drinking at the same moment?

CALLICLES: True.

SOCRATES: And if he is hungry, or has any other desire, does he not cease from the desire and the pleasure at the same moment?

CALLICLES: Very true.

SOCRATES: Then he ceases from pain and pleasure at the same moment?

CALLICLES: Yes.

SOCRATES: But he does not cease from good and evil at the same moment, as you have admitted: do you still adhere to what you said?

CALLICLES: Yes, I do; but what is the inference?

SOCRATES: Why, my friend, the inference is that the good is not the same as the pleasant, or the evil the same as the painful; there is a cessation of pleasure and pain at the same moment; but not of good and evil, for they are different. How then can pleasure be the same as good, or pain as evil? And I would have you look at the matter in another light, which could hardly, I think, have been considered by you when you identified them: are not the good good because they have good present with them, as the beautiful are those who have beauty present with them?

CALLICLES: Yes.

SOCRATES: And do you call the fools and cowards good men? For you were saying just now that the courageous and the wise are the good – would you not say so?

CALLICLES: Certainly.

SOCRATES: And did you never see a foolish child rejoicing?

CALLICLES: Yes, I have.

SOCRATES: And a foolish man too?

CALLICLES: Yes, certainly; but what is your drift?

SOCRATES: Nothing particular, if you will only answer.

CALLICLES: Yes, I have.

SOCRATES: And did you ever see a sensible man rejoicing or sorrowing?

CALLICLES: Yes.

SOCRATES: Which rejoice and sorrow most – the wise or the foolish?

CALLICLES: They are much upon a par, I think, in that respect.

SOCRATES: Enough: and did you ever see a coward in battle?

CALLICLES: To be sure.

SOCRATES: And which rejoiced most at the departure of the enemy, the coward or the brave?

CALLICLES: I should say 'most' of both; or at any rate, they rejoiced about equally.

SOCRATES: No matter; then the cowards, and not only the brave, rejoice?

CALLICLES: Greatly.

SOCRATES: And the foolish; so it would seem?

CALLICLES: Yes.

SOCRATES: And are only the cowards pained at the approach of their enemies, or are the brave also pained?

CALLICLES: Both are pained.

SOCRATES: And are they equally pained?

CALLICLES: I should imagine that the cowards are more pained.

SOCRATES: And are they not better pleased at the enemy's departure?

CALLICLES: I dare say.

SOCRATES: Then are the foolish and the wise and the cowards and the brave all pleased and pained, as you were saying, in nearly equal degree; but are the cowards more pleased and pained than the brave?

CALLICLES: Yes.

SOCRATES: But surely the wise and brave are the good, and the foolish and the cowardly are the bad?

CALLICLES: Yes.

SOCRATES: Then the good and the bad are pleased and pained in a nearly equal degree?

CALLICLES: Yes.

SOCRATES: Then are the good and bad good and bad in a nearly equal degree, or have the bad the advantage both in good and evil?

CALLICLES: I really do not know what you mean.

SOCRATES: Why, do you not remember saying that the

good were good because good was present with them, and the evil because evil; and that pleasures were goods and pains evils?

CALLICLES: Yes, I remember.

SOCRATES: And are not these pleasures or goods present to those who rejoice – if they do rejoice?

CALLICLES: Certainly.

SOCRATES: Then those who rejoice are good when goods are present with them?

CALLICLES: Yes.

SOCRATES: And those who are in pain have evil or sorrow present with them?

CALLICLES: Yes.

SOCRATES: And would you still say that the evil are evil by reason of the presence of evil?

CALLICLES: I should.

SOCRATES: Then those who rejoice are good, and those who are in pain evil?

CALLICLES: Yes.

SOCRATES: The degrees of good and evil vary with the degrees of pleasure and of pain?

CALLICLES: Yes.

SOCRATES: Have the wise man and the fool, the brave and the coward, joy and pain in nearly equal degrees? Or would you say that the coward has more?

CALLICLES: I should say that he has.

SOCRATES: Help me then to draw out the conclusion which follows from our admissions; for it is good to repeat and review what is good twice and thrice over, as they say. Both the wise man and the brave man we allow to be good?

CALLICLES: Yes.

SOCRATES: And the foolish man and the coward to be evil?

433

PLATO

CALLICLES: Certainly.

SOCRATES: And he who has joy is good?

CALLICLES: Yes.

SOCRATES: And he who is in pain is evil?

CALLICLES: Certainly.

SOCRATES: The good and evil both have joy and pain, but, perhaps, the evil has more of them?

CALLICLES: Yes.

SOCRATES: Then must we not infer, that the bad man is as good and bad as the good, or, perhaps, even better? Is not this a further inference which follows equally with the preceding from the assertion that the good and the pleasant are the same: can this be denied, Callicles?

CALLICLES: I have been listening and making admissions to you, Socrates; and I remark that if a person grants you anything in play, you, like a child, want to keep hold and will not give it back. But do you really suppose that I or any other human being denies that some pleasures are good and others bad?

SOCRATES: Alas, Callicles, how unfair you are! You certainly treat me as if I were a child, sometimes saying one thing, and then another, as if you were meaning to deceive me. And yet I thought at first that you were my friend, and would not have deceived me if you could have helped. But I see that I was mistaken; and now I suppose that I must make the best of a bad business, as they said of old, and take what I can get out of you. Well, then, as I understand you to say, I may assume that some pleasures are good and others evil?

CALLICLES: Yes.

SOCRATES: The beneficial are good, and the hurtful are evil?

CALLICLES: To be sure.

SOCRATES: And the beneficial are those which do some good, and the hurtful are those which do some evil?

CALLICLES: Yes.

SOCRATES: Take, for example, the bodily pleasures of eating and drinking, which we were just now mentioning – you mean to say that those which promote health, or any other bodily excellence, are good, and their opposites evil?

CALLICLES: Certainly.

SOCRATES: And in the same way there are good pains and there are evil pains?

CALLICLES: To be sure.

SOCRATES: And ought we not to choose and use the good pleasures and pains?

CALLICLES: Certainly.

SOCRATES: But not the evil?

CALLICLES: Clearly.

SOCRATES: Because, if you remember, Polus and I have agreed that all our actions are to be done for the sake of the good; and will you agree with us in saying, that the good is the end of all our actions, and that all our actions are to be done for the sake of the good, and not the good for the sake of them? Will you add a third vote to our two?

CALLICLES: I will.

SOCRATES: Then pleasure, like everything else, is to be sought for the sake of that which is good, and not that which is good for the sake of pleasure?

CALLICLES: To be sure.

SOCRATES: But can every man choose what pleasures are good and what are evil, or must he have art or knowledge of them in detail?

CALLICLES: He must have art.

SOCRATES: Let me now remind you of what I was

saying to Gorgias and Polus; I was saying, as you will not have forgotten, that there were some processes which aim only at pleasure, and know nothing of a better and worse, and there are other processes which know good and evil. And I considered that cookery, which I do not call an art, but only an experience, was of the former class, which is concerned with pleasure, and that the art of medicine was of the class which is concerned with the good. And now, by the god of friendship, I must beg you, Callicles, not to jest, or to imagine that I am jesting with you; do not answer at random and contrary to your real opinion – for you will observe that we are arguing about the way of human life; and to a man who has any sense at all, what question can be more serious than this – whether he should follow after that way of life to which you exhort me, and act what you call the manly part of speaking in the assembly, and cultivating rhetoric, and engaging in public affairs, according to the principles now in vogue, or whether he should pursue the life of philosophy, and in what the latter way differs from the former? But perhaps we had better first try to distinguish them, as I did before, and when we have come to an agreement that they are distinct, we may proceed to consider in what they differ from one another, and which of them we should choose. Perhaps, however, you do not even now understand what I mean?

CALLICLES: No, I do not.

SOCRATES: Then I will explain myself more clearly: seeing that you and I have agreed that there is such a thing as good, and that there is such a thing as pleasure, and that pleasure is not the same as good, and that the pursuit and process of acquisition of the one, that is pleasure, is different from the pursuit and process of acquisition of the other, which is good – I wish that you would tell me whether you agree with me thus far or not – do you agree?

CALLICLES: I do.

SOCRATES: Then I will proceed, and ask whether you also agree with me, and whether you think that I spoke the truth when I further said to Gorgias and Polus that cookery in my opinion is only an experience, and not an art at all; and that whereas medicine is an art, and attends to the nature and constitution of the patient, and has principles of action and reason in each case, cookery in attending upon pleasure never regards either the nature or reason of that pleasure to which she devotes herself, but goes straight to her end, nor ever considers or calculates anything, but works by experience and routine, and just preserves the recollection of what she has usually done when producing pleasure. And first, I would have you consider whether I have proved what I was saying, and then whether there are not other similar processes which have to do with the soul – some of them processes of art, making a provision for the soul's highest interest – others despising the interest, and, as in the previous case, considering only the pleasure of the soul, and how this may be acquired, but not considering what pleasures are good or bad, and having no other aim but to afford gratification, whether good or bad. In my opinion, Callicles, there are such processes, and this is the sort of thing which I term flattery, whether concerned with the body or the soul, or whenever employed with a view to pleasure and without any consideration of good and evil. And now I wish that you would tell me whether you agree with us in this notion, or whether you differ.

CALLICLES: I do not differ; on the contrary, I agree; for in that way I shall soonest bring the argument to an end, and shall oblige my friend Gorgias.

SOCRATES: And is this notion true of one soul, or of two or more?

CALLICLES: Equally true of two or more.

SOCRATES: Then a man may delight a whole assembly, and yet have no regard for their true interests?

CALLICLES: Yes.

SOCRATES: Can you tell me the pursuits which delight mankind – or rather, if you would prefer, let me ask, and do you answer, which of them belong to the pleasurable class, and which of them not? In the first place, what say you of flute-playing? Does not that appear to be an art which seeks only pleasure, Callicles, and thinks of nothing else?

CALLICLES: I assent.

SOCRATES: And is not the same true of all similar arts, as, for example, the art of playing the lyre at festivals?

CALLICLES: Yes.

SOCRATES: And what do you say of the choral art and of dithyrambic poetry? Are not they of the same nature? Do you imagine that Cinesias the son of Meles cares about what will tend to the moral improvement of his hearers, or about what will give pleasure to the multitude?

CALLICLES: There can be no mistake about Cinesias, Socrates.

SOCRATES: And what do you say of his father, Meles the harp-player? Did he perform with any view to the good of his hearers? Could he be said to regard even their pleasure? For his singing was an infliction to his audience. And of harp-playing and dithyrambic poetry in general, what would you say? Have they not been invented wholly for the sake of pleasure?

CALLICLES: That is my notion of them.

SOCRATES: And as for the Muse of Tragedy, that solemn and august personage – what are her aspirations? Is all her aim and desire only to give pleasure to the spectators, or does she fight against them and refuse to speak of their pleasant vices, and willingly proclaim in word and song truths welcome and unwelcome? Which in your judgment is her character?

CALLICLES: There can be no doubt, Socrates, that Tragedy has her face turned towards pleasure and the gratification of the audience.

SOCRATES: And is not that the sort of thing, Callicles, which we were just now describing as flattery?

CALLICLES: Quite true.

SOCRATES: Well now, suppose that we strip all poetry of song and rhythm and metre, there will remain speech?

CALLICLES: To be sure.

SOCRATES: And this speech is addressed to a crowd of people?

CALLICLES: Yes.

SOCRATES: Then poetry is a sort of rhetoric?

CALLICLES: True.

SOCRATES: And do not the poets in the theatres seem to you to be rhetoricians?

CALLICLES: Yes.

SOCRATES: Then now we have discovered a sort of rhetoric which is addressed to a crowd of men, women, and children, freemen and slaves. And this is not much to our taste, for we have described it as having the nature of flattery.

CALLICLES: Quite true.

SOCRATES: Very good. And what do you say of that

other rhetoric which addresses the Athenian assembly and the assemblies of freemen in other states? Do the rhetoricians appear to you always to aim at what is best, and do they seek to improve the citizens by their speeches, or are they too, like the rest of mankind, bent upon giving them pleasure, forgetting the public good in the thought of their own interest, playing with the people as with children, and trying to amuse them, but never considering whether they are better or worse for this?

CALLICLES: I must distinguish. There are some who have a real care of the public in what they say, while others are such as you describe.

SOCRATES: I am contented with the admission that rhetoric is of two sorts: one which is mere flattery and disgraceful declamation; the other which is noble and aims at the training and improvement of the souls of the citizens, and strives to say what is best, whether welcome or unwelcome, to the audience; but have you ever known such a rhetoric? Or if you have, and can point out any rhetorician who is of this stamp, who is he?

CALLICLES: But, indeed, I am afraid that I cannot tell you of any such among the orators who are at present living.

SOCRATES: Well, then, can you mention anyone of a former generation, who may be said to have improved the Athenians, who found them worse and made them better, from the day that he began to make speeches? For indeed, I do not know of such a man.

CALLICLES: What! Did you never hear that Themistocles was a good man, and Cimon and Miltiades and Pericles, who is just lately dead, and whom you heard yourself?

SOCRATES: Yes, Callicles, they were good men, if, as you said at first, true virtue consists only in the satisfaction of our own desires and those of others; but if not, and if, as we were afterwards compelled to acknowledge, the satisfaction of some desires makes us better, and of others, worse, and we ought to gratify the one and not the other, and there is an art in distinguishing them – can you tell me of any of these statesmen who did distinguish them?

CALLICLES: No, indeed, I cannot.

SOCRATES: Yet, surely, Callicles, if you look you will find such a one. Suppose that we just calmly consider whether any of these was such as I have described. Will not the good man, who says whatever he says with a view to the best, speak with a reference to some standard and not at random; just as all other artists, whether the painter, the builder, the shipwright, or any other, look all of them to their own work, and do not select and apply at random what they apply, but strive to give a definite form to it? The artist disposes all things in order, and compels the one part to harmonise and accord with the other part, until he has constructed a regular and systematic whole; and this is true of all artists, and in the same way the trainers and physicians, of whom we spoke before, give order and regularity to the body: do you deny this?

CALLICLES: No; I am ready to admit it.

SOCRATES: Then the house in which order and regularity prevail is good; that in which there is disorder, evil?

CALLICLES: Yes.

SOCRATES: And the same is true of a ship?

CALLICLES: Yes.

SOCRATES: And the same may be said of the human body?

CALLICLES: Yes.

SOCRATES: And what would you say of the soul? Will the good soul be that in which disorder is prevalent, or that in which there is harmony and order?

CALLICLES: The latter follows from our previous admissions.

SOCRATES: What is the name which is given to the effect of harmony and order in the body?

CALLICLES: I suppose that you mean health and strength?

SOCRATES: Yes, I do; and what is the name which you would give to the effect of harmony and order in the soul? Try and discover a name for this as well as for the other.

CALLICLES: Why not give the name yourself, Socrates?

SOCRATES: Well, if you had rather that I should, I will; and you shall say whether you agree with me, and if not, you shall refute and answer me. 'Healthy,' as I conceive, is the name which is given to the regular order of the body, whence comes health and every other bodily excellence: is that true or not?

CALLICLES: True.

SOCRATES: And 'lawful' and 'law' are the names which are given to the regular order and action of the soul, and these make men lawful and orderly: and so we have temperance and justice: have we not?

CALLICLES: Granted.

SOCRATES: And will not the true rhetorician who is honest and understands his art have his eye fixed upon these, in all the words which he addresses to the souls of men, and in all his actions, both in what he gives and in what he takes away? Will not his aim be to implant justice in the souls of his citizens and take away injustice, to implant temperance and take away intemperance, to implant every virtue and take away every vice? Do you not agree?

CALLICLES: I agree.

SOCRATES: For what use is there, Callicles, in giving to the body of a sick man who is in a bad state of health a quantity of the most delightful food or drink or any other pleasant thing, which may be really as bad for him as if you gave him nothing, or even worse if rightly estimated. Is not that true?

CALLICLES: I will not say No to it.

SOCRATES: For in my opinion there is no profit in a man's life if his body is in an evil plight – in that case his life also is evil: am I not right?

CALLICLES: Yes.

SOCRATES: When a man is in health the physicians will generally allow him to eat when he is hungry and drink when he is thirsty, and to satisfy his desires as he likes, but when he is sick they hardly suffer him to satisfy his desires at all: even you will admit that?

CALLICLES: Yes.

SOCRATES: And does not the same argument hold of the soul, my good sir? While she is in a bad state and is senseless and intemperate and unjust and unholy, her desires ought to be controlled, and she ought to be prevented from doing anything which does not tend to her own improvement.

CALLICLES: Yes.

SOCRATES: Such treatment will be better for the soul herself?

CALLICLES: To be sure.

SOCRATES: And to restrain her from her appetites is to chastise her?

CALLICLES: Yes.

SOCRATES: Then restraint or chastisement is better for

the soul than intemperance or the absence of control which you were just now preferring?

CALLICLES: I do not understand you, Socrates, and I wish that you would ask some one who does.

SOCRATES: Here is a gentleman who cannot endure to be improved or to subject himself to that very chastisement of which the argument speaks!

CALLICLES: I do not heed a word of what you are saying, and have only answered hitherto out of civility to Gorgias.

SOCRATES: What are we to do, then? Shall we break off in the middle?

CALLICLES: You shall judge for yourself.

SOCRATES: Well, but people say that 'a tale should have a head and not break off in the middle', and I should not like to have the argument going about without a head; please then to go on a little longer, and put the head on.

CALLICLES: How tyrannical you are, Socrates! I wish that you and your argument would rest, or that you would get some one else to argue with you.

SOCRATES: But who else is willing? I want to finish the argument.

CALLICLES: Cannot you finish without my help, either talking straight on, or questioning and answering yourself?

SOCRATES: Must I then say with Epicharmus, 'Two men spoke before, but now one shall be enough'? I suppose that there is absolutely no help. And if I am to carry on the enquiry by myself, I will first of all remark that not only I but all of us should have an ambition to know what is true and what is false in this matter, for the discovery of the truth is a common good. And now I will proceed to argue according to my own notion. But if any of you think that I arrive at conclusions which are untrue you must interpose and refute me, for I do not speak from any knowledge of what I am saying; I am an enquirer like yourselves, and therefore, if my opponent says anything which is of force, I shall be the first to agree with him. I am speaking on the supposition that the argument ought to be completed; but if you think otherwise let us leave off and go our ways.

GORGIAS: I think, Socrates, that we should not go our ways until you have completed the argument; and this appears to me to be the wish of the rest of the company; I myself should very much like to hear what more you have to say.

SOCRATES: I too, Gorgias, should have liked to continue the argument with Callicles, and then I might have given him an 'Amphion' in return for his 'Zethus'; but since you, Callicles, are unwilling to continue, I hope that you will listen, and interrupt me if I seem to you to be in error. And if you refute me, I shall not be angry with you as you are with me, but I shall inscribe you as the greatest of benefactors on the tablets of my soul.

CALLICLES: My good fellow, never mind me, but get on.

SOCRATES: Listen to me, then, while I recapitulate the argument: Is the pleasant the same as the good? Not the same. Callicles and I are agreed about that. And is the pleasant to be pursued for the sake of the good, or the good for the sake of the pleasant? The pleasant is to be pursued for the sake of the good. And that is pleasant at the presence of which we are pleased, and that is good at the presence of which we are good? To be sure. And we are good, and all good things whatever are good when some virtue is present in us or them? That, Callicles, is my conviction. But the virtue of each thing, whether body or soul, instrument or creature, when given to them in the best way comes to them not by chance but as the result of the order and truth and art which are imparted to them: am I not right? I maintain that I am. And is not the virtue of each thing dependent on order or arrangement? Yes, I say. And that which makes a thing good is the proper order inhering in each thing? Such is my view. And is not the soul which has an order of her own better than that which has no order? Certainly. And the soul which has order is orderly? Of course. And that which is orderly is temperate? Assuredly. And the temperate soul is good? No other answer can I give, Callicles dear; have you any?

CALLICLES: Go on, my good fellow.

SOCRATES: Then I shall proceed to add, that if the temperate soul is the good soul, the soul which is in the opposite condition, that is, the foolish and intemperate, is the bad soul. Very true. And will not the temperate man do what is proper, both in relation to the gods and to men? For he would not be temperate if he did not? Certainly he will do what is proper. In his relation to other men he will do what is just, and in his relation to the gods he will do what is holy; and he who does what is just and holy must be just and holy? Very true. And must he not be courageous? For the duty of a temperate man is not to follow or to avoid what he ought not, but what he ought, whether things or men or pleasures or pains, and patiently to endure when he ought; and therefore, Callicles, the temperate man, being, as we have described, also just and courageous and holy, cannot be other than a perfectly good man, nor can the good man do otherwise than well and perfectly whatever he does; and he who does well must of necessity be happy and blessed, and the evil man who does evil, miserable: now this latter is he whom you were applauding – the intemperate who is the opposite of the temperate. Such is my position, and these things I affirm to be true.

And if they are true, then I further affirm that he who desires to be happy must pursue and practise temperance and run away from intemperance as fast as his legs will carry him: he had better order his life so as not to need punishment; but if either he or any of his friends, whether private individual or city, are in need of punishment, then justice must be done and he must suffer punishment, if he would be happy. This appears to me to be the aim which a man ought to have, and towards which he ought to direct all the energies both of himself and of the state, acting so that he may have temperance and justice present with him and be happy, not suffering his lusts to be unrestrained, and in the never-ending desire to satisfy them leading a robber's life. Such a one is the friend neither of god nor man, for he is incapable of society, and he who is incapable of society is also incapable of friendship. And philosophers tell us, Callicles, that society and friendship and orderliness and temperance and justice bind together heaven and earth and gods and men, and that this universe is therefore called Cosmos or order, not disorder or misrule, my friend. But although you are a philosopher you seem to me never to have observed that geometrical equality is mighty, both among gods and men; you think that you ought to cultivate inequality or excess, and do not care about geometry.

Well, then, either the principle that the happy are made happy by the possession of justice and temperance, and the miserable miserable by the possession of vice, must be refuted, or, if it is granted, what will be the consequences? All the consequences which I drew before, Callicles, and about which you asked me whether I was in earnest when I said that a man ought to accuse himself and his son and his friend if he did anything wrong, and that to this end he should use his rhetoric – all those consequences are true. And that which you thought that Polus was led to admit out of modesty is true, viz., that, to do injustice, if more disgraceful than to suffer, is in that degree worse; and the other position, which, according to Polus, Gorgias admitted out of modesty, that he who would truly be a rhetorician ought to be just and have a knowledge of justice, has also turned out to be true.

And now, these things being as we have said, let us proceed in the next place to consider whether you are right in throwing in my teeth that I am unable to help myself or any of my friends or kinsmen, or to save them in the extremity of danger, and that I am in the power of another like an outlaw to whom any one may do what he likes – he may box my ears, which was a brave saying of yours; or take away my goods or banish me, or even do his worst and kill me; a condition which, as you say, is the height of disgrace. My answer to you is one which has been already often repeated, but may as well be repeated once more. I tell you, Callicles, that to be boxed on the ears wrongfully is not the worst evil which can befall a man, nor to have my purse or my body cut open, but that to smite and slay me and mine wrongfully is far more disgraceful and more evil; aye, and to despoil and enslave and pillage, or in any way at all to wrong me and mine, is far more disgraceful and evil to the doer of the wrong than to me who am the sufferer.

These truths, which have been already set forth as I state them in the previous discussion, would seem now to have been fixed and riveted by us, if I may use an expression which is certainly bold, in words which are like bonds of iron and adamant; and unless you or some other still more enterprising hero shall break them, there is no possibility of denying what I say. For my position has always been, that I myself am ignorant how these things are, but that I have never met any one who could say otherwise, any more than you can, and not appear ridiculous. This is my position still, and if what I am saying is true, and injustice is the greatest of evils to the doer of injustice, and yet there is if possible a greater than this greatest of evils, in an unjust man not suffering retribution, what is that defence of which the want will make a man truly ridiculous? Must not the defence be one which will avert the greatest of human evils? And will not the worst of all defences be that with which a man is unable to defend himself or his family or his friends? Next will come that which is unable to avert the next greatest evil; thirdly that which is unable to avert the third greatest evil; and so of other evils. As is the greatness of evil so is the honour of being able to avert them in their several degrees, and the disgrace of not being able to avert them. Am I not right Callicles?

CALLICLES: Yes, quite right.

SOCRATES: Seeing then that there are these two evils, the doing injustice and the suffering injustice – and we affirm that to do injustice is a greater, and to suffer injustice a lesser evil – by what devices can a man succeed in obtaining the two advantages, the one of not doing and the other of not suffering injustice? Must he have the power, or only the will to obtain them? I mean to ask whether a man will escape injustice if he has only the will to escape, or must he have provided himself with the power?

CALLICLES: He must have provided himself with the power; that is clear.

SOCRATES: And what do you say of doing injustice? Is the will only sufficient, and will that prevent him from doing injustice, or must he have provided himself with power and art; and if he have not studied and practised, will he be unjust still? Surely you might say, Callicles, whether you think that Polus and I were right in admitting the conclusion that no one does wrong voluntarily, but that all do wrong against their will?

CALLICLES: Granted, Socrates, if you will only have done.

SOCRATES: Then, as would appear, power and art have to be provided in order that we may do no injustice?

CALLICLES: Certainly.

SOCRATES: And what art will protect us from suffering injustice, if not wholly, yet as far as possible? I want to know whether you agree with me; for I think that such an art is the art of one who is either a ruler or even tyrant himself, or the equal and companion of the ruling power.

CALLICLES: Well said, Socrates; and please to observe how ready I am to praise you when you talk sense.

SOCRATES: Think and tell me whether you would approve of another view of mine: To me every man appears to be most the friend of him who is most like to him – like to like, as ancient sages say: would you not agree to this?

CALLICLES: I should.

SOCRATES: But when the tyrant is rude and un-educated, he may be expected to fear any one who is his superior in virtue, and will never be able to be perfectly friendly with him.

CALLICLES: That is true.

SOCRATES: Neither will he be the friend of any one who is greatly his inferior, for the tyrant will despise him, and will never seriously regard him as a friend.

CALLICLES: That again is true.

SOCRATES: Then the only friend worth mentioning, whom the tyrant can have, will be one who is of the same character, and has the same likes and dislikes, and is at the same time willing to be subject and subservient to him; he is the man who will have power in the state, and no one will injure him with impunity: is not that so?

CALLICLES: Yes.

SOCRATES: And if a young man begins to ask how he may become great and formidable, this would seem to be the way – he will accustom himself, from his youth upward, to feel sorrow and joy on the same occasions as his master, and will contrive to be as like him as possible?

CALLICLES: Yes.

SOCRATES: And in this way he will have accomplished, as you and your friends would say, the end of becoming a great man and not suffering injury?

CALLICLES: Very true.

SOCRATES: But will he also escape from doing injury? Must not the very opposite be true – if he is to be like the tyrant in his injustice, and to have influence with him? Will he not rather contrive to do as much wrong as possible, and not be punished?

CALLICLES: True.

SOCRATES: And by the imitation of his master and by the power which he thus acquires will not his soul become bad and corrupted, and will not this be the greatest evil to him?

CALLICLES: You always contrive somehow or other, Socrates, to invert everything: do you not know that he who imitates the tyrant will, if he has a mind, kill him who does not imitate him and take away his goods?

SOCRATES: Excellent Callicles, I am not deaf, and I have heard that a great many times from you and from Polus and from nearly every man in the city, but I wish that you would hear me too. I dare say that he will kill him if he has a mind – the bad man will kill the good and true.

CALLICLES: And is not that just the provoking thing?

SOCRATES: Nay, not to a man of sense, as the argument shows: do you think that all our cares should be directed to prolonging life to the uttermost, and to the study of those arts which secure us from danger always like that art of rhetoric which saves men in courts of law, and which you advise me to cultivate?

CALLICLES: Yes, truly, and very good advice too.

SOCRATES: Well, my friend, but what do you think of swimming; is that an art of any great pretensions?

CALLICLES: No, indeed.

SOCRATES: And yet surely swimming saves a man from death, and there are occasions on which he must know how to swim. And if you despise the swimmers, I will tell you of another and greater art, the art of the pilot, who not only saves the souls of men, but also their bodies and properties from the extremity of danger, just like rhetoric. Yet his art is modest and unpresuming: it has no airs or pretences of doing anything extraordinary, and, in return for the same salvation which is given by the pleader, demands only two obols if he brings us from Aegina to Athens, or for the longer voyage from Pontus or Egypt, at the utmost two drachmae, when he has saved, as I was just now saying, the passenger and his wife and children and goods, and safely disembarked them at the Piraeus – this is the payment which he asks in return for so great a boon; and he who is the master of the art, and has done all this, gets out and walks about on the seashore by his ship in an unassuming way. For he is able to reflect and is aware that he cannot tell which of his fellow-passengers he has benefited, and which of them he has injured in not allowing them to be drowned.

He knows that they are just the same when he has disembarked them as when they embarked, and not a whit better either in their bodies or in their souls; and he considers that if a man who is afflicted by great and incurable bodily diseases is only to be pitied for having escaped, and is in no way benefited by him in having been saved from drowning, much less he who has great and incurable diseases, not of the body but of the soul, which is the more valuable part of him – neither is life worth having nor of any profit to the bad man, whether he be delivered from the sea or the law-courts or any other devourer; and so he reflects that such a one had better not live, for he cannot live well. And this is the reason why the pilot, although he is our saviour, is not usually conceited, any more than the engineer, who is not at all behind either the general, or the pilot, or anyone else, in his saving power, for he sometimes saves whole cities. Is there any comparison between him and the pleader? And if he were to talk, Callicles, in your grandiose style, he would bury you under a mountain of words, declaring and insisting that we ought all of us to be engine-makers, and that no other profession is worth thinking about; he would have plenty to say.

Nevertheless you despise him and his art, and sneeringly call him an engine-maker, and you will not allow your daughters to marry his son, or marry your son to his daughters. And yet, on your principle, what justice or reason is there in your refusal? What right have you to despise the engine-maker, and the others whom I was just now mentioning? I know that you will say, 'I am better, and better born.' But if the better is not what I say, and virtue consists only in a man saving himself and his, whatever may be his character, then your censure of the engine-maker, and of the physician, and of the other arts of salvation, is ridiculous.

O my friend! I want you to see that the noble and the good may possibly be something different from saving and being saved: may not he who is truly a man cease to care about living a certain time? He knows, as women say, that no man can escape fate, and therefore he is not fond of life; he leaves all that with god, and considers in what way he can best spend his appointed term; whether by assimilating himself to the constitution under which he lives, as you at this moment have to consider how you may become as like as possible to the Athenian people, if you mean to be in their good graces, and to have power in the state; whereas I want you to think and see whether this is for the interest of either of us; I would not have us risk that which is dearest on the acquisition of this power, like the Thessalian enchantresses, who, as they say, bring down the moon from heaven at the risk of their own perdition.

But if you suppose that any man will show you the art of becoming great in the city, yet not conforming yourself to the ways of the city, whether for better or worse, then I can only say that you are mistaken, Callides; for he who would deserve to be the true natural friend of the Athenian demos, aye, or of Pyrilampes' darling who is called after them, must be by nature like them, and not an imitator only. He, then, who will make you most like them, will make you as you desire, a statesman and orator: for every man is pleased when he is spoken to in his own language and spirit, and dislikes any other. But perhaps you, sweet Callicles, may be of another mind. What do you say?

CALLICLES: Somehow or other your words, Socrates, always appear to me to be good words; and yet, like the rest of the world, I am not quite convinced by them.

SOCRATES: The reason is, Callicles, that the love of Demos which abides in your soul is an adversary to me; but I dare say that if we recur to these same matters, and consider them more thoroughly, you may be convinced for all that. Please, then, to remember that there are two processes of training all things, including body and soul; in the one, as we said, we treat them with a view to pleasure, and in the other with a view to the highest good, and then we do not indulge but resist them: was not that the distinction which we drew?

CALLICLES: Very true.

SOCRATES: And the one which had pleasure in view was just a vulgar flattery: was not that another of our conclusions?

CALLICLES: Be it so, if you will have it.

SOCRATES: And the other had in view the greatest

improvement of that which was ministered to, whether body or soul?

CALLICLES: Quite true.

SOCRATES: And must we not have the same end in view in the treatment of our city and citizens? Must we not try and make them as good as possible? For we have already discovered that there is no use in imparting to them any other good, unless the mind of those who are to have the good, whether money, or office, or any other sort of power, be gentle and good. Shall we say that?

CALLICLES: Yes, certainly, if you like.

SOCRATES: Well, then, if you and I, Callicles, were intending to set about some public business, and were advising one another to undertake buildings, such as walls, docks or temples of the largest size, ought we not to examine ourselves, first, as to whether we know or do not know the art of building, and who taught us? Would not that be necessary, Callicles?

CALLICLES: True.

SOCRATES: In the second place, we should have to consider whether we had ever constructed any private house, either of our own or for our friends, and whether this building of ours was a success or not; and if upon consideration we found that we had had good and eminent masters, and had been successful in constructing many fine buildings, not only with their assistance, but without them, by our own unaided skill – in that case prudence would not dissuade us from proceeding to the construction of public works. But if we had no master to show, and only a number of worthless buildings or none at all, then, surely, it would be ridiculous in us to attempt public works, or to advise one another to undertake them. Is not this true?

GORGIAS

CALLICLES: Certainly.

SOCRATES: And does not the same hold in all other cases? If you and I were physicians, and were advising one another that we were competent to practise as state-physicians, should I not ask about you, and would you not ask about me, 'Well, but how about Socrates himself, has he good health? And was any one else ever known to be cured by him, whether slave or freeman?' And I should make the same enquiries about you. And if we arrived at the conclusion that no one, whether citizen or stranger, man or woman, had ever been any the better for the medical skill of either of us, then, by heaven, Callicles, what an absurdity to think that we or any human being should be so silly as to set up as state-physicians and advise others like ourselves to do the same, without having first practised in private, whether successfully or not, and acquired experience of the art! Is not this, as they say, to begin with the big jar when you are learning the potter's art; which is a foolish thing?

CALLICLES: True.

SOCRATES: And now, my friend, as you are already beginning to be a public character, and are admonishing and reproaching me for not being one, suppose that we ask a few questions of one another. Tell me, then, Callicles, how about making any of the citizens better? Was there ever a man who was once vicious, or unjust, or intemperate, or foolish, and became by the help of Callicles good and noble? Was there ever such a man, whether citizen or stranger, slave or freeman? Tell me, Callicles, if a person were to ask these questions of you, what would you answer? Whom would you say that you had improved by your conversation? There may have been good deeds of this sort which were done by you as

457

a private person, before you came forward in public. Why will you not answer?

CALLICLES: You are contentious, Socrates.

SOCRATES: Nay, I ask you, not from a love of contention, but because I really want to know in what way you think that affairs should be administered among us – whether, when you come to the administration of them, you have any other aim but the improvement of the citizens? Have we not already admitted many times over that such is the duty of a public man? Nay, we have surely said so; for if you will not answer for yourself I must answer for you. But if this is what the good man ought to effect for the benefit of his own state, allow me to recall to you the names of those whom you were just now mentioning, Pericles, and Cimon, and Miltiades, and Themistocles, and ask whether you still think that they were good citizens.

CALLICLES: I do.

SOCRATES: But if they were good, then clearly each of them must have made the citizens better instead of worse?

CALLICLES: Yes.

SOCRATES: And, therefore, when Pericles first began to speak in the assembly, the Athenians were not so good as when he spoke last?

CALLICLES: Very likely.

SOCRATES: Nay, my friend, 'likely' is not the word; for if he was a good citizen, the inference is certain.

CALLICLES: And what difference does that make?

SOCRATES: None; only I should like further to know whether the Athenians are supposed to have been made better by Pericles, or, on the contrary, to have been corrupted by him; for I hear that he was the first who gave the people pay, and made them idle and cowardly, and encouraged them in the love of talk and money.

CALLICLES: You heard that, Socrates, from the laconising set who bruise their ears.

SOCRATES: But what I am going to tell you now is not mere hearsay, but well known both to you and me: that at first, Pericles was glorious and his character unimpeached by any verdict of the Athenians – this was during the time when they were not so good – yet afterwards, when they had been made good and gentle by him, at the very end of his life they convicted him of theft, and almost put him to death, clearly under the notion that he was a malefactor.

CALLICLES: Well, but how does that prove Pericles' badness?

SOCRATES: Why, surely you would say that he was a bad manager of asses or horses or oxen, who had received them originally neither kicking nor butting nor biting him, and implanted in them all these savage tricks? Would he not be a bad manager of any animals who received them gentle, and made them fiercer than they were when he received them? What do you say?

CALLICLES: I will do you the favour of saying 'yes'.

SOCRATES: And will you also do me the favour of saying whether man is an animal?

CALLICLES: Certainly he is.

SOCRATES: And was not Pericles a shepherd of men?

CALLICLES: Yes.

SOCRATES: And if he was a good political shepherd, ought not the animals who were his subjects, as we were just now acknowledging, to have become more just, and not more unjust?

CALLICLES: Quite true.

SOCRATES: And are not just men gentle, as Homer says? Or are you of another mind?

CALLICLES: I agree.

SOCRATES: And yet he really did make them more savage than he received them, and their savageness was shown towards himself; which he must have been very far from desiring.

CALLICLES: Do you want me to agree with you?

SOCRATES: Yes, if I seem to you to speak the truth.

CALLICLES: Granted then.

SOCRATES: And if they were more savage, must they not have been more unjust and inferior?

CALLICLES: Granted again.

SOCRATES: Then upon this view, Pericles was not a good statesman?

CALLICLES: That is, upon your view.

SOCRATES: Nay, the view is yours, after what you have admitted. Take the case of Cimon again. Did not the very persons whom he was serving ostracise him, in order that they might not hear his voice for ten years? And they did just the same to Themistocles, adding the penalty of exile; and they voted that Miltiades, the hero of Marathon, should be thrown into the pit of death, and he was only saved by the Prytanis. And yet, if they had been really good men, as you say, these things would never have happened to them. For the good charioteers are not those who at first keep their place, and then, when they have broken in their horses, and themselves become better charioteers, are thrown out – that is not the way either in charioteering or in any profession. What do you think?

CALLICLES: I should think not.

SOCRATES: Well, but if so, the truth is as I have said already, that in the Athenian state no one has ever

shown himself to be a good statesman – you admitted
that this was true of our present statesmen, but not true
of former ones, and you preferred them to the others;
yet they have turned out to be no better than our
present ones; and therefore, if they were rhetoricians,
they did not use the true art of rhetoric or of flattery, or
they would not have fallen out of favour.

CALLICLES: But surely, Socrates, no living man ever
came near any one of them in his performances.

SOCRATES: O, my dear friend, I say nothing against
them regarded as the serving-men of the state; and I do
think that they were certainly more serviceable than
those who are living now, and better able to gratify the
wishes of the state; but as to transforming those desires
and not allowing them to have their way, and using the
powers which they had, whether of persuasion or of
force, in the improvement of their fellow citizens,
which is the prime object of the truly good citizen, I do
not see that in these respects they were a whit superior
to our present statesmen, although I do admit that
they were more clever at providing ships and walls and
docks, and all that.

You and I have a ridiculous way, for during the
whole time that we are arguing, we are always going
round and round to the same point, and constantly
misunderstanding one another. If I am not mistaken,
you have admitted and acknowledged more than
once, that there are two kinds of operations which
have to do with the body, and two which have to do
with the soul: one of the two is ministerial, and if our
bodies are hungry provides food for them, and if they
are thirsty gives them drink, or if they are cold supplies
them with garments, blankets, shoes, and all that they
crave. I use the same images as before intentionally, in

order that you may understand me the better. The purveyor of the articles may provide them either wholesale or retail, or he may be the maker of any of them – the baker, or the cook, or the weaver, or the shoemaker, or the currier; and in so doing, being such as he is, he is naturally supposed by himself and every one to minister to the body. For none of them know that there is another art – an art of gymnastic and medicine which is the true minister of the body, and ought to be the mistress of all the rest, and to use their results according to the knowledge which she has and they have not, of the real good or bad effects of meats and drinks on the body. All other arts which have to do with the body are servile and menial and illiberal; and gymnastic and medicine are, as they ought to be, their mistresses.

Now, when I say that all this is equally true of the soul, you seem at first to know and understand and assent to my words, and then a little while afterwards you come repeating, 'Has not the state had good and noble citizens?' and when I ask you who they are, you reply, seemingly quite in earnest, as if I had asked 'Who are or have been good trainers?' and you had replied 'Thearion the baker, Mithoecus, who wrote the Sicilian cookery-book, Sarambus, the vintner: these are ministers of the body, first-rate in their art; for the first makes admirable loaves, the second excellent dishes, and the third capital wine.' To me these appear to be the exact parallel of the statesmen whom you mention. Now you would not be altogether pleased if I said to you 'My friend, you know nothing of gymnastics; those of whom you are speaking to me are only the ministers and purveyors of luxury, who have no good or noble notions of their art, and may very likely be filling and fattening men's bodies and gaining their approval, although the result is that they lose their original flesh in the long run, and become thinner than they were before; and yet they, in their simplicity, will not attribute their diseases and loss of flesh to their entertainers; but when in after years the unhealthy surfeit brings the attendant penalty of disease, he who happens to be near them at the time, and offers them advice, is accused and blamed by them, and if they could they would do him some harm; while they proceed to eulogise the men who have been the real authors of the mischief.'

And that, Callicles, is just what you are now doing. You praise the men who feasted the citizens and satisfied their desires, and people say that they have made the city great, not seeing that the swollen and ulcerated condition of the state is to be attributed to these elder statesmen; for they have filled the city full of harbours and docks and walls and revenues and all that, and have left no room for justice and temperance. And when the crisis of the disorder comes, the people will blame the advisers of the hour, and applaud Themistocles and Cimon and Pericles, who are the real authors of their calamities; and if you are not careful they may assail you and my friend Alcibiades, when they are losing not only their new acquisitions, but also their original possessions; not that you are the authors of these misfortunes of theirs, although you may perhaps be accessories to them. A great piece of work is always being made, as I see and am told, now as of old, about our statesmen. When the state treats any of them as malefactors, I observe that there is a great uproar and indignation at the supposed wrong which is done to them; 'after all their many services to the state, that they should unjustly perish' – so the tale runs.

But the cry is all a lie; for no statesman ever could be unjustly put to death by the city of which he is the head. The case of the professed statesman is, I believe, very much like that of the professed sophist; for the sophists, although they are wise men, are nevertheless guilty of a strange piece of folly; professing to be teachers of virtue, they will often accuse their disciples of wronging them, and defrauding them of their pay, and showing no gratitude for their services. Yet what can be more absurd than that men who have become just and good, and whose injustice has been taken away from them, and who have had justice implanted in them by their teachers, should act unjustly by reason of the injustice which is not in them? Can anything be more irrational, my friends, than this? You, Callicles, compel me to be a mob-orator, because you will not answer.

CALLICLES: And you are the man who cannot speak unless there is someone to answer?

SOCRATES: I suppose that I can; just now, at any rate, the speeches which I am making are long enough because you refuse to answer me. But I adjure you by the god of friendship, my good sir, do tell me whether there does not appear to you to be a great inconsistency in saying that you have made a man good, and then blaming him for being bad?

CALLICLES: Yes, it appears so to me.

SOCRATES: Do you never hear our professors of education speaking in this inconsistent manner?

CALLICLES: Yes, but why talk of men who are good for nothing?

SOCRATES: I would rather say, why talk of men who profess to be rulers, and declare that they are devoted to the improvement of the city, and nevertheless upon occasion declaim against the utter vileness of the city: do you think that there is any difference between one and the other? My good friend, the sophist and the rhetorician, as I was saying to Polus, are the same, or nearly the same; but you ignorantly fancy that rhetoric is a perfect thing, and sophistry a thing to be despised; whereas the truth is that sophistry is as much superior to rhetoric as legislation is to the practice of law, or gymnastic to medicine. The orators and sophists, as I am inclined to think, are the only class who cannot complain of the mischief ensuing to themselves from that which they teach others, without in the same breath accusing themselves of having done no good to those whom they profess to benefit. Is not this a fact?

CALLICLES: Certainly it is.

SOCRATES: If they were right in saying that they make men better, then they are the only class who can afford to leave their remuneration to those who have been benefited by them. Whereas if a man has been benefited in any other way, if, for example, he has been taught to run by a trainer, he might possibly defraud him of his pay, if the trainer left the matter to him, and made no agreement with him that he should receive money as soon as he had given him the utmost speed; for not because of any deficiency of speed do men act unjustly, but by reason of injustice.

CALLICLES: Very true.

SOCRATES: And he who removes injustice can be in no danger of being treated unjustly: he alone can safely leave the honorarium to his pupils, if he be really able to make them good – am I not right?

CALLICLES: Yes.

SOCRATES: Then we have found the reason why there

is no dishonour in a man receiving pay who is called in to advise about building or any other art?

CALLICLES: Yes, we have found the reason.

SOCRATES: But when the point is, how a man may become best himself, and best govern his family and state, then to say that you will give no advice gratis is held to be dishonourable?

CALLICLES: True.

SOCRATES: And why? Because only such benefits call forth a desire to requite them, and there is evidence that a benefit has been conferred when the benefactor receives a return; otherwise not. Is this true?

CALLICLES: It is.

SOCRATES: Then to which service of the state do you invite me? Determine for me. Am I to be the physician of the state who will strive and struggle to make the Athenians as good as possible; or am I to be the servant and flatterer of the state? Speak out, my good friend, freely and fairly as you did at first and ought to do again, and tell me your entire mind.

CALLICLES: I say then that you should be the servant of the state.

SOCRATES: The flatterer? Well, sir, that is a noble invitation.

CALLICLES: The Mysian, Socrates, or what you please. For if you refuse, the consequences will be –

SOCRATES: Do not repeat the old story – that he who likes will kill me and get my money; for then I shall have to repeat the old answer, that he will be a bad man and will kill the good, and that the money will be of no use to him, but that he will wrongly use that which he wrongly took, and if wrongly, basely, and if basely, hurtfully.

CALLICLES: How confident you are, Socrates, that you

will never come to harm! You seem to think that you are living in another country, and can never be brought into a court of justice, as you very likely may be brought by some miserable and mean person.

SOCRATES: Then I must indeed be a fool, Callicles, if I do not know that in the Athenian state any man may suffer anything. And if I am brought to trial and incur the dangers of which you speak, he will be a villain who brings me to trial – of that I am very sure, for no good man would accuse the innocent. Nor shall I be surprised if I am put to death. Shall I tell you why I anticipate this?

CALLICLES: By all means.

SOCRATES: I think that I am the only or almost the only Athenian living who practises the true art of politics; I am the only politician of my time. Now, seeing that when I speak my words are not uttered with any view of gaining favour, and that I look to what is best and not to what is most pleasant, having no mind to use those arts and graces which you recommend, I shall have nothing to say in the justice court. And you might argue with me, as I was arguing with Polus: I shall be tried just as a physician would be tried in a court of little boys at the indictment of the cook. What would he reply under such circumstances, if some one were to accuse him, saying, 'O my boys, many evil things has this man done to you: he is the death of you, especially of the younger ones among you, cutting and burning and starving and suffocating you, until you know not what to do; he gives you the bitterest potions, and compels you to hunger and thirst. How unlike the variety of meats and sweets on which I feasted you!'

What do you suppose that the physician would be

able to reply when he found himself in such a predicament? If he told the truth he could only say, 'All these evil things, my boys, I did for your health', and then would there not just be a clamour among a jury like that? How they would cry out!

CALLICLES: I dare say.

SOCRATES: Would he not be utterly at a loss for a reply?

CALLICLES: He certainly would.

SOCRATES: And I too shall be treated in the same way, as I well know, if I am brought before the court. For I shall not be able to rehearse to the people the pleasures which I have procured for them, and which, although I am not disposed to envy either the procurers or enjoyers of them, are deemed by them to be benefits and advantages. And if anyone says that I corrupt young men, and perplex their minds, or that I speak evil of old men, and use bitter words towards them, whether in private or public, it is useless for me to reply, as I truly might: 'All this I do for the sake of justice, and with a view to your interest, my judges, and to nothing else.' And therefore there is no saying what may happen to me.

CALLICLES: And do you think, Socrates, that a man who is thus defenceless is in a good position?

SOCRATES: Yes, Callicles, if he have that defence which you have often acknowledged he should have – if he be his own defence, and have never said or done anything wrong, either in respect of gods or men; and this has been repeatedly acknowledged by us to be the best sort of defence. And if any one could convict me of inability to defend myself or others after this sort, I should blush for shame, whether I was convicted before many, or before a few, or by myself alone; and if I died from want of ability to do so, that would

indeed grieve me. But if I died because I have no
powers of flattery or rhetoric, I am very sure that you
would not find me repining at death. For no man who
is not an utter fool and coward is afraid of death itself,
but he is afraid of doing wrong. For to go to the world
below having one's soul full of injustice is the last and
worst of all evils. And in proof of what I say, if you have
no objection, I should like to tell you a story.

CALLICLES: Very well, proceed; and then we shall have
done.

SOCRATES: Listen, then, as storytellers say, to a very
pretty tale, which I dare say that you may be disposed
to regard as a fable only, but which, as I believe, is a
true tale, for I mean to speak the truth. Homer tells us
how Zeus and Poseidon and Pluto divided the empire
which they inherited from their father. Now in the
days of Cronos there existed a law respecting the
destiny of man, which has always been, and still continues to be in heaven – that he who has lived all his life
in justice and holiness shall go, when he is dead, to the
Islands of the Blessed, and dwell there in perfect
happiness out of the reach of evil; but that he who has
lived unjustly and impiously shall go to the house of
vengeance and punishment, which is called Tartarus.

In the time of Cronos, and even quite lately in the
reign of Zeus, the judgment was given on the very day
on which the men were to die; the judges were alive,
and the men were alive; and the consequence was that
the judgments were not well given. Then Pluto and
the authorities from the Islands of the Blessed came to
Zeus, and said that the souls found their way to the
wrong places. Zeus said: 'I shall put a stop to this; the
judgments are not well given, because the persons who
are judged have their clothes on, for they are alive; and

there are many who, having evil souls, are apparelled in fair bodies, or encased in wealth or rank, and, when the day of judgment arrives, numerous witnesses come forward and testify on their behalf that they have lived righteously. The judges are awed by them, and they themselves too have their clothes on when judging; their eyes and ears and their whole bodies are interposed as a veil before their own souls. All this is a hindrance to them; there are the clothes of the judges and the clothes of the judged.

What is to be done? I will tell you: in the first place, I will deprive men of the foreknowledge of death, which they possess at present: this power which they have Prometheus has already received my orders to take from them: in the second place, they shall be entirely stripped before they are judged, for they shall be judged when they are dead; and the judge too shall be naked, that is to say, dead – he with his naked soul shall pierce into the other naked souls; and they shall die suddenly and be deprived of all their kindred, and leave their brave attire strewn upon the earth – conducted in this manner, the judgment will be just. I knew all about the matter before any of you, and therefore I have made my sons judges; two from Asia, Minos and Rhadamanthus, and one from Europe, Aeacus. And these, when they are dead, shall give judgment in the meadow at the parting of the ways, whence the two roads lead, one to the Islands of the Blessed, and the other to Tartarus. Rhadamanthus shall judge those who come from Asia, and Aeacus those who come from Europe. And to Minos I shall give the primacy, and he shall hold a court of appeal, in case either of the two others are in any doubt: then the judgment respecting the last journey of men will be as just as possible.'

From this tale, Callicles, which I have heard and believe, I draw the following inferences: death, if I am right, is in the first place the separation from one another of two things, soul and body; nothing else. And after they are separated they retain their several natures, as in life; the body keeps the same habit, and the results of treatment or accident are distinctly visible in it: for example, he who by nature or training or both, was a tall man while he was alive, will remain as he was, after he is dead; and the fat man will remain fat; and so on; and the dead man, who in life had a fancy to have flowing hair, will have flowing hair. And if he was marked with the whip and had the prints of the scourge, or of wounds in him when he was alive, you might see the same in the dead body; and if his limbs were broken or misshapen when he was alive, the same appearance would be visible in the dead. And in a word, whatever was the habit of the body during life would be distinguishable after death, either perfectly, or in a great measure and for a certain time. And I should imagine that this is equally true of the soul, Callicles; when a man is stripped of the body, all the natural or acquired affections of the soul are laid open to view.

And when they come to the judge, as those from Asia come to Rhadamanthus, he places them near him and inspects them quite impartially, not knowing whose the soul is: perhaps he may lay hands on the soul of the great king, or of some other king or potentate, who has no soundness in him, but his soul is marked with the whip, and is full of the prints and scars of perjuries and crimes with which each action has stained him, and he is all crooked with falsehood and imposture, and has no straightness, because he has lived without truth. Him Rhadamanthus beholds, full of all deformity and disproportion, which is caused by licence and luxury and insolence and incontinence, and despatches him ignominiously to his prison, and there he undergoes the punishment which he deserves.

Now the proper office of punishment is twofold: he who is rightly punished ought either to become better and profit by it, or he ought to be made an example to his fellows, that they may see what he suffers, and fear and become better. Those who are improved when they are punished by gods and men, are those whose sins are curable; and they are improved, as in this world so also in another, by pain and suffering; for there is no other way in which they can be delivered from their evil. But they who have been guilty of the worst crimes, and are incurable by reason of their crimes, are made examples; for, as they are incurable, the time has passed at which they can receive any benefit. They get no good themselves, but others get good when they behold them enduring for ever the most terrible and painful and fearful sufferings as the penalty of their sins – there they are, hanging up as examples, in the prison-house of the world below, a spectacle and a warning to all unrighteous men who come thither.

And among them, as I confidently affirm, will be found Archelaus, if Polus truly reports of him, and any other tyrant who is like him. Of these fearful examples, most, as I believe, are taken from the class of tyrants and kings and potentates and public men, for they are the authors of the greatest and most impious crimes, because they have the power. And Homer witnesses to the truth of this; for they are always kings and potentates whom he has described as suffering everlasting punishment in the world below: such were Tantalus and Sisyphus and Tityus. But no one ever described Thersites, or any private person who was a villain, as suffering everlasting punishment, or as incurable. For to commit the worst crimes, as I am inclined to think, was not in his power, and he was happier than those who had the power.

No, Callicles, the very bad men come from the class of those who have power. And yet in that very class there may arise good men, and worthy of all admiration they are, for where there is great power to do wrong, to live and to die justly is a hard thing, and greatly to be praised, and few there are who attain to this. Such good and true men, however, there have been, and will be again, at Athens and in other states, who have fulfilled their trust righteously; and there is one who is quite famous all over Hellas, Aristeides, the son of Lysimachus. But in general, great men are also bad, my friend. As I was saying, Rhadamanthus, when he gets a soul of the bad kind, knows nothing about him, neither who he is, nor who his parents are; he knows only that he has got hold of a villain; and seeing this, he stamps him as curable or incurable, and sends him away to Tartarus, whither he goes and receives his proper recompense.

Or again, he looks with admiration on the soul of some just one who has lived in holiness and truth; he may have been a private man or not; and I should say, Callicles, that he is most likely to have been a philosopher who has done his own work, and not troubled himself with the doings of other men in his lifetime; him Rhadamanthus sends to the Islands of the Blessed. Aeacus does the same; and they both have sceptres, and judge; but Minos alone has a golden sceptre and is seated looking on, as Odysseus in Homer declares that he saw him 'holding a sceptre of gold, and giving laws to the dead'.

Now I, Callicles, am persuaded of the truth of these things, and I consider how I shall present my soul whole and undefiled before the judge in that day. Renouncing the honours at which the world aims, I desire only to know the truth, and to live as well as I can, and, when I die, to die as well as I can. And, to the utmost of my power, I exhort all other men to do the same. And, in return for your exhortation of me, I exhort you also to take part in the great combat, which is the combat of life, and greater than every other earthly conflict. And I retort your reproach of me, and say, that you will not be able to help yourself when the day of trial and judgment, of which I was speaking, comes upon you; you will go before the judge, the son of Aegina, and, when he has got you in his grip and is carrying you off, you will gape and your head will swim round, just as mine would in the courts of this world, and very likely someone will shamefully box you on the ears, and put upon you any sort of insult.

Perhaps this may appear to you to be only an old wife's tale, which you will contemn. And there might be reason in your contemning such tales, if by search-ing we could find out anything better or truer: but now you see that you and Polus and Gorgias, who are the three wisest of the Greeks of our day, are not able to show that we ought to live any life which does not profit in another world as well as in this. And of all that has been said, nothing remains unshaken but the saying, that to do injustice is more to be avoided than to suffer injustice, and that the reality and not the appearance of virtue is to be followed above all things, as well in public as in private life; and that when any one has been wrong in anything, he is to be chastised, and that the next best thing to a man being just is that he should become just, and be chastised and punished; also that he should avoid all flattery of himself as well as of others, of the few or of the many: and rhetoric and any other art should be used by him, and all his actions should be done always, with a view to justice.

Follow me then, and I will lead you where you will be happy in life and after death, as the argument shows. And never mind if someone despises you as a fool, and insults you, if he has a mind; let him strike you, by Zeus, and do you be of good cheer, and do not mind the insulting blow, for you will never come to any harm in the practice of virtue, if you are a really good and true man. When we have practised virtue together, we will apply ourselves to politics, if that seems desirable, or we will advise about whatever else may seem good to us, for we shall be better able to judge then. In our present condition we ought not to give ourselves airs, for even on the most important subjects we are always changing our minds; so utterly stupid are we! Let us, then, take the argument as our guide, which has revealed to us that the best way of life is to practise justice and every virtue in life and death. This way let us go; and in this exhort all men to follow, not in the way to which you trust and in which you exhort me to follow you; for that way, Callicles, is nothing worth.